HALE YES

Facebook fun with Tom and Friends

Tom Hale

Visit my website at www.haletales.com

Printed in the United States of America

First Printing: March 2019

ISBN: 978-1-7946-1837-4

This book is dedicated with respect, gusto, and glee to the effervescent Maxine Pope.

I am far from the first to admire her strength, savvy, and sense of humor. I had to get in a long line.

She brings out the best in the rest of us. She brings it out and makes it better.

Ms. Pope is the kind of friend everyone wants. She is the example we all need. She has kept me going and pondering and laughing for years. Even when I didn't think I could. Even when I didn't want to but needed to. And I do so very much appreciate her.

Humor, Human Escapades, and Higher Wahoo: That's what this book is about.

What makes you smile out loud? What sets your brain to twinkling? What puts fizz in your existence? The posts, prompts, and ponderings contained herein will heighten those experiences. Or so I've been told.

Don't take my word for it. Take Ms. Maxine Pope's word for it:

"The tales and the stories are a treat that can only be appreciated by people who are programmed to be lighthearted and serious at the same time."

Better yet, don't take anyone's word for anything. Try it for yourself.

This mischief was instigated by my amigo of many moons, Rev. Steve Adkison:
"Hey Mertz (nickname), you might consider compiling all of your Facebook musings into a book. A theologian friend of mine did that with his theological musings and it is excellent."

Mine are not theological musings, but many are amusing.

I don't have all the answers, but I do have some pretty good questions.

Above all, this book is about personal relationships, finding common ground, and getting along. Speaking of which, the following friends had a great deal to do with this project:

Steve Adkison (Sky Pilot)
Alex Aldridge ("It's 11:11, make a wish.")
Tiffany Billingsley
Dana Crisp
Jim Genandt
John Hale
Chris Heigle
Teresa Duett Howell
Jackie James ("WTFB.")
Paige Laws
Teressa Lee ("The better it gets, the better it gets.")
Maxine Pope
Jeff Slatton
Gayla Stidham

If not for each one, one way or another, this book would not have happened. I do mighty much love and appreciate them.

But I'd rather help than watch. I'd rather have a heart than a mind. I'd rather expose too much than too little. I'd rather say hello to strangers than be afraid of them. I would rather know all this about myself than have more money than I need. I'd rather have something to love than a way to impress you.

~Po Bronson (*What Should I Do with My Life?*)

WALKING HOME

*I look at my posts and have to fight off
depression, and then this pops up. Thanks, Tom,
for always making my day better.
~Sandy Allen*

"We're all just walking each other home." ~Ram Dass

Would it help if I thought that you hung the moon?
Would that make you whistle a happier tune?
Would it shine up your smile and rekindle your eyes?
If I gave you credit for every sunrise?
Would your heart leap a little if somehow you found
That someone thought you made this world go around?
Would it trigger a giggle or give you a buzz?
Would it help to know that one somebody does?

A friend told me about a woman who can "take thrift
shop items and turn them into gold." She takes other
people's discards, mends them, decorates them, and
transforms them into something more valuable.

That launched a pondering:

Some of our fellow travelers find themselves in life's
bargain bin. Some were donated, some hopped in
voluntarily. (Perhaps we've all been there at one time or
another in one way or another.) For whatever reason, they

are convinced that they're not worth as much as they once were.

We can help restore them with a welcoming gesture, an encouraging word, a listening ear. With a little attention and kind assistance from us, they can be worth even more than they were before.

"It's the Golden Rule, right?"

Sure. Plus, that's just the kind of folks we want to be.

"People of good will."

Jeff brought me the crossword puzzle every morning. He didn't have to do that but he did. He brought me the puzzle and a pen.

I'd mentioned that I enjoyed doing the Sunday crossword, in ink because I seldom made a mistake. That may have been true a week or two before, but not then. Then, I would just sit and stare at them. Even the dinky weekday puzzles were befuddling. Maybe if one of the clues had been a three-letter word for "Your name." Maybe not. Jeff still brought them. Sometimes he'd make a good-natured observation that my progress was not exactly lending credibility to my self-proclaimed proficiency.

Jeff was showing me kindness and confidence. At the same time, he was gently challenging me to, as we said on the river, come ahead on it.

Jeff and everyone else at the hospital did many things to mold me back into some semblance of a human being. I'm sure that Jeff's crossword puzzle therapy did as much as, maybe more than, anything else to get me back on my feet.

I'll never forget it. And I try to remember that we can all, to some extent, do what Jeff does. We can show kindness toward and confidence in someone who needs it. Who needs it? We all do from time to time.

You display the outward signs of one in a dither, on the verge of a tizzy. What's up?

"Someone pushed all my buttons."

What are you, a robot? Last time I checked, I have only one button, a belly button. And I don't make it a habit to let just anyone push it.

"You know what I mean."

Not sure I do and afraid I might. If we're talking metaphorical buttons, disconnect them. Folks can push a disconnected button until their poker is pooped and it won't do a thing.

"How do we disconnect them?"

The same way we wired them: with our chosen responses. Or, since they're your buttons, you can reroute them.

"Reroute them?"

Certainly. You can reroute your Bugs-Me Button to where it activates your Shrug-Off Center.

"I'm still not sure—"

It may help to start with this question: Which are easier to control, your thoughts, actions, and attitudes or everyone else's?

"Never criticize, condemn, or complain." Those words are written on a sticky note stuck to my computer screen; it's one of the first things I see each morning. Never criticize, condemn, or complain. It's a personal goal. Earlier in the week, I was doing a good bit of all three about a situation over which I have no external control. I was venting to my friend and coworker, Jackie. She's a good listener. After I rattled on for what to her must have seemed like days, I asked if she had any ideas.

In a calm, matter-of-fact voice (like a vocal shrug), she said, "You'll have to practice what you preach."

Then it got funny. The blood pressure lowered. The mind shifted into neutral. A solution was found.

We can't control everything that happens, but we can control how we respond.

For a while a while back, I was trying to persuade folks to focus on what we all have in common instead of all the divisive, meanspirited, logically flawed flapdoodle. Again, I heard Jackie's voice telling me to practice what I preach. So, I have tried to do just that and post things that most everyone can identify with. Positive things.

Facebook is fun. We've known some of our friends along the way. Others we didn't meet until they were pretty much set in their ways; through old photos and comments from their other friends and family, we get clues to who they were before they got that way. Some of us go way back. All of us have a way to go.

The way we were, in large part, determines the way we are, but the way we are is not static. With new friends and new perspectives, we may be more open to new ways. We can agree or disagree—both of which are helpful—but we, if we'll admit it, are not there yet. Our friends, old and new, can help us make way and mend our ways. When we like folks and enjoy their company, we're at liberty to say, "I may not support your position, but I see your point." We can freely concede, "Maybe you see something I missed. That would not be unprecedented."

Money may talk, but civility sings.

We know we're not supposed to judge others. We also know that's easier said than done, so what do we do?

I've found that it helps to ask myself if I've ever acted like the person who has triggered my indignation. Have I ever driven like a crazed loon—tailgating, zipping past some "Idiot!" who has the audacity to be going the speed limit? Have I ever been in such a hurry that I forgot my manners? Have I ever allowed pain—physical, mental, spiritual—to make me snippy? Have I let borrowed trouble, worry, or dread wreck my mood? Have I ever been so locked in on what I want that I didn't consider what anyone else wanted? Yikes, yes.

When I turn it back on me, I'm no longer judging the other person; I'm at least trying to understand the other person. Does it always work? No. Does it help when I remember to do it? Yes...most times. Perfection doesn't seem to be in the cards, but improvement is possible. And fun.

Creature comforts: I'm all for and grateful for them. But they're no yardstick for contentment. Stuff cannot be swapped for serenity. Once the new wears off, toys do not correlate with joys.

If money is the be-all and end-all, congratulations. A person with a part-time (20 hours per week), minimum wage job in the USA is in the top 20% of the richest people on the planet. We have the luxury of time. Time to explore, ponder, and participate. Time to take a class, read a book, join a church. Time to reflect and prioritize.

A fabulous vacation or a great date has little or nothing to do with where we went. It has everything to do with who we went with. "Fabulous" and "great" are defined from within.

Used properly, our wealth can be a supplement to, but never a substitute for, the things we really want. The Holy Grail is not power over others. The top prize is peace of mind.

Mom would sometimes say, "Don't look at me in that tone of voice." I knew exactly what she meant. So do you.

I've seen what I consider credible research revealing that at least 70 percent of what we "hear" in any conversation is body language and tone of voice. When the nonverbal cues are missing—email, text messages, this particular post—we can be easily misunderstood. One time, Mark Twain's wife tried to shame him by repeating every profanity he had just uttered (he didn't realize she was within earshot). He told her that she had the words right, but not the tune.

We all instinctively know a fake smile when we see one (the eyes don't participate) and a fake laugh when we hear one (the tune is off). We may only perceive it subconsciously, but we know. We are easy to read.

What we "say" to everyone with whom we come in contact communicates our real motives, our true intentions. I don't need to carefully choose my words nearly as much as I need to carefully monitor my thoughts.

"Ma'am, I'm sorry, but you can't park here."

It was summertime. There were no other cars in the lot next to the sorority house. It was just across Maple Street from my building at the University of Arkansas. Anyway, I was only going to be a few minutes. It made perfectly good sense to me to park there.

It made no sense to the campus police work-study student. She'd likely been trained to be on the lookout for desperados like me.

When she saw that I was not a ma'am—all she'd initially seen was my long hair through the back window—she apologized.

She was right about the parking, though. Technically, I was not allowed.

We'd both made assumptions that proved to be ill-founded. No big deal. We laughed about it and parted on friendly terms.

It can be easy to misread folks and jump to conclusions based on any number of things. That's okay and to be expected. It doesn't have to be a big deal, and it won't be as long as we see it for what it is, maybe even laugh about it, and part on friendly terms.

"When one door closes, another door opens." That's good news if we're on an elevator. If we're trying to go somewhere in the car or lock up for the night, it's Twilight Zone time.

Is the glass half full or half empty? Depends. If it's only half full of iced tea, then by all means top it off. If it's half empty of some nasty-tasting medicine, hey, we're making progress. Are we talking about a shot glass or an hourglass? (If it's a looking glass, either way is rather disconcerting.)

Max Planck said, "When you change the way you look at things, the things you look at change." Just because he said it, that doesn't make it true. The proof is in whether or not what he said matches our experiences. Has anything ever happened to you that at first seemed bad but turned out to be good? Is there any reason to think that won't continue to be the case?

An about-to-be-born baby might think her world is ending, and that one is. Ah, but she can stretch and breathe and holler in the next one. Feels great. And she can see. Oh, my, what wonders. (Nine months, give or take, seemed like a long time, and it was; as far back as she could remember.)

After a brief frolic in this world, with all its ups and downs, the next step is just as necessary, every bit as unavoidable. (One hundred years, give or take, seems like a long time, and it is from this POV.) There is no reason whatsoever to think that the next one won't be just as dazzling, just as fun. I'd feel safe betting even more so.

A woman I used to work with came in one day all freaked out, exhibiting a first-class case of the heebie-jeebies. "Have you ever seen a hairy caterpillar!?"

Sure, I'm from east Arkansas and grew up in the desert; I've seen all kinds of—

"I mean with horns?! Yellow, black, red—I bet they're poison! Are they poison?"

I wouldn't think s—

"Scared the hell out of me! I felt it crawling on my toe! I snap-kicked and flicked it off into the grass. (Fanning herself) My heart's beating so fast! That's got to be a bad sign!"

Take a deep—

"I can't breathe!"

Never mind.

A month or so later, she came in beaming, almost dancing. "This is my lucky day!"

Why's that?

"A blue butterfly landed on my shoulder! Just like in Cinderella!"

Well, how about that? I guess most of us can, at times, seem pretty creepy on our way to what we will become.

It was a summer night on Highway 80, just outside Monroe, Louisiana. It was darker than Marie Laveau's to-do list. This stretch of road had been recently repaved; it was shiny black and the lines had not yet been painted. It was raining hard. I was driving a VW bug, one of the older ones with the six-volt system. The headlights were just bright enough to highlight the fact that I couldn't see a thing. Where did the side of the road end and the muddy bank begin? It was hard to tell. Until I found myself sliding down it.

Sliding sideways. Would the car stop before it hit a snag or a rut and flipped? Yes, and it came to rest in the weeds. There'd been no other traffic in either direction for a long time. After what seemed a year or two, I saw headlights approaching. I flashed—okay, "flash" is an undeserved flattery; "weakly winked" would be more accurate—my lights.

The truck stopped. Someone told me to hang on. A little while later, a guy came back with a tractor and a chain and hauled me up.

They invited me to follow them to their house for breakfast while we waited for the rain to stop and the sun to rise.

Those guys didn't know me from Adam, yet they went out of their way to help me on my way. I've noticed over the years that most folks are like that. We enjoy helping and readily will. If it's demanded, we balk. If it's forced, we resist. If it's requested or obviously needed, nothing can stop us.

I once heard a guest speaker tell her against-all-odds success story. Again and again she credited people who made her feel like she had value. It's surprising how little it takes to make another person feel worthwhile instead of marginalized. Eye-contact ("I see you."); a simple greeting ("How's it goin?"); common courtesy (no grand gesture, just good manners); undivided attention (let the phone buzz).

Every social ill, every physical ill, perhaps cannot be cured, but they can be, to some extent, relieved and made a tad more tolerable by a simple kindness. Our uplifting actions toward down-and-outers may someday be part of someone else's success story.

El Paso used to have a fairly nice bus station. About as nice as most airports are nowadays. Not as big as an airport, of course; not as confining or authoritarian, either. It was a pleasant place to be. Greyhound and Trailways busses rolled in and out around the clock. It was downtown, not far from the San Jacinto Plaza.

The Plaza was the hub for the city busses. Several of us would go to the Plaza during the day. We'd sing our goofy songs and pass the hat—or an empty Bugler Tobacco can. Bored people sitting on long benches, waiting for the bus, were a perfect audience. They had little else to amuse them. They all had change. They were easy to please. We did okay. Sometimes, we'd have to compete with a preacher up on the concrete stage; that was fun too. The Plaza looks a lot different now. So do we.

We liked to go to the bus station around two in the morning. We'd sit in the coffee shop, eat chewy lemon pie, drink coffee that looked like maybe it had dandruff floating on it, and listen to the jukebox. Most of one wall was a window. Interesting view. A traffic light on a timer. The light would go from red to green, but nobody was waiting, so it didn't matter. They must have washed the city busses somewhere close by. Every now and then, we'd see one pass, dripping water, its tires hissing on the asphalt. No other traffic except maybe a stray taxi. Brook Benton on the jukebox. "Rainy Night in Georgia."

It was a soul bath of an atmosphere, a snug lonesome, tailor-made for daydreaming and writing bad poetry. We were anchorless, not a care in the world, and just as happy, like Mom used to say, as if we had good sense.

Sometimes, all it takes is good news from someone who knows what they're talking about. Nine years earlier, I'd gone to a dentist in another state. He told me that my choices were to either buy a new Cadillac or get my teeth fixed. And the first step would be (an expensive and painful procedure). Not able to afford a new Cadillac and not interested in anything painful, I blew it off.

When there was no choice left but to go, I picked out a local dentist, the choice based solely on his radio commercial. When I showed up for the appointment, I was petrified and felt like a neglectful goon.

Step one was to see the hygienist. She took X-rays, poked around, and basically said, "Yeah, we can fix that." She was so confident and casual. She and the dentist worked up a long-term treatment plan. I was feeling about 80% more calm. I said, "I guess the first step is (an expensive and painful procedure)." She frowned and said, "No, you don't need that." Make that 99%.

The hygienist not only knows what she's talking about, she knows how to say it in a way that puts phobic folks like me at ease. When we fear the worst, it helps to double-check with the best.

(Many visits later, we're about halfway through the treatment plan. The dentist is excellent; so is everyone else in the office. There's been no pain; I never dread a visit. And the expense? Well, I could have instead bought a used Toyota, one that needs a little work.)

Suggestion for folks just starting out: Go for the passion instead of the paycheck.

So often when I ask a student why she or he chose a particular major, the first answer given is because it pays well. Without a corresponding enthusiasm, a paycheck will not be enough. No matter how much money we make, we get used to it, even bored with it rather quickly. It's called hedonic adaptation. The new soon wears off. Our passion and enthusiasm for the things we love, the things we really care about, the things we're innately good at, do not wear off. We're always eager to learn more about and get better at them. People who merely have a job, no matter how well it pays, count the hours until quitting time, count the days until the weekend, and count the years until retirement. People who have a passion often don't care (may not even know) what time it is or what day it is, and they have no desire to retire. A master mechanic is not going to stop working on engines. Folks will be seeking his expertise until his dying day, and he will gladly give it. A songwriter is not going to stop writing songs when she's 65, wouldn't dream of it. A retired nurse will often volunteer and will continue to be a healer until she's wheeled out. A paycheck is not the best reason to do anything.

The good news is that there's money at the top of every field, and who rises to the top?

Good work, good manners, and a sense of humor.

Those are not prize-winning attributes; they are what we reasonably expect. It's breaking even. No gold stars for doing what we're supposed to do in the first place.

When I make a mistake—and I'm really good at that—it doesn't help to be raked over the coals. It helps when someone shows me how to correct it (and perhaps admits to making a similar error). It shows that they know I want to do better and demonstrates confidence that I can.

Years ago, I sent a bulk email to the entire faculty and staff. I'd edited it but, in my haste, failed to do a final proofreading. It contained an egregious grammar gaffe. A little later, one of the English teachers sent me a link explaining subject-verb agreement, along with a winking smiley face. She knew that I knew better and was good-naturedly reminding me that knowing better and doing better do not always go hand-in-hand. It made me smile out loud.

Humor greases the skids. It helps us get our point across without being coarse. Besides, it's dang near impossible to trust someone who never smiles or laughs— a real one where the whole self participates.

Good work, good manners, and a sense of humor do not warrant a gold star, but there is a reward: They help us get along with just about anyone.

Early, Lord, one winter morn in the Arkansas delta, a nine-year-old boy awoke with a fervent desire: Stay home from school that day. Far better to lay on the couch and watch gameshows on TV.

The boy's mother relented. Yes, if he was that ill, he'd best stay home, inside, all day. It did seem to the boy that Mom hadn't put up much of a fuss about it this time. She didn't even feel his forehead.

Mom went to a window and raised the shade to reveal the first snow I'd ever seen. And plenty of it. Other kids were already outside wallowing in their good fortune. They didn't have to go to school, either. While I, by my own insistence, was too sick to join them.

That was one long day.

It was a dazzling jigsaw puzzle with thousands of intricate, interlocking pieces. Upon completion, however, the beauty and the symmetry were ruined because one small piece was missing.

It was not affiliated with the wizard; it made no contribution to the rainbow. It was a nondescript green piece, just an anonymous part of the pasture. It would have blended in and gone largely unnoticed, yet when it was missing, that's where the viewer's eye was drawn. It wrecked the whole picture.

What happened to that piece? Was it left out of the box? No. Was it lost? Sort of. That little piece was convinced that it was the wrong shape, the wrong size, the wrong color. It screwed up its edges by trying to alter them so they'd fit in somewhere else, destroying itself in a vain attempt to be what it was not, and in the process, depriving another piece of its rightful place. It wanted to be noticed and now it was. And no other piece could replace it.

You and I, day to day, are doing okay. We work and play, party and pray with people who don't vote like we do and who don't always prefer, or even totally approve of, our flavor of religion. We do not always agree, nor should we, but we trust them. We trust their intentions. And we know we need that balance in order to arrive at an intelligent answer. We know that we do not know it all. They don't vote like we do or worship like we do, but we crave their company and we'll cry at their funeral. That doesn't make us special, that makes us sane. That makes us smart. That makes us civilized.

Most of the most successful people who have ever lived on our planet have not kept their methods secret. They explained, in books, speeches, and recordings, exactly how they did it.

Success does not necessarily mean money, although that can certainly be a part of it. The big prize, the Holy Grail, however, is Peace of Mind.

Money cannot buy happiness, true. Neither can poverty. Once our basic needs are met, money has little to do with it. We know or know of wealthy folks who are happy as can be. We know of others who, no matter how much they have in the bank, are ill at ease to say the least, folks for whom mere money wasn't enough to quite fill the glass once the fizz settled. Mother Teresa was not a rich property owner, but she was certainly successful.

When we read and listen to successful people share their secrets, certain themes come up again and again. One common theme is doing what we do as a service to others. Zig Ziglar put it this way: "You can have everything in life you want, if you will just help other people get what they want."

Makes sense, doesn't it? As we know, it is more fun to help people than to hurt them. If we want Peace of Mind, a fun, meaningful life is a good place to start.

What do we say about something that no longer physically exists? Do you have a photo of yourself from a year ago? If so, please look at it or hold it in your mind. Ninety-eight percent of your atoms have been replaced since that picture was taken. The person in that picture no longer physically exists, yet here you are. Creation never ends; we are never finished, even when we think we have evidence that says otherwise. Are we there yet? Not hardly.

A friend recently posted something about how saying something nice to someone can, for them, last a lifetime.

My skeptical eyebrow reached for the ceiling. But hang on a sec; could I think of anything anyone ever said to me that has made the trip? Immediately.

The lifetime part could be disputed since technically I'm not yet dead, but one remark has lasted a mighty long time. A friend wrote in my high school year book, "To God's last happy man." I've not seen the guy since (that was back in 1492), and he's not on Facebook, but the comment has stuck with me lo these many years.

15

"To God's last happy man." For all I know, he wrote the same thing in everyone's book; even so, it has served as a mental life raft when I was anything but. (What's God's last happy man doing in the gutter? Get on up outta there.) It has served as a challenge, something to try and live up to. It has served me well. It probably didn't take him 15 seconds to write it, but I'll never forget it.

The staying power of our words. Wow. I'd never much thought about it until now. And—here's the hard part— don't you know the same is true for our not so kind comments? Can we do a recall? Can we get them back? No. They're out there, out there doing their dirty work. Can we avoid them in the future? Man, if anything was ever worth a try. Since our words are a reflection of what we're thinking, we can exercise some control over that.

(This analogy is not original. Wayne Dyer and others have used it. This is just my version.)

Projector on.

The first slide is of a garbage dump. Rancid, nasty; you can almost smell it. Humans compete with wild animals for scraps of food. The next slide is a collage of photos representing success and contentment—receiving a diploma, shaking hands to accept a job offer, dancing, a grinning baby, flying down the road on a motorcycle, events that trigger wide-eyed wonder.

There is nothing wrong with the light. The light is functioning perfectly, but it can only project on the big screen what we put in front of it.

We want to choose our slides carefully. Problems or solutions? What we hate or what we love? What we are against or what we are for? What we've lost or what we want? Either way, we can't blame the light; it's just doing its job.

(There is no shortage of less-interested others standing by to pick our slides for us.)

The note is kept where I see it every day as a reminder. Got it years ago: "Thank you. Housekeeper Stephanie."

I've been in mighty many hotel rooms and had never thought to leave a tip for the folks who take care of the room. It was a Facebook post—I forget whose—that put me wise to the practice. It was just a dollar, but she left a thank-you note. It really is the thought that counts, isn't it? "Someone noticed me and what I do."

There's some what's-in-it-for-me for the tipper too. I did not want to be in that hotel or in that town. I was eagerly leaping on every opportunity to feel irritated and put-upon. That simple note changed everything. My attitude did a 180. And it only cost a dollar. The next day, I left a lot more. Because I left with a lot more.

We can get better results and have more energy simply by reframing what we say and think.

"What are you selling?"

Nothing, just pondering something Wayne Dyer said.

"What did he say?"

Everything we are for empowers us. Everything we are against weakens us.

"What do you make of that?"

We don't have to change our minds about anything; we just say it and think about it in terms of what we want instead of what we don't. For example, we're not against ignorance; we are for education. We are not against poverty; we are for prosperity. We are not against potholes; we are for smooth roads. When we think about and act on what we are for, it gives us more energy—physically, mentally, spiritually.

"And you believe that?"

I believe it's worth a try.

"What about the better results part?"

Who are you more likely to support? Some down-in-the-mouth complainer who hates everything or someone who has a plan, a vision? One person says, "It sucks to have to drive all the way to Penciltucky to cross the river." Another person says, "Let's build a bridge." Which is more appealing?

"Misery loves company."

Maybe so, but ambition is more fun to hang around with.

"When you change the way you look at things, the things you look at change." ~Max Planck

When we paint with too broad a brush, we obscure the details. A broad brush is fine for painting a barn, but not a portrait. Too broad a brush disallows authentic definition.

"Ain't that just like a (fill-in-the-blank)?" Some, maybe. Certainly, not all.

"The (fill-in-the-blanks) are ruining everything." Many of them have made my life better.

"Typical (fill-in-the-blank)!" That's not been my experience.

Do you personally know anyone—of any faith, philosophy, or persuasion—who is all good or all bad? I don't. I'm not.

Before we can paint an accurate picture, we have to get to know individuals (details) well enough to understand their motives, their circumstances, their fears, their hopes & dreams. That takes time and effort. That leaves no room for lazy thinking, emotional shortcuts, or stereotypical smears.

Any blanket statement leaves someone's toes sticking out.

"Isn't that awful?!"

Of course it is. What can we do about it?

"Repost and perpetuate the outrage! Respond with that scowling mad-face icon! Use lots of exclamation points!"

Is there something we can do to help douse the flames instead of fanning them?

"We can flood Facebook with fluffy animals! Like and share if you really care! Shout Amen and click it again!"

Facebook has billions of users. I doubt you and I could flood Facebook with anything. No doubt a small group can change the world; as Margaret Mead said, it's the only thing that ever has. But it has to start with something that makes sense.

"Sign the petition demanding that bad stuff be banned!"

How about this: I stop allowing people who want me to buy something or vote for something to define the Real World? I'll define the real world by what I really see and what I really experience day in and day out. I'll do my best to cut other folks some slack and treat everyone like I want to be treated.

"Doesn't sound too exciting."

Maybe not, but it's actually more fun than anxiety and high blood pressure.

There are over seven billion folks on our fine planet. Sounds like a lot, 'eh? There's no way to accurately count, but a best guess is that there are at least 37 trillion cells in your body. Safe to say there are more cells in a person than there are persons on Earth.

How long would we last if our individual cells acted like we do as individual people? What would happen if our cells didn't see themselves as part of, and affected by, the whole? They all have their individual roles to play, and necessarily so, but they do it in service to, in support of, all the others.

The pretty little eye cells might find liver cells creepy. "They're the wrong color and they excrete that bile stuff. Yuck!" Of course, we know that if the liver cells were not true to themselves, the whole body, including the pretty little eye cells, would perish.

Big toe cell: "Them brain cells don't act right. Think they're so smart up there in their ivory skull. And the bleedin heart cells? I could do without all that nonsense." (Keeping in mind that a big toe that doesn't do its job can throw the whole being off balance. We need them all to do what they do and not try to imitate each other.)

Do brain cells tell jokes about butt cells?

Instead of competing and trying to be what we're not, instead of downplaying or aggrandizing others, we might be better off to just be ourselves and do our part in a spirit of cooperation. What happens when cells do not cooperate?

You had your water tested: It was not pollution free?
Boo-hoo, too bad for you, but what's that got to do with me?
How is that my problem? How come I should care?
I live here; my water's clear; and you live over there.
You say you've seen some prowlers? Someone vandalized your truck?
My thoughts and prayers are with you; may God grant you better luck.
I'll mind my own business; I have my own goals to meet.

Hale Yes

I can't be bothered with the woes of those who live across
the street.

Drugs and crime, filth and grime: how can they live that
way?
People gettin shot and folks who have no place to stay.
They're lazy and they're crazy and they have no common
sense.
I shouldn't have to see them. I say we build a fence.
Those people act like animals; those people ain't no good.
If God loved them, they'd be livin in a better
neighborhood.
Yeah, it's sad as Hell, but I won't let it get me down
Because they live in another part of town.

Budget cuts are shuttin down your schools? You're
unemployed?
Your job got outsourced? Yeah, I can see why you're
annoyed.
They say poverty builds character and ignorance is bliss.
Here's a self-help tape; cheer up and listen to this.
Unsafe roads and bridges and a crumbling overpass?
Good thing you can't travel, then—you can't afford the
gas.
You're in my prayers; I'll thank the good Lord I don't
share your fate,
But it's really no concern of mine; you're in another state.

Your whole town got blown to smithereens? Sucks to be
you.
You have no place to go? So what do you want me to do?
You lost everything; you had to leave behind your stuff?
Hey, man, the tough get goin when the goin gets tough.
Say what? The Good Samaritan? Yeah, I love that guy.
We tell that tale in Sunday School, but how does it apply?

21

I empathize with all you guys, feel bad about your wars,
But you're from another country, and this one isn't yours.

It's been so nice to see you. Have a nice day. Bye.
I have other fish to fry, and you've got rivers to cry.
Come to our Bible study (it's my sacrifice for Lent);
We're discussing how what Jesus said ain't what he really
meant.
Before you come, bone up on Matthew, Chapter twenty-
five.
That last part will make you laugh out loud and glad to
be alive.
I know you're in a bind; I know your prospects are grim,
But it's no sweat off my salvation if you sink or swim.

An informal observation: Most folks making small talk
tend to lead with what's wrong.
"I've got that (fill-in-the-blank) that's going around."
Or suffering some seasonal malady—autumn allergies,
dearth of sunlight in the winter, too much sun in the
summer, spring fever.
The alarm went off too early. Weekends (no matter
how long) go by too fast; and now, of course, it's Monday.
I wonder if we'd be as sick, tired, and stressed, if we
didn't talk about it so much. Are we feeding it, honoring
it, making it worse? Are we frontloading excuses in case
we screw up? Would it help if our small talk was bigger?
What if we focused on the things (most things) that are
going right? Misery may love company, but can
contentment also draw a crowd?
Want to try a quick experiment? Which of the
following statements makes you feel better?
"I hate Mondays." "We get paid this week."
Which one merits the most attention?

"Yeah, but..."

It's always positive. It always gets a grin, from those who pick it up and those who hear it. Leaning against a bookshelf behind my desk, within easy reach, is a guitar. Folks from every corner of the Ivory Tower—maintenance, administration, students, support staff, and professors— have picked it up and played it. If you saw them going about their daily doings, you might never guess they possessed such talent. We've been treated to rock & roll, bluegrass, gospel, and country.

It's a festive looking instrument with a cowgirl motif; it even gets smiles from those who don't know a C chord from a kite string. A cowgirl guitar: It may not be the most useful or practical office supply, but the stapler never elicited that kind of enthusiasm.

Maybe we should write our own job descriptions. The official ones can be boring and vague, worded as uninspiring CYA exercises to appease the state/federal Department of Employment Stuff. But why are we really there? To get a paycheck, certainly. Most of us wouldn't show up, at least not as often, if we weren't getting paid, but what gets us out of bed and on the road each morning? Forget the jargon and the often-overblown job titles. What is it we really do?

When we think about it, every one of us does something that makes other folks' lives better. We help each other survive, celebrate, and succeed. That's no small calling. Everything that enhances our wellbeing is imagined, designed, made, sold, delivered, maintained, decorated, or taught—provided—by someone. We need them. They need us.

When someone asks, "What do you do?" think it over. Earl Nightingale said that our rewards in life, financial and otherwise, will be in direct proportion to our service to others. When we believe that, when we act on that, writing our own job descriptions gets easy and fun.

For example:

Mechanic: "I help people pick up their kids from school. I make it possible for them to get to and from their entertainments and obligations."

Store Clerk: "I provide luxuries, necessities, and a pleasant demeanor; all of which contribute to the pleasure and attitudes of the customers."

Teacher: "I throw wide the windows of wonder and let in the fresh air of fascination and possibilities."

What's yours?

A guy was complaining this morning about how he could not get to sleep last night, so bummed was he after watching the local news.

I'm not sure what good it does to watch that stuff. If we do watch it, let's not let it be the last thing we focus on. Whatever we have on our minds while falling asleep, our brains will take and play with while we snooze. It will probably help to give it something positive, entertaining, or interesting. Something favorable rather than frightening. Since it's dang near impossible to be anxious and grateful at the same time, we could drift off to dreamland while reviewing the people and things we are glad we have in our lives. We could replay a happy moment. Anything that negates the hate and perpetuates the Wahoo; anything that sends fear to the rear and lets fun cut in front of the line. Don't take dread to bed; take hope instead.

Sally kept misspelling the same word. She blamed the pencil. New pencils, no matter how finely sharpened, still made the mistake. "Must be a defective batch."

One day, a friend taught Sally how to spell the word correctly. Once her mind had accurate information, the pencil's performance improved markedly.

Simon kept misreading people. He found them irksome. He blamed their politics and their religions. New people he met were equally ill informed. "You can't fix stupid."

One day, a friend taught Simon to look for what he had in common with other folks instead of dwelling on their differences and revealed to him the magic words for getting along: Empathy and Respect. Once his mind had accurate information, other people's behavior improved markedly.

Any meaningful change has to first take place on the inside.

(Just say know.)

You and I, for whatever else we might be, are physically mostly water.

That same water, in its time, may have been part of a raging river, Niagara Falls, or a wave off Waikiki. It might have struggled through a rusty radiator or stood stagnant in a mud puddle. It could have kept Noah's Ark afloat or helped destroy a village as a tsunami participant. That mud puddle water fell from the sky. It was, perhaps, part of an Old Faithful blast that evaporated in midair and then took a most delightful journey. Sometimes it was part of a tourist destination, posing for pictures. Sometimes it was flushed. Sometimes it hung dripping from a gutter as the sun freed it from its icicle trap. The sweat from our labor may show up next in a cold bottle of club soda. We are always taking on water to replace lost water. "Do you recycle?" Constantly. Holy water, firewater, bilge water, you name it; from the Ice Capades to the ice machine at the Rat-Tacky Motel; from

Steamboat Willie to boiled weenies: Been there, done that, washed the T-shirt.

In an interview (12/25/16) on *Face the Nation* (CBS), John Dickerson asked Stephen Colbert, "If you had to do a focus group, what would you ask people?"

Colbert said, "What makes you most hopeful?"

That got me to pondering. What makes me most hopeful? "Most" is a tough call. There are so many things.

Knowing that what we're doing here on this planet is not even close to being all there is to it, that's a load off.

Realizing that our thoughts, the ways we choose to process things, are what determine our moods, perhaps our very sanity, that's liberating. We've all seen folks with way more disadvantages, who've been dealt far sorrier cards, rise above it and be happy, productive, inspiring people.

A big one is noticing that, as we go about our daily doings, it's not us against them. Sure, if it's a ballgame or an election, we have our preferences, but when we need help—to commiserate or celebrate—we can count on "them." It doesn't matter who we root for or who we voted for; that's not why they are there for us.

Gads, we're all goofy as an outhouse rat in our own way; we all have our blind spots, but our vision clears, we can see just fine when it comes to the things that matter most.

An honest look reveals that we have far more blessings than bummers. Most hopeful? Don't know. But I do know that there are a lot more reasons to be hopeful than not.

"Truth is not necessarily a function of factuality." Rob Riggs, GM of Radio Free Texas, said that to me many years ago, and it didn't make a lick of sense. Five minutes on Facebook is enough to convince me that maybe Rob was right, at least to some extent. Seems nothing is so farfetched that someone, self included, won't buy into it. It has little to do with facts; those are easy enough to check—entire websites are devoted to it. Sometimes, it seems, we tend to believe things not because they are true, but because we want to. Sometimes we'd rather react than research.

"Our outlook on life is a kind of paintbrush, and with it we paint our world. It can be bright and filled with hope and satisfaction, or it can be dark and gloomy—lugubrious." ~Earl Nightingale

"Every person takes the limits of their own field of vision for the limits of the world." ~Arthur Schopenhauer

"The great obstacle to progress is not ignorance but the illusion of knowledge." ~Daniel Boorstin

"Since we all create our habitual reality tunnels, either consciously and intelligently or unconsciously and mechanically, I prefer to create for each hour the happiest, funniest, and most romantic reality tunnel consistent with the signals my brain apprehends. I feel sorry for the people who persistently organize experience into sad, dreary, and hopeless reality tunnels, and try to show them how to break that bad habit, but I don't feel any masochistic duty to share their misery." ~Robert Anton Wilson

There's a guy I know who collects railroad antiques. One day, on one of the auction sites, he saw some playing cards, the kind that the railroads used to offer to passengers to pass the time. It was a rare pack and he wanted it. The price was discounted because one of the cards was gone.

When the cards arrived, my friend sorted them into suits to see which one was missing. One of the cards felt thicker than the others. It was soon obvious that two of the cards were stuck together. They came apart easily, revealing that all 52 were indeed there and in good shape.

What a fine metaphor. Might we all, from time to time, sell ourselves short, cheapen our value, because of something that we perceive to be missing—or something some less-interested other told us is missing? A thorough inventory may reveal that we really are playing with a full deck. We might just be stuck, hung up on something that conceals our true identity.

"There's so much hate and anger."

(Am I perpetuating it or looking for ways to alleviate it? Am I helpless or helpful?)

"People haven't been this divided since I don't know when."

(What am I doing to unite? I can't just blame "them." Some of this is on me.)

We've all seen how one dinky candle flame can displace a disproportionate amount of darkness. We don't have to bulldoze the darkness out the door; we don't have to wrestle it to the exit; we don't have to fight it or force it; all we need to do is shine a little light.

In much the same way, one little positive act or thought can displace a lot of negativity. One person, even a stranger, can do something nice and it can make our day, put the other nonsense in perspective. It may not seem like much, but it's something we can all do, something powerful. And fun. There are enough folks groaning and bellyaching, right? Got a light?

Chronic pain does not bring out the best in anyone. It can cause folks to be short-tempered and longwinded. When we realize that they live with their pain every minute of every day, and that it even disrupts, confuses, and sabotages their sleep, we can more easily overlook and understand if they tend to make everything all about them.

Chronic pain—physical, mental, spiritual—does not bring out the best, but there's still some best in there and we would do well to honor that.

How do we bring it out, that best that's still in there? Sometimes we can't. But we can allow it to bring out the best in ourselves.

Odd are, they're frightened, angry, disappointed. Their quest for relief may manifest itself in some unflattering and counterproductive behaviors. We can pull back that curtain (à la Toto in *The Wizard of Oz*) and see them, remember them, for who they really are, who they were before they got that way.

Perhaps the most powerful thing we can do is just be there. Be there and listen. Be there and trust the relationship.

Who you gonna call? Goat Dusters.

Hannibal was a recent arrival and learning to talk when the original *Ghostbusters* movie came out and the theme song was everywhere. While the rest of us responded with "Ghostbusters!" he was hearing and singing "Goat Dusters!" It was mighty cute.

We go with what we know, don't we? Our frames of reference or our preferences don't always match the meaning; our comprehension sometimes doesn't align with the intention, but we sing along just as enthusiastically.

Odds are we've all been misinterpreted and misrepresented at one time or another. Sometimes it's cute. Sometimes it's catastrophic.

On any given day, any political candidate can say or do something that will thrill millions and appall as many more. I know and like some folks on the far right and some on the far left. Far as I can tell, we could all, with a straight face, accurately echo Eric Burdon and the Animals: "I'm just a soul whose intentions are good. Oh, Lord, please don't let me be misunderstood."

("So, next election, who you gonna call?"

Well, after I give my goats a good dusting, I'm gonna call Dial-A-Prayer.)

Hannibal Atticus Hale. To me, it seemed a fine name, a name with meaning.

I was on a towboat that dang near sank just upriver from Hannibal, Missouri. That was my cue to get off the river and hasten myself to Austin, Texas. Among the many hoots and flashes of magic that transpired in that trippy town was a series of events that resulted in Hannibal's existence.

His first name, in addition to the Mark Twain connection, represents something that seems like a negative becoming just the opposite. When the boat started taking on water in the middle of the night, we were sounding alarms and standing by to cut the barges loose with us on them. At the time, it didn't appear to belong in the plus column.

Atticus: For Atticus Finch.

Bonus: His initials are HAH.

I always told Hannibal that his name was one that I picked, but if ever he didn't like it he could choose his own name. If he found one that was a better fit for him, and stuck with it, I'd have it legally changed.

When he was five, he changed it. He preferred to be known as...Stompy Root Beer. Others were tried on along the way, some of them quite good, but he's always gone back to the original. How we identify ourselves and what we answer to is always a choice. Today, if you see

Hannibal and his back is turned, you can get his attention by calling out, "Mr. Root Beer." or "Hey, Root Beer Boy." He will respond with a smile.

Not every Tom, Dick, and Harry is named Hannibal. When a name that different comes along, it can, to some folks, be a bit disconcerting. When my charming and delightful son, Hannibal, was younger, my great-grandmother kept referring to him as Christopher.

Someone asked her, "Grandma, why do you call him Christopher?" She said, "Because I never can remember Hamilton."

With one of those helium-quality balloons, you can make a water balloon as big as a bowling ball. If you first put in a few drops of food coloring, add the water, then put it in the freezer, it makes an excellent swimming pool bomb (peel off the balloon before dropping...you might not want to use yellow dye). Those dinky dime-a-dozen balloons can burst if they get bigger than a pear.

When we stretch ourselves, creating more room for Wahoo and less for getting derailed by the common inconveniences, we can make quite a splash.

How do we do that? How can we increase our capacity?

Physically: Walk, run, lift, or bend a little more each week. It releases the feel-good endorphins and helps put things in perspective.

Mentally: Learn something new or more about a current passion. When we're excited, about a hobby or a career, we don't have much time to fret the foofaraw.

Spiritually: Pray, meditate, or sit under a tree—better yet, in a tree—and ponder. Focus on the things in your plus column. It's almost impossible to be grateful and anxious at the same time.

Anyone reading this has reasons to celebrate something. Cue the balloons. What kind of balloons? Those that yield a happy, refreshing surprise or a disappointing pop on the faucet?

It can sometimes seem like we're steel marbles, born/launched into a huge, noisy, flashy pinball machine. There are probably rules; it likely makes sense on some level, but we're so busy being bumped and bounced from one obstacle/opportunity to another that it often doesn't seem so. Sometimes we randomly roll through a gate or land in a dip that awards bonus points, and we're happy to take full credit for it. Other times we ramble right down the middle, where no corrective actions can reach us, with nothing to show for our efforts but a lost chance, a waste of time. Of course, it's not our fault.

Eventually, we have a happy and disconcerting realization: We're the ones working the flippers. Happy because we now have some control. Disconcerting because we can no longer blame it all on some ineffable bigger other. Happy because we know we can always put in another quarter and try again. (And do everything we can, just short of tilting the contraption.)

Some people, no matter what else is going on, make the world shine and our own lives sparkle. Day in and day out, we need them. And they're always there, just being themselves and making the rest of us smile, often right out loud. Sometimes, they're the answered prayer that shows up in our spiritual inbox and may go unnoticed among all the spam. Sometimes they're the conversation that gets interrupted because a plastic rectangle vibrates nearby— "I gotta take this." But they're also the ruby slippers that guide our steps and patiently wait for us to wise up and click our heels.

Now and then, when all the dreck is deleted, when the plastic rectangle is turned off and charging, we relax, pay attention, and say, "Hey, cool shoes!"

I'm outrageously blessed and mighty glad to know a few such folks.

We didn't pass a hat; we passed an empty Bugler tobacco can. Nickels and dimes make a more prosperous sound rattling around in a tin container. We had a captive audience on the Plaza Square in downtown El Paso. That was the city bus hub. People sat waiting on long benches with few amusements—no phones to stare at yet—so our tacky little songs provided a welcome diversion. Okay, "welcome" might be stretching it a bit, but at least a bizarre curiosity. Have you ever noticed how much a person's enunciation improves when cussing?

During the winter months, we took our offerings indoors. Swinging doors. We'd play for tips and free beer.

In one particular bar—I'll never forget it—a patron said, "I'll give y'all five bucks if you'll shut up and plug the jukebox back in."

Five dollars went a long way in those days. That was hamburger, cigarette, and gas money home.

Flash forward a few decades. The instruments and lyrics have changed, but the lesson still applies: On occasion, if we're lucky, our words and actions are beneficial and appreciated. Sometimes we're more valuable when we hush and stop.

My worst day looks like a holiday when stood next to Viktor Frankl's typical day in a Nazi concentration camp. Why did he make it out when so many did not? How did he convince others, hell bent on suicide, to stick around? Not by promoting the pursuit of happiness—it was way too late for that—but by pursuing meaning.

A doughnut and a cup of coffee can make me happy. For a little while. The "what" has to be constantly replenished and can distract from all else. The "why" provides lasting satisfaction, even in circumstances that are anything but happy. If we pursue only happiness, the chase never ends. It's exhausting. When we pursue meaning, happiness stops running from us.

One of my favorite cartoons is Charlie Brown walking away after a baseball game and asking, "How can we lose when we're so sincere?"

Wayne Dyer said something akin to "If anyone has to lose in order for me to win, I haven't won anything of lasting value." (Couldn't find the exact quote.)

Certainly, keeping score is entertaining and fun, but it's ephemeral. Some team wins the championship; happy hugs are exchanged, Gatorade is dumped, confetti is dropped, trophies are awarded and posed with. Next day, everyone—especially fans of the opposing team—is talking about next year. Without Googling: Who won the Super Bowl, the World Series, or any Oscar three years ago? (Some will know; most won't.) It doesn't last.

If I can win something that benefits all concerned, that's something to celebrate. If I can rise above blaming others for my lot in life and take responsibility for it, we're all better off. If I can defeat my insecurity and my need to judge others, a lot of folks will gain. If I can overcome apathy and replace it with empathy, everyone I come in contact with wins. If I can get over myself and get to know folks with opposing views (not to change their minds, but to try to understand where they're coming from), nobody loses.

Competition can be fun. Cooperation can be fun and then some. Even if we're not there yet, if we are sincerely trying to improve, there are no losers.

Hale Yes

The temperature outside was 12 degrees when I made the shift from horizontal to fairly vertical this morning. Don't know when I've ever appreciated the heater more. It was 12 degrees outside. But I was inside. Inside with electricity and sweet comfort blasting from the vents. Inside with electricity to spur the pot to action; all I had to do was add water and coffee.

This snug dwelling, the electricity, the water and the coffee (don't forget the donuts), the print and Internet entertainments, this pleasant Sunday: How was it all possible? Easy. I cashed in a few Monday mornings to pay for it.

For the life of me, I just can't complain about going to work on a Monday. Bills will continue to be due. Coffee and donuts will continue to need replacing. Good news: After checking the calendar, I see there's no shortage of Mondays, no scarcity of new opportunities. Lucky me.

What a grand aroma: A fresh pot of coffee brewing. I usually make the coffee by myself, but this morning I had a slew of helpers. During each step, I tried to imagine the other people that made it happen.

The filter: How many were involved in the manufacturing, shipping, and selling? Impossible to say.

The water: I have no idea who and what all is involved in the engineering, treatment, and pipe maintenance that brings it into the house and out the spout. The water bill? Yes, I'll gladly pay it. Saved me a trip to the creek.

The coffee: Juan Valdez and his donkey were there, along with some truckers, forklift drivers, and a parade of pros responsible for donkey, truck, and forklift upkeep.

And the coffee maker, and the electricity ... You get the picture.

Independent? By no means. I can't even have a cup of coffee unless hundreds (thousands?) of folks cooperate.

In some old TV western—I forget which one—the hero, through no fault of his own, fell on hard times. To cover his losses, he accepted a job piloting a wagonload of liquid nitroglycerin to a mining camp. The hazard pay was worth the risk. Hit a bump too hard and he's history. He spent the trip sweating, clearing large stones from the path, and praying some sidewinder didn't spook the horses.

That's sort of how it feels posting anything these days. No matter what we say, someone can take it wrong or take offense. We can remove stones from the path, but those unseen chips on assorted shoulders (some of them quite large) are often difficult to detect. Even so, we must keep moving, proceeding with caution, choosing our words carefully, thinking before we act. And it's good practice. We'll get along better if we apply it to every person and every situation we encounter.

There are worse things than getting blown to smithereens. Like not trying at all.

"Did you have a good day?"
There are many ways we could gauge what a good day means. "Yeah, I had a nice lunch and didn't screw up so bad that anyone yelled at me." "I got there and back without losing my mind, came home and kicked my shoes off, so yes."

Worthy goals, certainly, but it might be fun and more fulfilling to aim a little higher, dive a little deeper. What other measuring stick could we use to evaluate the value of a day?

Perhaps this one: "Did I make anyone's life better today?"

It can be tempting to chime in and chirp along with the impotent criticism choir. That's too easy. We all know what the problems are. Might I feel better at the end of the day if I offered, seriously researched, or cooperated with possible solutions?

"Did I make anyone's life better today?"

I'll bet you did. Sure, we'd all like to sleep later and oh Lord, it's Monday; forget all that. Focus instead on how you've made other folks' lives better. If you sold them a hamburger, provided accurate information, repaired their vehicle, delivered their mail, helped them heal, or just about anything else, you made someone's life better. You made a much-needed contribution and greased the skids of progress. The woman who cut my hair and the guy who sold me the tie I wore to the interview helped me get that job. I did not do it, could not have done it, by myself. If you contributed a smile or a kind word, you did us all a favor.

Would it help things along if we saw others and ourselves in that light? Can't hurt to try.

Have a good day.

An ad for an El Paso newspaper appeared on my Facebook page. Of all the magic and moon howls that happened in the Sun City, the first thing that came to mind was how the desert smells after a summer rain. It smells like being fully alive feels. It smells like anything is possible and anything goes. It smells like Let's Dance. If we could capture it in a cologne, we'd call it Essence of Yes.

After a summer rain, the lizards get livelier (some to the point of leaping); the coyotes get wilier; the rattlers add shake and roll to their repertoire. And wildflowers pop up. Oh, my, what an eye carnival. Dazzle times ten. Where have they been hiding all this time?

It didn't take much rain at all—which is good because we didn't get much—to bring out the best in every living thing.

The capacity for joy and a sense of purpose are planted in each of us from the get-go. They may lie dormant for decades, but they're there. It doesn't take much to release them. Just a little bit of belief in ourselves, just a little bit of bravado, just one step in a positive direction. They can be triggered by a simple compliment or a brief show of faith from a trusted other. You and I have the power to make it rain, for ourselves and for everyone we interact with. Criticism and complaints have left many plenty parched. Let's water the Wahoo.

It's interesting and a tad sad: Someone who has a peace sign or a unicorn as their profile picture while they spout anger, hate, and derision in their comments and posts.

Call it a hunch or a character flaw, but I'm willing to bet that nothing is going to be settled by who comes up with the best insult. Peace isn't likely to happen until we're willing to listen to each other and admit that maybe there's an outside chance that we don't know everything. If you want to change my mind, don't tell me what an idiot I am—for some reason, folks tend not to respond well to that. Tell me why your idea makes more sense, why it's better, fairer, for all concerned. That's something we're all interested in. If someone leads with anger and hate, I don't want their opinion on anything, not even a chicken salad recipe.

We create peace and goodwill one-on-one as we go about our daily doings. A diatribe or a sarcastic cartoon will not hasten the process. We should stand our ground, of course. And while we're standing there, we can plant a garden or dig a deeper hole.

"I'm so angry and so frightened, and way too lazy to work through it."

Have you tried hating foreigners?

"Yes, and that does help—a little."

How about blaming Obama or Reagan?

"I've been neglecting that lately."

Then get back on that horse. C'mon, man. You got this!

"Hell, yeah!"

How are things in the...how to put this delicately...in the, you know, r-e-l-i-g-i-o-n department?

"Pretty good. I found a group that goes along with everything I already like and denounces the stuff I don't like or am no good at."

Doesn't that ease your fear and assuage your anger?

"Are you kidding?"

What's the problem?

"What's the problem? I'll tell ya what's the problem: Not everyone agrees with me, that's what's the problem! Those damn MethoBapTerians are ruining it for everybody, being all inclusive and neighborly. Holy shi—"

Have you been keeping up with the news?

"Yes. I watch KWTF. But that's the only one; all the others are nothing but fake news and alternative facts. I keep KWTF on 24/7."

Does that make it better?

"Have you seen what's going on in the world? No, of course it doesn't make it better! If anything, it makes it worse!"

Is there any way to turn it off?

"Not that I'm aware of."

Have you read *The Little Prince*? Remember what the fox said?

"What did the fox say?"

"One sees clearly only with the heart. The essential is invisible to the eye."

"Get over it."

I'm not sure that's a good idea. I kind of need it, as a map and a reminder. I don't want to forget the seemingly logical circumstances that led up to it. I need to remember and be on guard against the part I played in it. I can't just erase it and move on because I don't ever want to do that again. How can we improve if we blow off the very reasons we so desperately need to?

"Okay, then rise above it. That way, you can still see it, but let it help steer instead of stifle."

Rise above it: I like that.

There's gold in them thar skulls.

The placebo effect is nothing to sneeze at. It can cause real chemical changes in our brains.

Dr. Ted Kaptchuk heads up the Harvard placebo program. They are not looking for the if (they know it works) but the how. One thing they've noticed is that placebo treatments offered by kind, empathetic folks are much more effective.

"It's valuable insight for any caregiver: patients' perceptions matter, and the ways physicians frame perceptions can have significant effects on their patients' health."

Likewise, every interaction we have with another person is an opportunity to make them (and ourselves) feel better...or worse. When we feel better, we tend to act better, and isn't that the goal? If we sneer, turn up our noses, or spout some tacky remark, that triggers harmful chemicals (in their brains and ours). A smile, a nod, or a polite remark launches the good stuff. Ranting and chanting may be invigorating, but they do little toward the changes we want to see. That energy might be better spent sowing and growing. (Just say "know.")

If we want to protect the environment, the best place to start may be with our social environment.

The Cave of Wonders, it appears, awaits us there between our ears.

His workshop is filled with the best state-of-the-art, cutting edge tools. Every time a new gizmo hits the market, he's first in line to buy it.

He has a first-class rasp, a Swiss Army drill, a silver hammer, a fancy planer, the latest lathe, and a saw with 20/20 hindsight. He replaced his old standard with a pneumatic. He has everything ... well, almost.

One thing is still missing: The desire to build something.

"Life is dull only to dull people." ~Earl Nightingale

I'm gratified and grateful to report that I do not personally know any dull people. They're out there, to be sure, but they tend to flee from us, don't they? I really enjoy people who:

Stand up for what they believe in. We don't always agree, and that's good because, since I don't know everything, I need and want input from trusted others. From history and from experience we know that no one person, no one philosophy, can ruin or long control everything because bold souls with opposing views will not sit still for it. That's fun and reassuring. It's certainly not dull. I really enjoy people who:

Bark at the moon. Dull people don't know how to—or are afraid to—just turn loose and go crazy every now and then. Even when circumstances make it physically impossible to kick up our heels, we can still do it mentally, and that's where the real action is and always has been, anyway. I really enjoy people who:

Jerk a knot in my tail when necessary. It takes a real Friend, a real Pastor, or a real Teacher to do that. Self-improvement is anything but dull.

"Your guys are awesome!"

When it comes to the what-does-what-why-and-how of an automobile, I don't know a dipstick from a door handle. What I do know is where to go for help. The mechanics know that they could tell me anything and I'd be obliged to believe them. They have never told me something was wrong that wasn't. What they charge has been consistently less than their estimates. They are always prompt and polite. A little extra is no big deal; that's just the way they do things.

How did I luck onto these folks? Easy: someone I trust recommended them.

A little while back, a coworker needed some mechanical work done. She got an estimate of $1200.00 from some other outfit. Whew! I encouraged her to see my mechanic pals before forking over that kind of cash. She did. My folks did the work for $400.00. She sent me an email, the contents of which make up the first sentence of this post.

True story: Aaron was born in Florida. One day, when he was about six or seven years old, he was playing outside when something bizarre started to happen. This strange...stuff...was falling out of the sky. Aaron hastened his wide-eyed self back indoors and excitedly asked his aunt, "What is that?!"

She looked out the window. Then laughed. "That's snow."

What a fine metaphor, 'eh? Something we've never experienced can be baffling, a ton of fun, or even disconcerting. No matter how it affects us, we cannot deny it exists. I try to keep Aaron's story in mind whenever someone tries to tell me all about the *real* world.

How's it going?

"(shrug) Same old same old."

Gads, even if it was true I'd never admit it. Nothing, including the atoms, the very building blocks of our bodies, is ever the same day to day or even moment to moment. We are constantly getting new chances, new cards, new clues. If we're not seeing them, maybe it's because our focus is too narrow.

Our old pal, Zig Ziglar, reminded us that the best way to get what we want is to help other folks get what they want. That's good news because most people love to help. So, what is it we want? When we tally the trappings, all the things, all the prestige, all the symbols of security, they add up to Peace of Mind. That's all we're seeking.

Most people love to help. It's equally true that most people are reluctant to ask for it. How can we help if they won't tell us what they need? Easy. They want and need the same things we do.

No one is going to be better off if I complain and disdain, if I lead with greed instead of gratitude. It's not going to help if I harp about the weather or what day of the week it is. Once our basic needs are met, we humans thrive on Love, Worth, and Recognition. I bet we can find ways today to include those in our conversations and actions.

What we plant is what we will harvest. It can be no other way. What we reward, we get more of. We're all angry about and hurt by something. We're all afraid of something—whether we admit it or act like a dang fool trying to hide it.

No matter what it is that angers, hurts, or frightens us, let's cut to the chase, be still, and ask ourselves, "Do I want more of it?"

If we do, then let's just keep doing what we're doing. If not, let's take a step back and acknowledge that hate breeds hate. Violence begets violence. Fear spawns fear. Kindness is contagious too.

Kindness does not mean condoning. It means listening, acknowledging, empathizing. It means taking the time to at least try to understand what the other person has experienced, believes in, and aspires to.

When we do that, we usually find that the other person merely wants the same things we want. We can help each other get it. We may not have a clue how to get there, but we're far more likely to find the way if we cooperate instead of blocking the path and shredding the map.

We three wee lads were just going about our business, playing outside, when what did we see—could it be? — yes, indeed. A dollar bill. Oh, my. We were rich. Serendipity-doo-dah and then some.

A dollar went a long way back then. It seemed we would never tire of refreshing and congratulating ourselves.

Reflecting on that greenback bonanza got me to pondering. What, these days, can evoke that same smile-out-loud bonus joy?

An unexpected, unrequested kindness, like that dollar, goes a long way. Hearing a real-deal, can't-help-it laugh from anyone at any age, that can make your day. A summer night in the New Mexico desert, how close the stars seem and how many there are, that peace forever just a recall away. You, no doubt, have your own Wahoo igniters.

The best and lasting things, the good feelings and fond memories, cannot be bought. Not even for a dollar.

We have this grand and healthy insistence that the Good Guys always win. We don't much care for movies and books where they don't. And we do our best to interpret "real" life likewise.

We're often easily distracted. When we shine our focus in the wrong direction, it can seem difficult to tell who the good guys are. It can get murky; it can get downright surreal when we divide anything into us and them.

There will always be someone from any political persuasion, any belief system, any team, any race, who will go out there, act a fool, and perpetuate the stereotype. You and I know that the extremists do not represent the whole because the ones from that group with whom we interact don't act like that.

The Good Guys are us. As long as we can work, shop, eat, laugh, and TCB with each other, we'll be okay. Perhaps the most heroic, the most patriotic, the Godliest thing we can do is to simply get along. As long as we continue to do that, the rest will sort itself out. The so-called leaders will have to follow suit; they'll have no choice. The Good Guys are not easily fooled by the memes, the media, and the maniacs.

During new student orientation, I saw a former student, a guy who was in a concurrent class I did at the alternative high school a few years ago. I was mighty glad to see him coming to college; I called him by name and told him so. His eyes got big. He said, "You remember me?" He was surprised. And pleased.

You and I would likely be more taken aback if someone did not remember us than if they did. Another reminder that, once our basic needs are met, we humans thrive on love, worth, and recognition. And that some folks get so little of it that it comes as a surprise.

No matter what line of work we're in, you and I have daily opportunities to teach lessons far more valuable than the three Rs. Eye contact and a friendly greeting go a long way. They cost nothing and benefit all concerned. Heck of a deal.

(In Pirate School, they taught us the three ARRRs.)

It was a 30-mile, two-lane commute to the college. Eventually, every curve and every cow became familiar. One morning there was something new: Freezing fog. It was dazzling, downright magical, watching it accumulate on the antenna. It made for a fun trip. At an early morning meeting, a colleague, referring to the freezing fog, said, "Wasn't that awful?!" The same event that fascinated me frightened her.

Another time, I was thrown into what seemed an impossible teaching situation. I went whining from person to person seeking sympathy. When the project failed, as it surely must, at least they'd understand what I'd been up against. One woman, a true friend, didn't play along. Her eyes lit up and she said, "What a wonderful opportunity. This is stuff they can't teach in grad school. Those students are lucky it's you instead of someone who doesn't give a [hoot]. Besides, how can we ever teach critical thinking if we ourselves can't do it?"

That changed everything, and it turned out to be some of the most fun I've ever had. All it took was a shift in perspective and a vote of confidence.

In both situations, the circumstances were the same for all concerned. What made it good or bad, welcome or worrisome, was how we thought about it.

"The only difference between a flower and a weed is a judgement." ~Wayne Dyer

(Some folks wish dandelions would go away. Others make a wish and blow the fuzz off.)

Having a positive attitude doesn't mean walking around with a vacuous grin and putting smiley face stickers on everything. It means more than merely singing "Don't worry; be happy." Having a positive attitude means putting more energy into finding solutions than fretting about the problems. In *On Course* terms, it means approaching life as a Creator instead of a Victim.

It's not pie in the sky; it's the willingness to bake a cake from scratch.

And it's just more fun to be around folks who are imaginatively constructing instead of impotently complaining.

On Course by Skip Downing advocates approaching life as a Creator instead of a Victim. It sometimes reminds me of Wendy Bagwell's story about when he and his group found themselves unwittingly performing at a church where they were handling snakes. "I said, 'Just look around and find out where the back door is.' She said, 'I already looked, and there ain't none.' I said, 'Reckon where do they want one?'"

Now and then, we all find ourselves in those seemingly impossible situations. We know we can't stay there, but there's no obvious way out, no back door. What matters is that we keep looking for one and, if necessary, are willing to make one. (Just between you, me, and the sledgehammer, it's really kind of fun, isn't it?)

All of our essentials, all of our luxuries, and all of our entertainments are available because mighty many people collaborated to get them manufactured, shipped, and sold.

We probably do not know every person who played a part in the process. If we did know them, we might not understand or even like some of them. That's okay. It's not necessary or important that we understand or like them. What is necessary and important is that you and I supply our piece of the puzzle and appreciate everyone who does the same. What is necessary and important is that we cooperate. Participate, appreciate, and cooperate. That leaves little time or inclination for side trips down the low road.

When Hannibal was going to spend some time with my folks, we would usually meet halfway at a restaurant just off the freeway.

One time when we were all loaded and about to head out, Hannibal hopped out of my parents' car and trotted over to me. I rolled the window down. He said, "You know how to get out of here, right?"

He wasn't trying to be funny. He was genuinely concerned. He'd been with me on more than one occasion when I got back on the road headed in the wrong direction. Instead of an internal compass, I was given a Magic 8-Ball with a single message: "Reply hazy try again." Hannibal was only six years old, but I'd long since learned to trust his sense of direction.

Sometimes it seems like we are going the right way, and it takes a well-meaning trusted other to convince us otherwise.

Hale Yes

Last Friday afternoon at the grocery store, a short, elderly woman asked a tall young man—a stranger—if he would "Reach me that box of seasoning on the next shelf up?" He did, and they exchanged pleasantries. (I would have been happy to fetch it for her, but *tall* and *young* aren't exactly bullet points on my résumé.)

Those are the kind of folks I mostly run into, day in and day out. There was no discussion of politics, just two people interacting civilly.

There have always been lunatics at the fringes. They get their 15 minutes then go away. Some in the cheaper media, click-bait cons, and way too many FB posters would have us believe that these knotheads represent the norm. They may trigger a knee-jerk response before our brains engage, but we know better.

We can surrender our peace to a pack of strangers, that's a choice. We can choose blind outrage or see it for what it is. We can rail against and we can pray for. (I'm guessing that one of those choices will lead to lower blood pressure—and likely do more lasting good.)

As we all continue to advocate for our various causes, this approach might give us some extra energy and perspective to do so more effectively.

"Are you sure this is the right road, the best way?"

"Sure. Siri, Google Maps, and that guy at the gas station all agree."

As they top a hill, traffic is at a standstill. Flashing lights, various vehicles backed up for miles.

Trooper: "The bridge is out. You'll have to reroute. Turn around and take State Podunk Path 11."

"Well, diddley-dang!"

(Few miles later...)

"This is really a pretty drive, isn't it?"

"Yeah, and there's no grim-faced maniac on our bumper doing 90."

"Those people on the porch, they waved at us. They don't even know us."

"Have you ever wanted to just slow down, calm down, and hang around some folks who know who they are and give a hoot who you are?"

"Where were we going in such a hell-bent hurry?"

"Can't even remember. Let's stay here."

What seems like a major obstacle can be a re-routing (maybe even a shortcut) to where we really want to go.

"Today, sadly, hate appears to be winning."

That's from one of those pitiful posts that tries to make it sound like friendly folks are the underdogs. We're urged to copy and paste.

Hate appears to be winning? Hate does appear to be playing and scoring a few points here and there, but winning? Not even close.

Hate appears to be winning? I'm not seeing it. In my own little world, day in and day out, at home, at work, on the road, and in the stores, I can't remember the last time I saw an act of blatant hatred. What I do see, almost daily, is someone—often someone who has been unfairly stereotyped—trot ahead to open a door for me. "Here, let me get that." I see strangers interacting politely. When the chips are down, around the world, I see thousands of good people willing to help, hurrying to help in any way they can. Who's winning?

Hate winning? Impossible because hate is a loser's game.

Logistically and realistically, it could not possibly have happened. That didn't keep it from being repeated as fact down through the years. I knew and know it didn't happen because I just made it up out of thin air, a nine-year-old kid's attempt at humor. The more it was repeated, the truer it became. People who were not there shared vivid memories of it, and even spared me the burden of embellishing it. Three decades later, when I fessed up and admitted the fiction, the news was greeted with, "It did so happen; I remember it."

The metaphors flow like a mighty river. Reminds me of Mark Twain discussing his keen memory: "When I was younger I could remember anything, whether it happened or not."

Had it really happened, it would have been funny. Now, it's even funnier that it didn't.

A friend told me about a semi-regular feature that used to be on CBS. The segment was called "Everybody has a Story."

The notion intrigued me, so for the last couple of weeks I've tried hard to hush and hear. For the most part, it's true. Everybody has a story...or two or ten.

More important than the entertainment and inspiration of good stories, people need to tell them. Beyond that, people need to be listened to. We all love a good story and we all love to be heard.

Almost every time we do active listening exercises in class, a student will say or write that it was the first time anyone ever really listened to them. The first time. As sad as that is, what a grand thing to be able to do for someone.

"See your obstacles as opportunities."

That's not as easy as it sounds, to say the least, but we know from experience that it's worth the effort.

An obstacle can be a physical limitation or a limiting belief.

We can use our obstacles as excuses and legitimately so, but that wears thin. We can also use them to spark our creativity. "Okay, here's the situation. What can I do in spite of it?" We can look for and often discover alternatives. We can focus more on what we can do instead of leading with our limitations. We can be unwilling to allow our situation to sabotage our wellbeing. It can be fun (or at least interesting) and rewarding. We can use our obstacles to wall us in or to build our confidence.

We can acknowledge that our obstacles, our problems, do not make us unique. Everyone has them. Anyone who is alive on Planet Earth is dealing, has dealt, or will deal with something unsavory. We do not have to look far to find someone with whom we would not want to trade places.

It's more satisfying to be a thinker upper than a bogger downer.

For years, I wore Red Wing work boots. One day, at a little shop in El Paso, I found a little brass bell that had a most pleasant ding. Back home, I took a length of dental floss and tied the bell to one of my boot loops. No one could see the bell, but most could hear it, if only just barely. When someone noticed the bell, I could often see it in their eyes—distracted, curious. I don't know how many people asked me, "Do you have a cat?" (People who knew darn good and well that I didn't have a cat.) If someone mentioned hearing a bell, I'd sometimes pretend to not hear it.

The bell, especially after folks found out where it was, always received a happy reaction. Something pleasant, harmless, and unexpected. I like that.

"Anything that can go wrong will go wrong."

Well, aren't we a bluebird this morning? What kind of downer dog howl is that?

"It's Murphy's Law. You've heard of it?"

Sure, I've heard of it. I've heard of lots of stuff that doesn't make sense.

"Hey, man, it is what it is."

Okay, so what is it? Let's take a cue from our old pal, M.C. Hammer, and Break It Down.

"Please stop dancing like that."

Sorry, didn't think anyone was watching. Anyway, you said anything that can go wrong will go wrong?

"Right."

Anything? Day to day, most of the things that could go wrong, don't. When's the last time all four tires exploded? When's the last time your pen even ran out of ink? So "anything that can" is out.

Go wrong? How often has something that seemed to go wrong led to a lesson learned, an insight gained, a confidence strengthened, a new opportunity? Things going "wrong" is a vital part of the learning process. How many things did you get right the first time? We would not have Silly Putty, potato chips, or penicillin if something hadn't gone "wrong."

Law? It's not a law by any definition I can find. Moses never mentioned it, nor has any serious scientist. It's not on the books of any nation, state, or municipality.

What it is: Murphy's opinion. Don't know about you, but I'd like to get a second opinion.

Remember that George Jones song, "Who's Gonna Fill Their Shoes?" There are some good lines in that one. My favorite is "Who's gonna give their heart and soul to get to me and you?" The great ones, the hall of famers, are not and were not merely looking for praise, money, or a gold record. They do it because they love it, because it's what they do. They're acting on purpose instead of outcome, and they share it with a missionary zeal & a childlike joy. They give their heart and soul and let the chips fall.

There's not a hall of fame for what most of us do, and that's okay because that's not why we do it. "Who's gonna give their heart and soul to get to me and you?" That nurse you'll never forget. That teacher who made a difference. That stranger who helped you just because. That pastor who kept you in one piece when your world was falling apart. That convenience store clerk who started your day with a smile. That trucker who blasted his air horn for your kid. That librarian who turned you on to your new favorite writer. That letter carrier who risked heatstroke, hypothermia, and thunderstorms to keep your good news dry and bring it to your house. That mechanic who said, "Nah, it's just a two-dollar fuse" when you would have believed the worst. That nice woman at the college who took you under her wing and showed you how to navigate the system. That friend who said, "If you need anything" and really meant it. And on and on...

No one is going to fill George Jones's shoes. Or yours.

Of late, I'd rather stroll than stomp
Most days I'd rather rest than romp
Wild was fun, and so is tame
The pleasure level is the same

We discover wondrous things
When we spread or fold our wings
Raising hell is such a lift
Landing safe's an equal gift

The past's a blast with much to give
But it's a lousy place to live
Grin for then, but then return

Hale Yes

Still much to love and yet to learn

We're off to see the world, no doubt
Dig the treasure, jump and shout
Of all the fortunes we can find
The Holy Grail is peace of mind

"You can lead a horse to water, but you can't make it drink."

A thirsty horse will drink. Why would you want to make it drink if it's not thirsty? If it's dying of thirst and still won't drink, you have bigger problems. Blaming the horse will not help. Sounds like someone doesn't know their horse very well.

Using a cliché to explain or dismiss certain human behaviors is just as counterproductive. It's lazy. It's a refusal to find and confront the real concerns.

For example, a student without a thirst, a perceived need, for knowledge is not going to cooperate with much of anything we offer. "But we're giving them state-of-the-art technology." Big deal. They don't want it.

We're the professionals, so it falls to us to find out why, to identify the problems and address them. Is it a lack of motivation? A lack of confidence? A skills gap? A mindset? Could we explain something better or remove a barrier? We know how to do all that stuff, and at my school we do. Step one is getting to know them.

No doubt there are similar examples in every profession, every area of life. "We told them it was Truck Month. We had balloons and everything, but a lot of people still didn't buy one. What are they, just stupid?" Sounds like someone doesn't know their customer very well.

(Maybe there's a snake we missed in the creek and the horse has better sense than we do. "I ain't drinkin nothin till you get rid of that thing.")

ASSORTED SILLINESS

Tom, you always make people smile!
~Gayla Stidham

"You can't have your cake and eat it too."
Don't be silly. Of course you can.
"How so?"
If you eat it, you still have it; it just changes form and location. You still possess it.
"Yes, but for how long—if you get my drift."
You didn't say anything about having it forever. Point is, you can indeed eat it and still have it. All the ingredients will break down and nourish various parts of you. Those little egg atoms and milk molecules will be with you for quite some time. Besides, doesn't having it mean eating it?
"I'm not following."
If Aunt Bessie says, "Here, have a piece of cake," is she expecting you to sit there and stare at it, or does she intend for you to eat it? Be kind of rude not to. You cannot have a piece of cake without eating it.
"Just never mind, okay?"

I was named after my mother's father. My legal name is Grandpa.

One evening in the towboat galley, I told what I thought was a pretty good joke. A single member of the deck crew laughed and applauded. Everyone else just stared at me like I'd lost my mind. The joke bombed, never a fun thing. On the up side, I have heard the sound of one hand clapping.

Whew, that was close. Marie Laveau just tried to put a hex on me via text message. Fortunately spellcheck caught it.

True story: When we were kids, I had to sleep under my older brother's bed. John had the top bunk.

An article in *Inside Higher Education* contained this sentence: "'Cultural fears compound economic ones' under the combined demographic pressures of immigration and an aging citizenry."

An aging citizenry? When have we not had an aging citizenry? As far back as I can remember, there have always been people older than me. Of course, folks didn't live as long back then as they did in those days. Maybe that's what they mean. And these kids today are growing up so fast. I have a friend who recently turned 50. When I was her age, I was only 47. So, I guess it makes sense. Yeah, that aging population can really touch off some demographic pressure. Whew!

Did you ever wash your socks, T-shirts, and underwear in a motel sink then roll them up in the car windows and let them flap-dry as you drove?

"Ah, yes. I remember those youthful bygone days on the road."

Bygone? I'm talking about this morning.

"Great way to save some quarters."

It also makes your car easy to find in the parking lot.
"And it negates the expense of a car alarm."
Really. Nothing says "keep moving" like a damp pair of skivvies.

We are experiencing nitwit difficulties. Please stand by.
"Did you check to see if it's plugged in?"
Yes, it's plugged in!
"Try unplugging it."
Okay. How's that?
"I found your problem: it's unplugged."

A bright, young friend told me that a good way to keep an aging mind nimble is to do routine tasks in new and different ways. An example she gave is to "brush your teeth with your nondominant hand."
I tried that and it was interesting, but I still prefer a toothbrush.

There's a Halloween labyrinth in an Alabama cornfield. From the air, you can see that the layout is in the shape of the Baseball Hall of Famer known as "The Say Hey Kid." It's the Willie Mays maize maze.

What ever happened to good, solid, old-fashioned Biblical names? You hardly ever see a kid named Nahum anymore. Yeah, names used to mean something.
"What does Nahum mean?"
That's what singing horses do when they forget the words. Gads, didn't they teach you anything in school? With your kind indulgence, I'd like to suggest some other Biblical names, along with their meanings (all references KJV):

Zebedee: In ancient Babylonia, Zebedee was the Keeper of the Doo-Dah. (Matthew 4:21)

Shethar: Sailors in Biblical times paid little attention to adverb/pronoun order, even when speaking English. Shethar came from a familiar response our nautical friends gave to the question, "Where does she blow?" (Esther 1:14)

Zadok: Even Vulcans have Biblical names. (2 Samuel 8:17)

Parnach: Another Vulcan. (Numbers 34:25)

Keturah: Hey, Klingons too! (1 Chronicles 1:32)—check out the names of her kids.

Puah: Another Klingon. Puah was the son of Dodo. It just wasn't very intimidating: "I am Puah, son of Dodo!" The other kids gave him a really hard time. (Judges 10:1)

Shaashgaz: What Jumpin Jack Flash was back in the day. (Esther 2:14)

Eldad: Means "father" to someone who flunked Spanish I. (Numbers 11:26)

Raamah: The King of Lama-Ding-Dong. (Genesis 10:7)

Zerubbabel: That's someone who just drank a whole firkin of wine trying to say "Jerusalem." (1 Chronicles 3:19) (See also John 2:6)

Elzaphan: Same guy trying to say "elephant." (Exodus 6:22)

Rakkon: Ancient French for "raccoon." (Joshua 19:46)

Pekah: Official charged with keeping track of how many pickled peppers Peter Piper picked. (2 Kings 15:29)

Suppose you are blessed with triplets & suppose they're of the male persuasion. How about

Shem, **Ham**, and **Japheth**? (After Shem retired, it was Curly, Ham, and Japheth.)

Mibzar: A cousin of the Coneheads (1 Chronicles 1:53)

Jozadak: Something Drill Sergeants can yell in G-Rated movies. (Ezra 3:8)

Iphedeiah Shashak: That Drill Sergeant's really ticked! (1 Chronicles 8:25)

Maadiah: Comedy routine in which the part of a feisty elderly woman is played by a young man. (Nehemiah 12:5)

Yes, friends and neighbors, names used to mean something, and with your help they can again.

Next time you take a sick day and have to give a reason, tell them you had an ataraxia attack. "I'd better stay home; this might be contagious."

Vampires? Get outta here. But wait. I may have turned into one: I walked past a mirror and did not see my reflection. I did see a reflection, but it wasn't mine. It was some old guy. Gave me the willies, man. Had to sleep with the lights on.

Pringles has a new flavor—new to me, anyway: Tangy Buffalo Wing. I brought some to work. One of my office buddies walking past said, "What's that you're eating?"

I said, "Tangy buffalo chips."

As a thought, it gave me no pause, but as soon as I heard it aloud and it was too late to get it back...

On the bright side, no one else wanted any.

This will be a new word to some: Shing. What would you guess it means?

"That's easy: ♫ Shing a shong of shixpence, a pocket full of rye... ♪"

Nice try, but no. If you're from the Arkansas Delta, shing means she can. This afternoon at the convenience store, I was behind a woman with a small child. The kid was holding a couple of Tootsie Roll Pops. The woman told the little boy to "Put 'em on the counter so shing ring 'em up."

The only hard part of doing radio in El Paso and Austin was trying to lose my accent. It's always fun to be back where I speak and understand the native language. Nodameen?

A lot of folks do air quotes when they talk. You hardly ever see anyone making air italics.

When I was 10, we moved from the Delta to the Desert; east Arkansas to El Paso, Texas. The Sun City. It always cracked Mom up when someone said, "Yeah, but it's a dry heat..." She'd say something like, "Well, good Lord, so is a toaster oven. That doesn't make it any more comfortable."

Hale Yes

Back in Arkansas one time, someone asked if it ever snowed in El Paso. Mom said, "Yeah, but it's a dry snow, so you don't notice it."

This week on "Most Dangerous Catch," a local prophet was swallowed by a giant fish. According to witnesses, he was thus confined for three days and three nights before he was unceremoniously deposited on a beach in Nineveh.

We asked Jonah what was going through his mind during his watery ordeal.

The prophet did not immediately respond. He just looked at us like maybe he thought we were stupid or something.

Fun time at the Dentist's office yesterday afternoon. Couple of fillings. The Dentist poked around a while then said to his assistant, "C-4." I remarked that that sounded dangerous. He assured me it was just a shade—they try to match the amalgam to the surrounding atrocities. With the kind assistance of the nitrous oxide, I amused myself with the idea of a Dentist filling teeth with C-4. Next time you bite into a crunchy taco or clinch your teeth, your head blows off. That might make for a most effective diet/stress relief combo. Dare we risk an Oreo?

How goofy is it getting out there? I can tell you this: It's worse than it really is. Now and then, if I get to feeling too sane, I'll check the Yahoo "news" page. This morning, I was stopped dead in my tracks when I saw this sobering headline: "Costco has just made it more expensive for 35 million people to shop for giant mustard bottles."

Curse you, Costco! At first, I wasn't too choked up about it because my current giant mustard bottle is still half full. (Or is it half empty?) As comforting as that is, what about when it runs out around oh, say 2023? Will I be willing or even able to pay more for the next one? Am I facing a future that holds the unpleasant prospect of hotdogs with ketchup? Will I by then be too old to cut the mayo?

Few if any of us, and understandably so, are easily consoled when it comes to the cost of our condiments. Times like these put our faith to the test. Faith is a personal matter, and I'll not pretend to tell you where to place yours. As for me, I'm putting mine in Save-A-Lot.

Just for fun, I stopped by my doctor's office to ask him how *he* was feeling.

Monday is Goody Day at work. They've started a list of who plans to bring what. One reason for the list is to make sure that not too many folks show up with potato salad because, "let's face it, there are only so many ways to make the stuff."

Well, they've never had my special recipe: Couch Potato Salad. It's made only with ingredients that one can reach from or find behind the cushions of the sofa—cold pizza, popcorn, stray Milk Duds, Pop Tart parts, crust from a ... (sniff) ... baloney sandwich, Cheez Ballz, anything that doesn't have too much fuzz stuck to it. That's what I'm bringing.

These elitist knuckleheads gettin all nostalgic about old TV shows, drinkin out of a hose, and ridin in the back of a truck!

Well, not all of us were that lucky, mister. We didn't have a TV back then. If we wanted to see somethin in black & white, we had to discuss politics. And if we wanted to drink out of a hose, that's all we could do: want to. Ride in the back of a pickup truck? Ride? Hell, we lived in a flipped over pickup truck bed. I can tell you a thing or two about tailgatin. It's like my old grand-pappy used to say, he'd look at me and say, "Which one of them damn kids are you?"

We didn't need Silly Putty and hula hoops. We made our own fun. We made fun of each other.

This is fun, and I've yet to see it fail: The next time you and a friend are outdoors and other people are around—between classes, in a park, the Walmart parking lot, etc.—stop and look up. Keep looking up at the same spot. Other folks will stop and look up too. It's dang near irresistible. The activity can be embellished by pointing and making comments such as, "Oh, man." or "I ain't believin this." Or you can act like you're watching a skywriter. Spell it out: "S-U-R-R-E-N-D-E-R D-O-R-O-T-H-Y."

Free entertainment.

My uncle, Pat O'Reilly, had an important position at St. Mary's.
"Oh, really?"
No, O'Reilly.
"What was his responsibility at St. Mary's?"
He was in charge of the bells.
"In charge of the bells. What did he do with the bells?"
He tolled them.
"What did he tell them?"
He didn't tell them, he tolled them.
"He didn't tell them, he told them?"
That's correct.
"What happened when he told them?"
It made them clang.
"He'd tell them and they would clang?"
He didn't tell them to clang, he made them clang.

"How did he make them clang?"
By clinging.
"Your uncle would cling and the bells would clang?"
Yes. He'd cling to the rope and pull on it. That made the bells clang.
"Is he still in charge of the bells?"
No, he died.
"I'm sorry to hear that. How'd he die?"
One day he missed the rope.
"Who's in charge of the bells now?"
They hired his twin brother.
"Your uncle had a twin?"
Yes, but his brother no longer had one.
"They hired his twin because his brother was—"
That's right: He was a dead ringer.

I know some who like it hot. I know some who like it cold. But I've yet to meet anyone who likes it in the pot nine days old.

The last thing on my bucket list: Kick the bucket.

People axe me, they say, "Tom, what do you do to relive stress and anxiety?"

I tell 'em I don't want to relive it; I want to relieve it.

"That's what I meant. Dadgum autocorrect... Thanks, Obama!"

Relax, man. Here's what I do: Since it is impossible to be grateful and anxious at the same time, I mentally review a litany of all the things I am thankful for.

"But what about when the burdens of this ol' world weigh so heavy that they preclude that level of concentration?"

Plan B—and this always works: I carry with me, at all times, a helium-filled balloon (most florists have them).

Whenever I get tired of livin and scared of dyin, I take a deep breath of helium and sing "Old Man River."

Woman in the office: "Eighties hair is coming back."
Guy in the office: "I wish my Eighties hair would come back."

As a wee lad, I once got in trouble for writing my name, with a stick, in the fresh cement of a new sidewalk. When I got my degree from the University of Arkansas, class of '97—
"1897?"
1997! When I got my degree from U of A in 1997, they paid a state employee to etch my name in the sidewalk—they do that for all graduates.
Lesson: When we toot our own horn, it sounds a sour note. If we accomplish something, earn it, someone else will notice and do it for us. And do a much better job of it.

Another fun trip to the Dentist Office.
After the procedures, I told them I needed some nitrous oxide to go. I bet you can guess how well that worked.
When settling the bill, I explained that my new partial is actually a refill, so there should be a discount. There wasn't.
They make up for these inconveniences by being some of the nicest folks you'd ever care to meet. They all do an above and beyond job of everything, and make you feel welcome and comfortable all the while. Heck of a deal.

Event Planning in Heaven:
"This is going to be the best costume party ever. We were able to obtain a planet between Venus and Mars. This happening has a novel feature: It will last so long

that everyone will forget what's going on and start thinking it's the—for lack of a better term—real world. The fun will be not in guessing who everyone else is but in trying to figure out who *you* really are. There will be plenty of clues, but folks will interpret them any number of bizarre ways. It'll be such a hoot to see how we react without the security of knowing. I'd be willing to bet that many, if not most, of us will be tricked into thinking we're somehow better than the others, and we'll express it in the most outrageous ways—skin color, hoarded resources, gender (I'll explain what that means later; oh, it's hysterical)—and we'll use this new wrinkle we're calling 'twisted logic' to support our positions. We'll call our conclusions facts, seriously, while rarely digging deeper to see if how we construe the clues makes a lick of sense. You think the Dark Matter Fun House was weird? You ain't seen nothin yet."

Maybe I'm not perfect, but neither am I impeccable. Flaws? Sure, I have some, and ceilings too. These gray hairs are merely evidence that all the pigment abandoned ship because I'm so dang old. These scars? I earned them. Well, deserved them, anyway. Each of them tells a story— not a true story necessarily, but a story doesn't have to be true in order to be boring. Wrinkles? I prefer to call them smile maps, or gross disruptions in the space/time continuum.

"Cut! C'mon, man. This is supposed to be inspiring; it's meant to highlight all the advantages of being an old ... a person of advanced years, brim-full of life lessons and old-timey wisdom. Let's try it again, please. Take 37!"

Oh, if I knew now what I knew then, I could tell you a thing or two. For example, I could tell you my middle name without having to look at my license. I no longer care what others think of me because I probably won't remember it tomorrow anyway. People call us geezers and old fogies, but I prefer "Rusty Rascals" or "Antique-Americans."

"Cut! (fume, cuss, kick stuff). Look, this isn't gonna work. But thanks for coming in."

We had the best music and the best cars. We were the coolest generation.

"No, you didn't; and no, you weren't."

Says who?

"Just about everyone who's at least 20 years younger than you. Really, we appreciate you trying—"

I could tell about how we rode in the back of a pickup truck.

"It can't be that tricky."

We used to drink out of a dirty hose.

"Why?"

Well, the dogs had dibs on the mud puddles.

"It's a wonder you're still alive."

Yeah, let's work the miracle angle. Mine that vein.

"Can't you tell me even one advantage to being a...an Antique American?"

I'm having more fun than you are. I bet your blood pressure is through the roof.

"Why, you Rusty Rascal. You've just been yanking my chain, right?"

Only because you make it so easy.

Overheard at the masquerade ball:
"What happens incognito stays incognito."
Neato.

He said, "After a while, you reach a point of diminishing returns with these old things. The parts wear out faster than you can replace them—if you can even find them. At that point, it really is cheaper, in the long run, to just get a new one."

"Your mechanic said that?"

No, that was my doctor.

(There's been a recall on certain models. Airbags are deploying indiscriminately.)

Facebook is fun. In the old days, if I wanted to show a photo of what I had for lunch, I had to take a picture with my Instamatic camera, take the film to the drugstore, and wait dang near a week to get the pictures back. As often as not, the baloney was blurred and the bread was fuzzy. Okay, in all fairness, the bread really was fuzzy. Then pick the best picture, put it in an envelope, address the envelope, buy a stamp, lick the stamp, stick it on the envelope, and hand it over to a uniformed representative of the United States Government. It could take up to two weeks to get a friend's response. Still, there was a sweet misery in the delayed gratification, and the payoff was worth the wait when you ripped opened that letter and read the handwritten words: "Looks yummy!"

It's like my old grand pappy used to say: "Never be in so great a hurry that you can't take time to make haste."

"I'll tell you how the cow ate the cabbage!"

They chew their cabbage twice, right?

"Well, I don't! I tell it like it is!"

Tell the cows. Bet they'd love to know how to do it properly.

"You don't know which side your bread is buttered on!"

That's why I drop it. The buttered side hits the floor.

"I'll tell you one damn thing!"

Don't hold back. Tell me two damn things.

"Let me just give you a piece of my mind!"
No, thanks. I'd rather have peace of mind.

Some folks just can't be out suffered. Probably one in every office. No matter how bizarre things get in your life, they give you a been-there-done-that eye roll, smirk, and nod.

"I've got double pneumonia and a broken leg, but I've got that meeting at 9, so I thought I'd better be here."

Eye roll-smirk-nod. "Tell me about it. While you're at it, tell Noah about the flood."

"There was a gas leak in our neighborhood. My house blew up; my car caught on fire; I walked to work and got mugged along the way."

Eye roll-smirk-nod. "Hey, welcome to *my* world."

"I've been diagnosed with terminal epidermal. Their most optimistic prognosis is that I won't live past noon today."

Eye roll-smirk-nod. "If that was my biggest problem, I'd feel blessed."

Some folks just can't be out suffered. But it's fun to try.

5-10-15

Last Friday, a dog in Mountain Home, Arkansas ate 17 bullets and had to be taken in for emergency surgery. We contacted the vet via email. She told us that the first thing she had to do was check the dog's shot records. "Luckily he wasn't a Cocker Spaniel: we'd of had to remove his firing pin."

What kind of dog was it?

"Obviously a muzzle loader."

Was surgery really necessary?

"First, we tried to induce projectile vomiting, but that didn't work."

Couldn't you have—how to put this delicately? —just waited for nature to take its course?

"You're referring to an ammo dump. No, with that many, we were afraid he might bust a cap in his ass."

How's the dog now?

"He was fine last time I made my rounds."

In a situation like that, I guess you have to act quickly.

"That's right; gotta get the lead out."

For a while, I worked as a window washer, but it was just something to see me through.

Going over my FB friend list, I was pleased and gratified to find that there's not a normal one in the bunch. Also apparent was the happy fact that we all, at least once a year, have a birthday.

You are creative, unconventional folks. The things the rest do routinely? You find a better, or at least a different, way to do them. Surely you do not want to extinguish your candles the way everyone else does, so let me offer these alternatives:

A leaf blower.

Water balloons.

Get an IRS auditor to suck all the oxygen out of the room.

Beat them with a wet burlap bag.

Snip the wicks and freeze the flames for next year.

Cuss them out.

A bullwhip (blindfold optional).

Get Smoky Bear to whop them with his shovel.

Maxine Pope suggested inviting the Big Bad Wolf.

A well-charged seltzer bottle.

A handful of baking soda and a pan lid.

Stop, drop, and roll on the cake.

This morning, I posted a picture of the cowgirl guitar. Sandy commented, "There has GOT to be a story about this guitar."

Indeed there is, Sandy, and it's a story I've never told until now:

Kerri Oakley was a waitress at the Cowgirl Café in Santa Fe, New Mexico. I was with a group of 10. We were all impressed by how Kerri took our orders, including complicated substitutions, without writing anything down. I convinced Kerri that she could make more money teaching memory techniques to nursing students—they have to memorize every bone and muscle in the human body, and that's just for starters.

I lined up the events and we hit the road doing memory training seminars. Kerri taught me how to remember and even how to premember. She helped me improve my memory so well that I could remember things that happened before I was born (you might be surprised how off some of the history books are). This went on for a year.

At a pawnshop in Cheyenne, Wyoming, Kerri bought me a cowgirl guitar to commemorate how and where we met. We enjoyed sitting around the campfire and singing cowgirl songs. One day at dawn, Kerri said she had to go.

"How come?"

"I'm waking up. I'm dreaming this. It's been fun."

"But it's been a year. You've been dreaming for a year? That don't make no sense."

"No, silly. Nobody sleeps for a year. You know how flexible time is in a dream. Something that seems to last for hours can take mere seconds in waking time."

Well, I had to admit she was right. "I also know how quickly dreams fade once we wake up, no matter how hard you try to hang on to them. I don't want to ever forget this one."

She shrugged. "So take your guitar with you. It'll keep the memory fresh."

I tried not to smirk. Yeah, right. The scene faded into a pastel rainbow fog. Kerri Oakley was gone and I woke up in my own bed.

I walked, in the loosest sense of the word, in to the kitchen. There, leaning against the counter next to the coffee pot, was the cowgirl guitar. You wanna know what's weird? I picked up the guitar and played "Malagueña." No mistakes, no hesitation. Before I went to bed the previous night, the trickiest thing I could pick out was a halting, multi-blunder rendition of "Wildwood Flower."

That's the story about the guitar. To learn to play it well, I didn't have to go to the Crossroads, I just had to go to sleep.

One cool thing about FB is that people can't hijack your jokes or derail the conversation. They'll either read it to the end or they won't, but they won't step on the punchline. It's getting harder these days to set up a joke, especially if you pause for effect. No matter what you say, it reminds someone else of something, something they must tell you about and right now. Even a simple joke, like this one: A horse walks into a bar. The bartender says, "Hey, buddy, why the long face?" Should be easy, right? Here's how it's more likely to go:

A horse walks int—

"Oh, I love horses! When I was 8 or maybe 9—I was in third grade, but I started late because I was born in October. Go Libras, right? Anyway, we had the sweetest horse! Oh, I miss him. His name was Pandayho. That's Spanish for something; I don't remember what. I have a knack for foreign languages; I love 'em all, but probably French the most. Capiche? Anyway, you were saying?"

Yeah, a horse walks into a bar. The bartender says—

"You were a bartender, right? What's the best margarita recipe? How do they make those blue ones? Okay, so a horse goes to a bar? That's weird. And the bartender is talking to it? That's crazy."

It's a joke; it didn't really happen.

"Oh, I love jokes. Tell me one."

Knock-knock.

"Hey, do those religious people ever come around, knocking on the door on Saturday morning? I hate to be rude, but good Lord! I'm still in my pajamas. Did you know they still make 'em with feet in 'em for grown-ups? Yeah. They. Are. So. Comfortable! What's in a Harvey Wallbanger?"

Anyone who wants to improve their listening skills should spend some time in our office building. Listening will be your only choice. Forget saying anything. The women I work with will not allow you to get more than one word in edgewise. This is not a literal transcript, but a representative example of how a typical "conversation" might go:

"Someone said that in the 21st century you'd be considered illiterate if you couldn't learn, unlearn, and relearn. Who was that?"

I knew and tried to say so: "Alvin—"

"Oh, I loved the Chipmunks, especially that one about wanting a hula hoop."

"We took hula lessons when we were in Maui. It's a great workout. We stayed at the Royal Wahine. Their breakfast luau is to die for. They serve this dish called poi polloi. I'm taro-intolerant, but I could pick out the bits of pineapple and eat those."

"Surfing looks like fun."

(This was a good opening for an old joke about water skiing, but I knew better than to try.)

"'Book 'em, Danno.' I loved that show."

"Have you seen *Beauty and the Beast*, the new one? It is so good."

Anyone who wants to improve their writing skills should spend some time in our office building. Writing is the only way you can communicate. I sent them a one-word email: "Toffler."

By then, the subject had changed 19 times, so I had to explain in a follow-up email that included this postscript: "We wanted to try water skiing, but we couldn't find a lake on a hill."

(My office buddies are good folks and fun to be around.)

Our office building is perfect for a lazy person like me. I don't even have to finish my own sentences. All I've got to do is start one.

"Hey, did you see—"

"That dog on *Fido's Got Talent*? Wasn't that hilarious?"

"Who'd of thought a dog could—"

"Tap dance on the sidewalk at night with bottle caps on his feet, making sparks fly!"

"The bottle caps were held on—"

"With rubber bands."

"Where you—"

"Going for lunch? Subway. Want me to bring you back something?"

"How 'bout—"

"Tuna on chili-cheese bread. With jalapeños."

"And maybe—"

"A chocolate chip cookie. I had a cat named Cookie one time. She was the sweetest kitty. We found her in a dumpster out back of the liquor store. The poor thing just reeked of cheap whiskey, covered in snuff juice and sardine oil."

"There's a country song just waiting to be—"

"Written. I love Loretta Lynn."

"Ever hear Johnny Cash sing Coal Miner's—"

"Daughter? No! That would be awful."

"It did lack authen—"

"Ticity. I know, right? I mean, he was from Arkansas. There aren't any coal mines in Arkansas..."

It's easy to get ho-hum about something as common and readily available as chicken, but I saw an ad today for some really special fried chicken. What makes it so special? Are you sitting down? It's "Hand Breaded." I don't care where you're from, you gotta admit that's better than foot breaded. Amen?

As grand as that is, just a few more questions: Whose hands? Were they washed recently? Were they human hands? Were they handy-dandy or hand-me-down? Any finger lickin goin on? Thumbs up or thumbed noses? Any bird flipping involved? Did they knuckle down or knuckle under? Did they wear gloves? If so, were they plastic gloves or baseball gloves? Were they slaphappy or slapdash? Just trying to get a grip on this whole process.

Ever pull up to the drive-thru or try to phone in an order and you can't understand a word they're saying? Next time, don't get all in a dither, have fun with it. Try one of these:

Yeah, let me get a dust buster with extra calories.

I have a coupon for 15% off a free one.

I'd like something from your dollar menu: how about
four quarters?

Curly, Larry, and Moe fries—and a chili-cheese Sprite.

We'll have the same thing as the car behind us, and
they're paying.

A Whopper Junior and a Whopper Sophomore.

A large pizza with medium toppings—and can you
trim the crust?

Are your salads crouton-free?

Half pepperoni and half mushroom, half large and
half small.

A bed of lettuce and some of that stuff that dreams
are made of.

Two small mediums and a four-pronged
Nebuchadnezzar.

A large camel spin with a half twist and a triple
Salchow.

We're going green: We brought our own wrappers and
sack.

A more-than-happy meal.

In a recent survey of Harvard and MIT students, none
of them could find Atlantis on a map. Nor could any of
them plot a course for the Neutral Zone. (We need to get
back to the basics, folks.) Most surprisingly, not a single
one of these eggheads knew who put the ram in the rama-
lama-ding-dong or who put the dip in the dip-di-dip-di-
dip. Admittedly, what we really want to know is who put
the ding-dong in the dip, but first things first. Geez
Louise.

Some Facebook posters seem to find it difficult to get
our attention without resorting to hyperbole. And it's
almost always a letdown. Fairly reliable rule of thumb: All

caps or more than one exclamation mark = it's not really that funny, fascinating, or heart-rending.

Here are a few examples I've seen already today:

"You'll do a double take!!" (I already did a double take when I walked past the bathroom mirror.)

"Your jaw will hit the floor!!" (That seems like reason enough not to watch.)

"You won't believe what happens next!!!" (You're probably right. I don't even believe what's happening now.)

"Stop whatever your [sic] doing and watch this!!!!" (I wasn't doing anything...kind of hard to stop that.)

"This is the most touching/inspiring thing you'll see all day!!" (Let me guess: Someone used a 3-D printer to make a new tail for a bulldog.)

"Harvard graduates could not answer these 5 questions, but rhesus monkeys get them right every time!!! How smart are you?!!!" (I don't want my intelligence evaluated by anyone who uses more than one exclamation point.)

"Can you find the hidden frog?!" (Not if it's hidden well enough.)

"I can't stop laughing!!!!" (Unless you're reading about Texas politics or visiting a Colorado Welcome Center, you might want to seek professional help.)

"Fine, just fine." "Oh, pretty good, how about your own self?" Been mighty glad lately to run into some folks I haven't seen in a while. (Cousin Linda and I didn't totally block a whole aisle at the grocery store a while ago, but we made it a tight squeeze for the other jolly shoppers. It was good to get caught up with her a bit.) There's always the "How are you" question, and my responses, even as I said them, sounded pretty weak. Need at least one new one.

I pondered it on the drive home and settled on something Mom used to say: "We're just as happy as if we had good sense."

Perfume popular with the Camptown ladies: Eau de doo-dah.

Aspendale, our church camp, was about five miles SW of Cloudcroft, New Mexico. Our youth group from El Paso went there every chance we got.

Aspendale was the perfect setting for a visit with the Hay Man. At night, it gets darker than a licorice jellybean in Satan's sock drawer. You can't see your hand in front of your face—although you could see better if you'd move your hand from in front of your face.

Out from the main lodge, there were some smaller cabins. In one of those cabins, Harvey laid supine on a wooden table, covered with a blanket. Small candles lit the four corners of the table. At the end where Harvey's head was, he held two boots so that it looked like his feet sticking out. At the other end, he had a straw hat over his feet so it looked like that's where his head was.

With dim flashlights, we led small groups of volunteers (not for the squeamish or faint of heart) down the winding path to see the Hay Man. Gravel crunching under their feet and who-knows-what chattering, howling, and creeping though the nearby woods. It was spooky times ten ("Watch out for night snakes!").

Once inside, we directed their attention to the hat and told them they could ask the Hay Man anything, but they must be yes or no questions.

If the answer was no, Harvey would move his feet side to side. If the answer was yes, he'd tilt his toes back and forth so as to resemble a nod.

After a few questions, Harv would sit up, casually prop himself on one elbow, and say, "Hey, man."

Of course, it didn't scare anyone, nor was it meant to. Kind of like acting out a shaggy dog story.

Ice storm! Electricity out = no heat, lights, or coffee maker since Tuesday. Trees busting to pieces and crashing into the road, transformers exploding. Eerie and fun how dark and quiet it really is out there without any manmade distractions. Felt kind of like Daniel Boone— except he probably knew how to keep warm no matter what and how to trap beavers and survive. Took about five minutes for that fantasy to play out. Since then, I've been holed up at the Holiday Hotel. Got the happy news this afternoon that the power is back on! I'd already paid for another night at the hotel & it was too late to cancel, so yes, it's literally true: the lights are on but there's nobody home.

It was a pretty good day, over all. I did mind my p's but disobeyed my q's a couple of times when they weren't looking. Got the i's crossed and t's dotted, for the most part. Wrote some letters of recommendation: I recommended m and n since they're the middle two in the alphabet (and the most common mistake found by the proofreaders at the m&m's plant). We didn't quite make it from A to Z, but we skipped lunch to find X.

Can you get the kit without the caboodle? Or suppose your kit is still in good condition but your old, worn out caboodle needs replacing. Could you get just the one? You never see them advertised separately. Must you acquire the whole thing?

If your stock & barrel are password protected, is there really a need for the extra expense of a lock?

Have you ever used a whole ball of wax? Seems at least half of it ends up in the junk drawer. If you ever need it again and are lucky enough to find it—or even remember it's in there—it's got all kinds of fuzz, rubber bands, and who-knows-what stuck to it, so you toss it and go for a new one. Probably, most of us could make do with a quarter ball. Or we could go halves on one and split it.

There was a fellow on the San Michez online garbage sale site. He had a hook and two lines; wanted to swap one of the lines for a sinker. I had an extra sinker but no line. We both came out ahead. Win-win.

(These things tend to sort themselves out, even when we're out of sorts.)

A few minutes ago, I ordered from Amazon a CD of bagpipe music. It was delivered with a drone.

"Why are they always on their damn phones?!"
Uh...that's how they communicate?
"We just folded notes into little footballs and passed them to our friends!"
Their way seems quicker.
"But they do it during class!"
And when did you pass your paper footballs?
"That's different! Anyhow, the old ways were better!"
Is that why we see so many horses in the parking lot?

I know a psychic pirate; she wears a patch over her third eye.

(She can read your aurrrra! She also does piercings—charges a buck an ear.)

Super moon, 2016:

In lieu of a view of the moon, some folks were sticking flour tortillas in their windows. The similarities can be uncanny. There are, however, some risks:

Nearsighted cows have been known to attempt to jump over them. Which, of course, amuses your dog. (Say goodbye to certain flatware and hey to your diddle-diddle while your cat displays a feline affectation for Johnny Gimble.)

If left up too long, it will become a crescent roll.

You may see George Bailey twirling a rope in your yard. (And Van Morrison dancing.)

Not always, but every now and then, it will turn blue. (Which is fine for corn chips, but not a good sign for a flour tortilla.)

If the wolfbane is blooming, a passerby may turn into a werewolf, who then turns into a Taco Bell.

A family reunion of yore...must have been seven or eight years old. Just horsing around with some cousins... Next thing I know, Mom grabs my arm and spins me around so that we're nearly nose to nose. She's scowling and yelling, "You'd better straighten up and fly right!"

I wasn't sure what that was all about or even what it meant.

Naturally, Dad saw the whole thing from over where he was visiting with some uncles. He came over and asked me what I'd done to get Mom so fired up.

Saying "Nothing" or "I don't know" was out of the question, but I honestly did not know.

So, panic-stricken and sincere, I said, "Ummm...I wasn't flyin right."

"What the hell are you talkin about?"

"Yeah...I was flyin all crooked and stuff."

"Have you lost your mind?"

I said, "Hey! Get off my case! Why didn't you teach me to fly better? I didn't even know I could fly until just now. Is your real name Jor-El? Are we from the planet Krypton?"

Okay, I didn't really say that, just thought it. Something about Dad discouraged that kind of insolence.

That fun memory was triggered by a woman I heard at the grocery store telling her kid to straighten up and fly right. Good advice. Timeless. I gave the woman a sympathetic nod and said, "You have a point, ma'am. That was some less than facile flying. By the time I was his age, I didn't even need shoes anymore."

Okay, I didn't really say that...

On this day in 1896, the first x-ray machine was demonstrated in the United States.

A famous song was written to commemorate the occasion. Can you guess which one?

1.) I'm Looking Through You
2.) You Light Up My Wife
C.) Bone in the USA

At San Michez High School, traditions go way back. How way back? Our mascot is the wooly mammoth. New traditions are not easily greeted, but we booster club members petitioned to try one. We'd seen other schools fire a cannon whenever the home team scores; it looked like fun. Voting was close, but the upshot was to give it a go.

Finding a cannon wasn't easy, but nothing difficult ever is. It didn't work out so well.

Our basketball team would often score again before we could get the thing reloaded—especially the free throws.

On the plus side, we were made aware of some ventilation concerns in the gym.

It was a beautiful display of generosity. The cologne is undoubtedly exotic and expensive, but the guy didn't hold out on the rest of us; he wore enough to share with everyone in the building, and it lingered long after he'd left. I felt blessed to the point of puking.

I'm certainly no connoisseur of cloying outrages, and I'll be the first to admit it, but I believe the name of the fragrance is "Eau de Tell Me of an Uncloudy Day." Or maybe it's just that during the brief window of opportunity between when one's air passages seize and one frantically digs out one's rescue inhaler, one has the time and the inclination to sharply focus on one's mortality.

His benevolent sharing moved me. I desperately wanted to give something in return. But even if there'd been a horse whip handy, I had not the strength to put it to proper use.

♫ "Eau de tell me of a home far beyond the skies, eau de tell me of a home far away..." ♪

The rain is Tess, the fire's Joe, and they call the wind...well, it seems lately the wind has picked up, among other things, a few unflattering sobriquets.

Growing up in El Paso, high winds were a way of life, especially this time of year. What's the use of having all those tumbleweeds if there's nothing to animate them? It was not uncommon to see an armadillo chasing its shell. Once, while performing a roadside repair, I saw the jack blown right out from under a rabbit. We're talking windy, friends and neighbors. Wind that forces horn toads to hit only high notes. Lizards dare not leap lest they fly. Snakes are obliged to add shake and roll to their rattle.

Yuccas find little to laugh about. Tacos are delivered to your door, but not on purpose.

"What did they call the wind in El Paso?"

It's been a while, but "viento Maldito" comes to mind. (State parks in New Mexico came to visit us.)

I complained about having no heat until I met a man who had no temperature at all. Gave me the creeps.

He once lost a staring contest with a paranoid meth addict. He's the least interesting man in the world. "I don't always drink beer. Sometimes I do other stuff."

He has a tattoo that's misspelled. Well, hey, not every sappy sentiment can be a palindrome. He's the least interesting man in the world. "I don't always drink beer, but when I do, somebody else has to buy it. I can't even afford that cheap $#!+. Not even if it's on sale."

He can't even teach a new dog an old trick. He's the least interesting man in the world. "I don't always drink beer. Sometimes I laugh and it flies out of my nose before I can swallow it."

When opportunity knocked, he was afraid it was the cops and ran out the back. He's the least interesting man in the world. "I don't always drink beer ... wait, that's not exactly true; I pretty much all the time drink beer."

Yikes. While preparing a delightful gelatin dessert—gummy bears, marshmallows, rainbow colors—for our SpringFest celebration this coming week ("An Infestation of Fun"), I accidentally dropped my phone into the bowl and didn't notice until the concoction had chilled and set.

Fortunately, the phone still works, but when I answer it, I have to say, "Jell-O."

Meanwhile, if you receive a text from me that looks rather jiggly, just copy and paste it to the door of your refrigerator. It should stabilize and become legible as it dries.

Got a new dog, one of those weird crossbreeds. It's part pit bull and part dachshund: a pit wiener. It's an imaginary dog, but you'd never know to look at it.

Mom used to make cracker pie. Some call it mock apple pie. Anyway, you use crackers instead of apples. Every time she made it, Dad would take a bite and declare, "Tastes just like apples!" The way he carried on, you'd think it was a feat of magic Houdini could only dream about. I'd say, "Well, it's edible and okay, but it does not taste just like apples." I'd say that to myself, not out loud. When Dad said it tasted just like apples, that made it official and conflicting opinions were not gladly received.

It got me to wondering where else crackers could be substituted for apples.

Not as a meaningful maxim: "A cracker a day keeps the doctor away." "The cracker doesn't fall far from the tree."

A party game: Bobbing for crackers.

A party snack: Caramel crackers.

A feature in a creation story: "The Bible never specifically says what Adam and Eve ate, so what makes people think it was a cracker?"

A wandering pioneer nurseryman: Johnny Crackerseed.

A Roger Miller song: " ♫ God didn't make little green crackers...♪"

Nor as a New York City nickname.

And the story of William Tell might be told with less enthusiasm.

His real name was John Chapman. In the early 1800s, he planted so many acres of apple orchards that he earned the sobriquet Johnny Appleseed.

The apples Chapman/Appleseed planted were used primarily for—

"Pies?"

No.

"Fritters?"

No.

"Cobbler?"

No. Not for anything to eat.

"What then?"

Cider. Hard cider. It was the drink of choice among the settlers. It was safer than water and a popular alternative to beer, wine, coffee, and tea. Our frontier cousins were buzzin night and day.

"Perhaps they should have called him Johnny Applesauce."

Sometimes, when we just see the answer, we can make a pretty good guess what the question is (or at least what it's about). But not always. Read the answers and see if you can guess the question:

1. "A moo moo here and a moo moo there."
2. "My dog ate it."
3. "Woo pig!"
4. "Just a little something to see me through."
5. "Like shooting ducks in a barrel."
6. "The Crimson tied."
7. "A crackerjack idea."
8. "Outside the box."

9. "To the bat pole!"
10. "A banjo on my knee."

How'd you do?
Here are the questions:
1. "How should I distribute these moo moos?"
2. "What happened to all the dogfood?"
3. "What must I do if I want to date pig?"
4. "What kind of office window do you prefer?"
5. "Okay, I'm on the Shooting Ducks in a Barrel Facebook page. What now?"
6. "How come the Harvard game went into overtime?"
7. "What's it called when someone is plotting to commandeer your cracker?"
8. "On which side of the box should we print our logo?"
9. "What should we tie this bat to?"
10. "Did you get any other tattoos besides that fiddle on your elbow?"

"Did you have a good weekend?" It's always fun on Monday mornings to hear what the introverts and the extroverts consider a good weekend. See if you can tell which is which:

"Most enjoyable. I didn't leave the house. Got caught up on some letter writing, did 30 minutes of hibachi meditation and some frozen yoga. Had a couple of visitors, but they didn't stay long, thank goodness. Watched a fascinating documentary about Werner Heisenberg on Netflix—I'm still on the fence about the uncertainty principle."

"Super! We popped over to Disney World to run the Goofy 10K and the Montessori Pre-K.

On the way back, we swung by Andalusia where we got to help with the gazpacho harvest. Tis the season on the Iberian Peninsula. ¡Viva las cosas! We had a blast at the Great Pyramid of Giza. Here, look at these 900 cute pictures."

Looking for the perfect gift this holiday season? Consider one of these books by the Golly Rama:

Soul Soup for Chickens (*Cluckers at the Crossroads*); *Who Moved My Mountain Goat?*; *Self-Esteem for Dummies* (*an Idiot's Guide to Image Enhancement*); *How to Get from Here to Where You Are*; *Eeny, Meaning, Miny, Moe* (*Them's Hard Choices*); *The Seven Habits of Highly Effective Procrastinators*; *Nine Golden Keys that Won't Work on a Combination Lock*; *A Quiet Mind: The Power of Being Thoughtless*; *Hoot: You Gotta Give One to Get One*; *Revving in Neutral*; *How to Stop Dilly Dogging and Start Lollygagging*; *Hot Chakra with Marshmallows*; *Chop Your Own Beanstalk* (*Hit the Road Less Traveled, Jack*); *Drawing on the Right Side of the Paper*; *The Power of Positive Profanity*; *The Journey from Doubt to Believing Anything*; *The Happiness Bucket: Dip it into Your Well Being*; *Mindful Brain Washing*; *The Five People You Meet in Wal-Mart*; *Solitary Leapfrog: Get over Yourself.*

A penurious percentage of all proceeds goes to support the Rama Lama Ding Dong School.

Bats in our belfries? Sure, we're quite at home with that. But in our salads? I'd be willing to bet that no one, with the possible exception of Ozzy Osbourne, ever said, "Hey, you know what this salad needs? A bat."

"What the hell are you talking about?"

Some folks in Florida found a bat in their packaged salad.

"A Louisville Slugger? Seems they'd have seen—"

Not the baseball kind, the winged mammal ones. Though admittedly, the winged mammal ones, over the years, have inspired many an individual to swing a stick.

"That's just nasty."

On the upside, they did get into the Guinness record book. Never before has a salad been tossed so far and with such vigor.

"This is out of my league. We need to consult an expert."

I have Polk Salad Annie on the line.

PSA: "Oh, please. They found a bat in their salad? Well, waah. A gator got my granny, so I can't get too choked up about their little flying mouse encounter."

Thanks, Annie. Empathetic as always. Friends, I think we've all learned something here today. This is where laziness and expediency will get us. If those hungry Floridians could have been bothered to scrub their own produce and toss it in the Veg-O-Matic, odds are they'd have noticed any bats or other aberrant ingredients. It's like Smokey Robinson & The Miracles told us all those years ago: "You better chop around."

El Paso, Texas is not known for snow, but snow's been known to fall there. On one such occasion, our friends, Liz and Sue, built a snowman in their front yard.

It was a pretty good snowman—eyes, nose, smile, corncob pipe. That night a couple of us guys decided to surprise our friends by adding a row of buttons to their snowman, and we had just the thing: lemon drops. The yellow buttons looked nice sparkling in the moonlight.

El Paso, Texas is known for its sun; it's called The Sun City. The morning sun melted a bit of the snowman, just enough trickle to make the lemon drops dissolve and run.

Liz and Sue were indeed surprised. You can imagine what they thought we did, and what we never did convince them we did not do, to their snowman.

Do you like bald eggs?

"What the hell are you talking about?"

In my earlier days, I thought boiled eggs were called bald eggs. For two reasons: One, I learned to talk in a little Arkansas delta town. Enunciation was not our strong suit. Two, it made sense. A boiled egg, when peeled, exhibits no hair. Looks kind of like a bald head. The first time I saw "boiled egg" in print, I thought it was a typo.

No matter how firmly we believe them or what we grew up calling them, our labels are not always accurate, are they?

I try to remember that every time I crack an Easter aig.

Yeah, we get in a hurry sometimes. And when we do, we can mistake the hairspray for the underarm deodorant. Not saying it happened, but if you wave at me today and my return gesture seems to lack enthusiasm...

(My hair smells great, by the way.)

Did you ever play Ring and Run when you were a kid? It seems to be a popular prank among our friends at FedEx.

Last Saturday, I was deep in ponder about the meaning of meaninglessness (a.k.a. watching Netflix) when the doorbell rang rapidly thrice, followed by a Judgment Day worthy pounding on the door. I nearly jumped out of my skin.

I stepped out the side door. The FedEx driver had already backed out and was pulling away. He yelled, "I put it by the front door." He waited until I quick-moseyed around and saw the package. I couldn't read the dinky writing, but I was pretty sure it wasn't for me. "I think it goes to the neighbor." By then, the aforementioned neighbor was on the scene; he read the label and hollered for the FedEx driver to stop. The package wasn't for either of us.

I know those drivers are burdened and in a hurry and that most times they get it right. Even so, I found myself harkening back to typing class way yonder ago in high school. (Typewriters were a recent invention and so much faster than a goose quill.) It didn't matter if you could type 80 words per minute if every other line contained an error. It wasn't just speed that mattered; it was speed and accuracy.

This wisdom that's supposed to show up with advancing years: I've been wondering for at least a decade when mine is going to arrive. I may now have a clue. Perhaps it was sent via FedEx and was delivered to someone else.

An invitation to join AARP? No one that old at this address. A playful child still lives here, and an optimistic, bright eyed, devil-may-care young man, but no one who qualifies for AARP. Obviously a case of mistaken identity. They wasted a stamp. A letter from the Social Security Administration? Okay, where's the camera hidden? It's a hoax, right?

Mirror, mirror, on the wall; where do these folks get the gall? Wait, you're not my mirror. Impostor! What have you done with my real reflection? Give it back.

Mirror, mirror, that won't do.
I need a magic one of you.
One into which I can stare
And see who really lives in there.
(Kids these days, they...grow up so fast.)

Sure, we're curious about our past, but we also have bills due in the present and near future. We have strong ties and close relations with those folks.

I found an online outfit making a tempting offer: "The family tree. What's on your branch? Sell the ranch and find out!"

We didn't want to pay an arm and a leg for a limb, so we kept looking.

John recalled a woman on his old mail route who runs a home-based business called You-Who.

We had a nice visit, a deep philosophical discussion, and a cold Pepsi. We gave her ten bucks and a self-addressed, stamped envelope.

Yesterday, we received this hand-written response: "We looked up your family tree and saw that most of you are still living in it."

Sure, it's an old joke, but she's an old woman, so it's okay.

Fourth Estate sale. Everything must go!
Facts 50% off, and more!
Click-bait headlines have never been cheaper!
Huge discounts on seldom used journalism degrees from expensive schools!
Antique office furniture once used by proofreaders!
Random vowels: Buy one, get one free!
Like-new style manuals marked real down & stuff!
Low, low credibility!
Souls sold to the highest bidder.

Okay, maybe it was tacky to put dryer lint in a bag of cotton candy, but the look on that guy's face was priceless.

Hale Yes

A little music history: Bill Medley and Bobby Hatfield were singing with a group called the Paramours. One night in a bar, after one of their duets, a Marine yelled, "That was righteous, brothers!" As a result, on their first album, Medley and Hatfield called themselves The Righteous Brothers. I wonder what other group names might have come about, based on what a Marine yelled in a bar...

What's with all this stuff people have to have these days? We didn't have anything worth havin, and we were darn glad to have it. If you think pullin yourself up by your own bootstraps is tough, just try doin it barefooted. That'll let you know. We were hopeless, and we kept that hope alive. We didn't talk much, but when we did, we didn't say much either. Granny used to tell us, "The world is your oyster." We had no earthly idea what an oyster was, so we just nodded and said, "Oh, okay." Mammy told us, "You can be anything you want to be," then she tanned our hides when we were— "But Mammy, we wanted to be pirates and watermelon thieves." To get to school, we had to walk five miles, so we just didn't go. ("What are you, nuts? It's snowin out there.") Kids nowadays wouldn't know how to amuse themselves if they had nothin to play with but a stick. That requires a lot of imagination, or in our case none at all. No, life wasn't perfect, but neither were we, so it worked out pretty good.

EDUCATION

I look forward to your posts each day so keep them coming!
~Judith Mary Brock

"I have never let my schooling interfere with my education." ~Mark Twain...maybe. (This quote hasn't been confirmed, so we can't be sure who said it or who said it first. Doesn't matter. The notion alone has sufficient heft; verification would add no weight, no matter who said it. It rings a bell.)

Any serious teacher is also a student, getting a genuine education along the way. Grad school was my ticket to the show, but the things I really need to know I've learned while attempting to teach other folks something else.

(Obviously, no real names are used when telling student stories.)

One thing we know for sure: We never know.

It was the first day of class. I was waiting by the door to have a quick word with the professor, who was also my advisor. Another student approached me, held up a can of Dr. Pepper, and said, "Do you mind if we have drinks in here?"

I said, "No, man. I don't care if you bring a keg of beer and pizza, long as you bring enough for everyone."

He grinned. "Really?"

"Wouldn't bother me a bit."

It was my first semester at the community college. I was quite a bit older than most of the other students. The guy had mistaken me for the teacher. It was all I could do to see myself as a maybe graduate, but a teacher? I could not, in my wildest, imagine that.

Life, like any good book, contains surprises and a bit of clarity in each new chapter. No matter what seems to be going on now, keep turning the pages.

When speaking, most folks clip along at around 150 words per minute. That may sound like a lot, but our brains can listen to 450-500 words per minute, about 3 times as fast. No matter how interested we are in what the speaker is saying, no matter how much we want or need the information, to our brains, it's ... as ... if ... there ... are ... huge ... gaps ... between ... the ... words. That's plenty of time for our minds to wander, and they will. That's just what they do. So, we make a conscious decision to listen; when our minds drift, we know why. We try to keep them on a friendly leash and gently guide them back. When our students get sidetracked, we see it for what it is and don't take it personally. I've found it helps to explain this on day one and have a non-threatening signal reminding them to refocus. The signal, accompanied by a smile or wink, is usually enough. It's something we're all in on, something we all do. No one is being chastised, just reminded. If we bellow, bark, or bang a gong, they may be quiet, but they'll sit there seething. That seems rather counterproductive.

"They don't listen!"

Oh, but they do. Just not so much to our words. According to the article referenced below, folks only pick up on about 7 percent of the words we say. The rest, what they really "hear," is how we say it—38 percent tone of voice and 55 percent body language.

"UCLA research has shown that only 7 percent of communication is based on the actual words we say. As for the rest, 38 percent comes from tone of voice and the remaining 55 percent comes from body language."

We have good reason to reevaluate what we say, how we say it, and why. All of it comes through loud and clear.

It also explains why online "conversations" can be easily misinterpreted. Emoticons and acronyms help, but the tone of voice part is usually missing—unless it's a video.

Experienced speakers know how to draw applause or an "amen" simply by how they say it. Watch/listen for it; it's rather fun.

Article: "8 Great Tricks for Reading People's Body Language" by Travis Bradberry, entrepreneur.com, May 18, 2016

In addition to GED classes, I was supposed to teach something called life skills. The curriculum was boring and belittling. So, I took the topics and presented them as stories, stories I wrote featuring the students and using their names. They loved the stories. I dared not show up on any day without a new one. It was fun and one of the few ways I'd found for getting and keeping their attention.

Laura got one of the highest scores I've ever seen on the GED, more than enough to qualify for a college scholarship.

Our job guy got her an apprenticeship at a local firm, helped her get suitable clothes, etc. I wish you could have seen her when Laura stopped by one morning on her way to work. She looked as crisp and poised as any professional you've ever seen. There was a light in her eyes and a bounce in her walk. She radiated confidence and competence.

We didn't see or hear from Laura for a while. I entertained the notion that she was somewhere impressing professors on her way to an MBA.

Years later, I saw her in a convenience store. At least I thought it was her...and prayed it wasn't. That woman looked like a meth infested nightmare. I waved; she stared right past me. I paid for my coffee and left.

After I started the car, someone knocked on the window. I rolled it down.

There was no light in her eyes. Her enunciation was minimal, but I understood what she said:

"I still have your stories. I still read them."

That encounter broke my heart and crushed my spirit. Okay, I allowed it to—everything is a choice.

These days, I choose to hang on to the last four words she said: "I still read them."

Who knows? Maybe someday one of those goofy little tales will make a positive difference. Maybe someday I'll consistently practice what I preach. Hey, anything's possible.

A successful team must be balanced. Years ago, I worked with a project at a junior college in Oklahoma. The director, Jim, was like me, only more so. At the interview—one of those committee things with strangers around a conference table—there came the inevitable "Do you have any questions for us?"

I said, "Okay, I've read the jargonized job description, but what do you really expect from the person who is chosen for this position?"

Jim said, "We want you to hallucinate and experiment."

I knew I was home. "I'm your guy."

Our staff meetings could and did often devolve into comedy routines and rabbit chasing. I thank God every day for Sidney. She kept Jim and me on a leash and forced us to focus & TCB. It would not have worked if not for Sidney. And work it did. We got excellent results.

Everyone on the crew, all five of us, learned a lot from each other. These days, we live in four different states, but we are all still in touch via Facebook. That's mighty nice.

(Sidney and I are 180-degree opposites in just about every measurable way. One time, we both completed a rather extensive personality inventory. Our scores were identical. I'll never forget her reaction: All the color drained from her face; she looked horrified. She said, "I can't be like you!"

Turns out she wasn't. The thing was scored on a Likert Scale. Five was Strongly Agree or Most Like Me; one was Strongly Disagree or Least Like Me. I had it backward and marked my responses accordingly. Sidney was so relieved. Cracked me up...still does.)

Envy: The green-eyed monster. Most would agree it's not a desirable trait. It can be healthy to admit our jealousies to ourselves, but they're not something we usually want to parade down Main Street. Still, to this day, there's one I cannot shake. Who knows why some folks get these rare opportunities and others don't? Maybe the planets line up just right; perhaps it's karma; could be God's will or blind luck. Whatever the reason, fate sure shined on a friend of mine.

He was a psychology professor. He took a stack of assignments home to grade. He left them on his desk and went to the kitchen for a cup of coffee. When he returned, he found his new puppy—he of the sharp teeth and little discipline—had chewed the papers to a pulp. Thus, my buddy had the once-in-a-lifetime fortuity to stand before the class and tell them, "My dog ate your homework."

We talk a lot about motivation and goals. It's helpful and fun to identify and keep an eye on them. They give us something solid to hang on to, especially when circumstances are less than desirable.

Leo was in a class I taught at the University. He was from a town that's little more than a wide spot in an Arkansas road. He was the first person in his family to go to college. It took him longer to get there than it does most students, but there he was.

When the semester began, Leo could walk but just barely and with the aid of crutches. A month later, he was in a motorized wheelchair.

Leo never missed a class. On the days we met, I stood in front of the building and watched him make his way across campus—sweat dripping in August, rain and snow falling on him in the later months. Even if he'd had an umbrella, he could not have held it. The obvious pain in his eyes competed with the smile on his face. The smile always won, at least it did whenever I saw him.

Leo did not need to explore his motivation or his goal. He already had them firmly locked in.

Motivation: "To set a good example for my nieces and nephews."

No idea whether or not anyone else was inspired by his example, but we certainly were. And still are.

Goal: "To graduate before I die."

There are worse things than not meeting an Earthly goal. Like never having one in the first place. Like waking up each morning with no purpose other than to do it all again. There are better things too. Like getting out of here and on to a far better place, a place where we can dance and sing and laugh in a manner that's worthy of our spirit.

My first job out of grad school was at a large university. Outside each office, there hung an official piece of plastic announcing the occupant's name and degree—Suzy Cue, Ph.D.; Jim Dandy, M.A.; Pat Hand, M.S., etc.

They gave me a form for my nameplate. "Fill this out and send it to Campus Printing." They're leaving it up to me? Let the games begin.

My actual degree is an M.Ed., but according to my official piece of plastic, it was the office of "Tom Hale, B.F.D." Gosh, how'd that happen?

Got a lot of comments on that. My favorite was a colleague who asked, "Is that a Bachelor of Fine Arts?" Close enough.

She went from being on academic probation to a successful 2.5 semester. I asked her what made the difference. She'd taken to heart and applied some advice I'd given in class several times. Only she didn't get it from me. She was taking a break between classes, smoking a cigarette and commiserating with some colleagues. A friend on the maintenance crew planted the idea in her mind. Voila! It rang a bell.

It wasn't the first time she'd been told, but it was the first time she'd *heard* it. I have three degrees printed on pieces of pretty paper—summa cum laude and hey lawdy mama—none of which guarantees I'm a better teacher than the maintenance man. Student success and retention are part of everyone's job description.

Years ago, when I worked at the University of Arkansas, one of the campus organizations asked if I'd do a workshop for them. Of course. Be glad to. They told me when and where.

I thought I knew where the building was. I left my office, toting materials and equipment, with 20 minutes to spare. When I arrived, uh-oh, wrong building. I had no idea how to find the right building. I spotted a friend and asked him. Sure, he knew, and we were not close to it. He agreed to walk with me. A clock chimed. Rats.

My friend asked, "What's your workshop about?"

I didn't want to say but saw no way around it, so I told him.

My friend tried not to laugh, but neither of us could hold it in for long.

You can imagine how much credibility I had showing up late and trying to pass myself off as an expert on time management.

Long ago, in a state far away, I worked at a community college. Their Business & Industry division did staff development trainings for outfits in the area. I told the appropriate VP that I'd like to get in on that— have some fun, pick up a few extra bucks. A month or so later, she told me they needed someone to do a session for a factory in a nearby city. She gave me the date, time, and name of the contact person.

I got my routine together and journeyed forth at the appointed time. When I got there, I asked to see Mr. So-and-So. The receptionist said, "He's out today."

I was introduced to Mr. So-and-So's secretary, Wanda, who had no knowledge of the proposed activity. She escorted me to the room where I was told the event was to take place. It was still trashed from a previous meeting. I called my folks. Yes, it was scheduled for today, due to start in about 10 minutes. Wanda called all around the plant; no one knew a thing.

On my way out, Wanda asked, "What was it you were going to talk about?" My response didn't hang in the air for a second before we were both laughing, but it was true: "Effective Communication."

Whenever I meet current or prospective students who do not know what they want to major in or what career they want to seek, I refer them to our Career Counselor. I also ask them this: What do you want to know? What question or questions do you want answered between now and the time you leave this fine planet? Is there a field you could go into where someone would pay you to look for your answers? (That idea probably came from Skip Downing; I really don't remember.) It's a fun exercise at any stage of life.

Teaching single moms, most of whom did not want to be there in the first place, how to write an essay was a fun challenge. They needed to be able to write a credible essay in order to pass the GED test. I was running out of ideas.

One day, Pootessa (not her real name) came in late as usual, threw her backpack on the table, and announced, "All men suck!"

I walked to the board, uncapped a marker, and said, "Tell me about it."

"Well, they just suck, all of them."

Can you give me some reasons why you say all men suck?

She certainly could, many and rapidly. I had to stop her. "Just give me the top three."

"Well, they're lazy. They won't help with the kids. They take everything and give nothing."

I wrote those on the board, leaving plenty of space. I uncapped another marker, a different color, and asked, "Can you give me some examples?"

Pootessa was off to the races again. "Slow down. Just give me three examples of each category."

She did. I wrote them on the board under their respective headings.

I said, "There's your essay. It's that easy. Tack on an introductory paragraph and a summary paragraph. Every time you explain a different reason why all men suck, like when you switch from them being lazy to not helping with the kids, that's where you start a new paragraph. Use complete sentences; punctuate and spell correctly."

For our practice essays, I let them write about anything they wanted. We would each write an essay, I'd make copies, then we'd read them aloud and suggest corrections. They loved to find mistakes in my essays— not all of them were on purpose.

How do you teach essay writing or anything else? Make it fun and interesting.

My favorite part of theater is all the hard work that goes on behind the scenes. Building the sets, the lighting, the sound, the long nights of after-hours rehearsals, skipped meals and missed cues. It requires dedication and a constant focus on the desired outcome. Sometimes goodwill and relationships get strained—hey, none of us are at our best when we are dog tired or ill, but we're still there, doing what we can—and mended. Mostly, there's fun and camaraderie and appreciation of our talented peers. Week after week after week of preparation. The payoff comes when the curtain goes up and the audience is pleased.

That's much the same thing we've been doing all summer. The curtain goes up next Monday. It's the first day of classes for the fall semester. It's Welcome Week for our students—for some it's welcome aboard, for some it's welcome back.

Each of them is doing their own behind the scenes work for their big production. Week after week after week of preparation. They'll laugh and cry and cuss and grow. The payoff will come when they walk out on the stage to receive their diplomas. They'll get some excellent direction along the way. And I guarantee the audience will be pleased.

Student who was absent the class before: "Did y'all do anything last time?"

My reply: "Of course not. We were all so bummed by you not being here that we just sat with our hands folded and wept for an hour. The title of the course may be English Composition, but we know that it's really all about you."

Nontraditional students (usually older, having to work their way through college, etc.) have some problems the traditional students do not. I was dang near 40 when finishing up my BA in psychology. One of the problems I had would not have been necessary if I had really been the grownup I fancied myself to be.

I took a class called social psychology. Dr. Whozit, at least 10 years younger than me, was telling us stuff that, according to my experience, was balderdash. All indignant and self-righteous, I dropped the class. Then I discovered two things: 1) The class was required for my degree. 2) Dr. Whozit was the only one who taught it. Uh-oh.

The professor, when given a fair chance, turned out to be a great guy and a staunch ally. It's all I can do to figure simple percentages, but he loved statistics. When I did my senior research paper, he ran nine-way Villanovas, tai chi squares, Golden Coral correlations, and everything else. He made me look smart. And he did it voluntarily, no strings attached. That is one of the most valuable lessons I've learned along the way.

Years ago, a nontraditional student came into the Advising Center. She'd tested into Beginning Algebra. It was my task to tell her that she needed to take Beginning and Intermediate before attempting College Algebra. She scowled and said, "Won't that put me behind?" I said, "No, you're already behind. This will help you get caught up."

We were no longer the bad guys who were making her take classes that would not count toward her degree. We were the good guys who were helping her get where she wanted to go. She didn't quite smile, but she did nod and accept the responsibility.

A little reframing does not alter the outcome, but it can make it taste better.

During hot weather, especially if there's a heat advisory or warning, it always helps to talk and complain about it. There's something about futile carping that refreshes the mind, body, and spirit.

"That's not been my experience."

As much as so many of us go on and on about it, you'd think it did some good, but it doesn't seem to help, does it?

During a particularly miserable spell in Oklahoma, the weather was all anyone could talk about. I was walking across campus and saw a colleague coming toward me on the sidewalk. As we met, I said, "Hey, Dave. Where are you?" He frowned, shook his head, and said, "It sure is."

I made a mental note to ask Dave to facilitate the next listening skills workshop.

Perhaps my frames of reference could use some updating.

Our building is not that large, but the multiple hallways going off in all directions can be confusing the first few times.

A prospective student, visiting the campus for the first time, stuck his head in the office and asked me, "How do I leave?"

I said, "You can check out any time you like, but you can never leave."

He bestowed upon me a blank stare.

I prompted him: "Hotel California?"

He shook his head. Not connecting.

"Come on, man. I'll show you."

(♬ "There must be some way out of here," said the joker to the thief...♪)

Today I'll get to visit with a group of high school counselors. That always triggers memories. I especially remember my freshman year of high school...because I had two of them. Flunked the first one. The following year, I ran for Student Council as the freshman representative. Ran on my experience. None of the other candidates knew half as much as I did about being a freshman.

Brother John created some most entertaining posters that we plastered all over campus. Got a lot of votes.

I never took high school seriously and resented having to be there. I barely graduated (my American Government teacher gave me a D. I did not earn it; she gave it to me. Take it. Go. Get outta here.) I was on what I think back then was called the goon track.

The senior counselor told me I was not college material, and she was right: A master's degree is as far as I ever got. To be fair, she was right for that particular time. But I do wish she'd have mentioned that it wasn't a chronic condition, that my problem was more attitude than aptitude. I believed her; she was an authority figure—had a fancy piece of paper on her wall and everything.

It wasn't until 18 years later that another group of authority figures (with similar pieces of fancy paper) at a community college convinced me that I could be college material. I met some real teachers and some above-average mentors and advisors. They were knowledgeable; they were patient; they were generous and friendly. They launched me on a grand adventure that continues to this day.

Perhaps we should not focus so much on whether a student is college material and put our energy into making colleges student material. That's the kind of folks I work with now. They get it. It's a joy and a refreshment. The opinions we accept, from ourselves and others, can make all the difference.

I wanted the class to hear a song that reinforced a concept we'd been discussing. The instructions were: "Please listen as best you can."

Almost immediately, some of the football players picked up the beat and began drumming on their desk tops. Before long, some of them were up and dancing. That led to laughing and showing off for each other.

When it was over, one of the older students announced loudly and indignantly, "I pay good money and devote my time for this class, and I do not appreciate it when people cannot even follow simple directions!"

I told her that they were indeed following directions. "If you recall, the instructions were to 'listen as best you can.' For now, that's the best they can do. They'll get better." And they did.

Most of the guys appreciated it: Acknowledging and expressing confidence in them without condoning their behavior.

Indifferent (most), disruptive (most—at one time or another), and downright rude (more than a few). What on Earth had I gotten myself into?

I'd volunteered to conduct a concurrent class (earn high school and college credit at the same time) at the alternative high school (students who weren't allowed, for one reason or another, to attend the regular school).

It was a long semester.

When it was all said and done, when the grades were turned in (not exactly the academic success I'd idealized) and nothing was on the line, I went back for one last meeting with them—to debrief, see if there was anything I could have done differently.

"Any questions, comments, suggestions?"

One of them, one of the main troublemakers, spoke up: "Yeah, I got something I'd like to say."

I braced myself and gave him a nod. "What's on your mind?"

He said, "Thank you for doing this for us."

If I live to be a thousand … Not the academic success I'd idealized. Something far, far better.

No hot water. I made that happy discovery when it was shower time at a motel in Oklahoma City. Called the front desk. They'd tell the maintenance guy when he came in at nine that morning. I had to attend an all-day training session at eight.

It was a suite, and there was a stove. Okay, fire up all the burners, turn on the oven, tough it out long enough to get quick soaped and rapid rinsed. When I hopped out, shivering and cursing, the smoke alarm was blaring like the opening act for Gabriel's Judgment Day trumpet performance. (Seems the stove hadn't been cleaned lately.) That was a mood lifter.

By fast-forwarding other morning rituals, I made it to the university on time. This was shaping up to be one sorry day. It was one of the best days.

Among other things, I learned a critical thinking exercise that is not only fun but effective. Even the most reluctant students—everything from resentful to don't give a hoot—find it nearly irresistible. Believe it or don't, but I've seen students voluntarily ignore their phones during this activity. It's more interesting than mindlessly texting. There's no way to Google the answers because we generate them. I like to call it a brain warmup for a day of learning.

I've had a ball of fun sharing it with educators at five national conferences (St. Louis, Dallas, Los Angeles, Las Vegas, and Disney World). The most rewarding experience was when a student at an alternative high school greeted me with, "Mr. Tom, I need to warm up my brain."

We never know what a day may bring...or turn into.

For three semesters, I taught a class at the alternative high school. They could get high school and college credit if they passed the class. If they passed? If I could get their attention.

The students were not the least bit shy. One day, one of them interrupted me to ask, "Mr. Tom, has your hair always been that white?" That got a big laugh.

I put on my most serious face, sat on a corner of the desk, took off my glasses, and stared at the floor for a few seconds. When they were quiet, I looked up and said, "No, it hasn't. My hair was jet black until I had that dream. When I woke up, it was the color you see now. That's how frightening it was. But enough of that, let's get back to coordinating conjunctions."

Not a chance. They demanded to know about the dream.

"I still have a hard time talking about it. It really shook me up. Please, let's just skip it and get back on topic."

When donkeys fly!

"Okay. It was one of those dreams that sticks with you all day, one that's so vivid, so real, you have a hard time distinguishing it from the waking world. I kept hoping it would fade, praying it would fade, but it would not. It shook me to my very foundation. In this dream (shudder), I experienced what life would be like without an education."

The conference was in Santa Fe, New Mexico. Most everyone else I met there, including a few from my own university, chose to fly into Albuquerque, rent a car, and drive I-25 north (over an hour) to Santa Fe. I chose the Santa Fe Municipal Airport.

It was like pulling up in the backyard of someone's adobe house. The taxi drivers were sitting on their cars, smoking and swapping lies. No lines, no nonsense. Easy in, easy out. Just a hop, skip, and a honk from the hotel. The main thing is we all got there. True, I flew on a smaller (more fun) airplane, but with far less hassle and far more friendliness.

It reminds me of the differences between large universities and community colleges (I've worked for and attended both). Community colleges are usually more convenient, less expensive, and easier to navigate. Both can get you where you want to go. Both can be a life-changing hoot, no doubt. Looking back on my own experience, including grad school, I have to acknowledge that the deepest learning and the single most valuable class I ever took happened at the community college.

Once upon a yonder ago, I facilitated a bridge program, prep for folks considering college. Among other fun things, we covered study strategies.

One day, a woman was telling us about how much money she made selling plasma twice a week. The talked about the who, what, when, where, and how of it all, including periodic bonuses.

The other students exhibited perfect successful student behavior. They took careful notes, they listened closely, they asked pertinent questions. I tried to tell them what a good job they were doing, but could not get a word in edgewise. So, I listened and took notes too.

At our next class meeting, I gave them a lengthy quiz over the ins and outs of selling plasma. They all scored at least 90 percent.

I asked them why they remembered so much and did so well on the quiz. One of them looked at me like I was the most clueless creature ever to hatch and said, "We were talking about money!"

I said, "If you'd use those same techniques and invest that much interest in an algebra class, you would do very well."

Another student rolled her eyes and told me, "You don't get paid for taking algebra."

I said, "I do."

The looks on their faces indicated that some explanation was required.

"Well, not for just taking it but for taking and passing it. If I had not passed college algebra, I could not have earned a bachelor's degree. Without a BA, I could never have gone on to get the degree that qualifies me for my current job. I get paid twice a month for taking algebra."

Community College, many moons ago: While mapping out the next semester, my academic advisor said, "You've got to take Dr. Mott's Vocabulary Building class." He explained that the class would not count toward my degree, but I should take it anyway. My advisor, as had many members of the faculty & staff, had taken Dr. Mott's class and found it a real eye-opener. Most students, especially we nontraditional ones, are leery of anything that involves extra time or expense, but my advisor had never steered me wrong. I trusted the guy.

Oh, my. To this day, decades later, Dr. Mott's Vocabulary Building Class is the single most valuable course I've taken at any level. Certainly, we learned a lot about Greek and Latin roots, prefixes, and suffixes. We were taking notes from the time we came in until it was time to go ("Copious notes always in this class!"), but of equal value was getting to be around Dr. Mott for three hours a week. At the time, teaching was the furthest thing from my mind. When that opportunity came along, Dr. Mott was the teacher I tried most to emulate—not so much his style, that would wear me out, but the enthusiasm he had for the subject and his obvious concern for each student. Dr. Mott warned us all semester that his final was, in his words, "a hirsute wooly booger." No student had ever aced it. I told him I'd be the first. He just smiled. I missed two.

When the time came for grad school, an entrance exam was required. We could either take the Graduate Record Examinations (GRE) or the Miller Analogies Test (MAT). The GRE has a math section, not exactly my strong suit. The MAT is just words and how they relate.

Kind of like a puzzle. On the MAT, I scored high enough and then some. I have to share credit for that with Dr. Mott. There were quite a few words that I'd never seen on the test, but I was able to make educated guesses.

Along with admission to grad school came the offer of a Teaching Assistant gig; it would cover expenses and pay a monthly stipend. Yeah, but teaching? Who, me? Once again, Dr. Mott, his class, and his example, paid off big. It would take a couple more decades to tell about all the good things that have resulted from that experience.

No one had ever aced Dr. Mott's final (Vocabulary Building). I was determined to be the first. I was locked in, focused, a studying machine, right up to the last minute...and then some. I looked at the clock. The test started in five minutes! No problem: I only lived fifteen minutes from campus. Fifteen minutes if the traffic was right. It wasn't.

I slid into the lot, did a ticket-worthy job of parking, and trotted toward the building.

Coming toward me on the sidewalk, headed in the opposite direction, I saw a classmate, Kim. Kim was very bright, an A student. Had she given up so soon? Had she finished that quickly? (You know how your brain can rev in neutral when you're in panic mode.)

I said, "Kim! How was it?"

"How was what?"

"Dr. Mott's final!"

"Uh, it's tomorrow."

Oh...sure, I knew that...I just like to be early is all...

(Didn't ace it, by the way. Not quite.)

"Never, never, never allow the horrendous, deleterious evils of indolence, procrastination, and ennui to gain a tenacious grip upon you."

Dr. Mott wrote that on the chalkboard at the beginning of each class. He explained that if you say something three times, you really mean it, that it's important, that you want to remember it.

Much of the first day was spent with each of us standing and introducing ourselves. As we did, he stood beside us and repeated our name three times. I wrote it off, at first, as an interesting eccentricity. I later realized it was his way of showing that each of us was important and that he wanted to remember us. And he really meant it, as I discovered 12 years later.

I was back in the area and decided to walk around the campus, a little trip down memory lane. It was summertime, so I didn't expect to find many folks hanging around. Sure enough, I ran into Dr. Mott. He didn't hesitate to call me by name—how many hundreds of students had he met in the meantime? Over the decades, I've visited with quite a few of Dr. Mott's former students and they all say the same thing—whether they run into him on campus, in Walmart, or anywhere else: Something akin to, "He remembered my name and other things about me."

If we want to bring out the best in someone, step one is demonstrating that who they are is important, that they matter. Pitiful as it sounds, so many of our students don't get much (if any) of that anywhere else. Show them that they matter, then they'll listen to the rest of what we have to say.

You wouldn't know it to walk by, but on the bookshelf behind my desk there's a little shrine, a tribute to the spirit of Education. There's a textbook, a box of chalk, and two sticks.

The textbook: Arithmetic and Algebra (beginning algebra). This is from the class that gave me the confidence to continue on the long path toward college algebra, a necessary milestone, a dragon to slay, on the way to a dream. Fear of algebra kept me out of college for 18 years. I never got it in high school and graduated on an "alternate track." All it took was the right teacher, a teacher who knew how and who took the patient time to explain the subject in a way I could understand it. Mrs. Jan Haven showed me what a real teacher is. As much as I needed the money, I did not sell the book back at the end of the semester. It meant too much; it represents something far more valuable than a few bucks.

The box of chalk: We don't use chalkboards much anymore. Most are whiteboards or Smart Boards or something else that's been invented since last time I looked. Dr. Mott filled at least two chalkboards at every class gathering and often erased the first one and started over ("Copious notes always in this class!"). It wasn't just *what* he was, it was just as much *who* he was. What a positive difference he made in so many lives. God only knows how many miles of chalk he spun into gold during his career. Dr. Mott was retired by the time I came full circle and hired on at the same community college. I was assigned an office. Someone said, "That's Dr. Mott's old office." Then why isn't it bronzed and roped off? Gads. I sat back down in the chair, feeling like a total impostor, and went through the desk drawers. I found a box of chalk.

Two sticks: I picked up the sticks along a path at the Bon Secours retreat center just outside Baltimore, Maryland. Beautiful place. It's where I met Dr. Skip Downing, author of *On Course*. It was my first four-day *On Course* Workshop. What an eye-opener that was and continues to be. You can start a fire with two dry sticks. It's not easy, but it can be done. That, to me, is an excellent metaphor for what so many of our students experience. Getting where they want to go is not easy, but it's definitely doable. *On Course* shows them how. The structures and strategies one learns at an *On Course* workshop change lives and last a lifetime.

Your brain will always agree with you. That's its job.
You: I can't do math.
Brain: Never could, never will.
Y: I can do math.
B: You can already tell time and make change for a dollar. You're on your way!
Y: There's no way.
B: None whatsoever.
Y: I'll find a way.
B: Here's a map and a flashlight.
Y: I hate it here.
B: I'll find plenty of reasons.
Y: I love it here.
B: I'll find plenty of reasons.
Y: Most people are awful!
B: There goes one now!
Y: Most people are good.
B: I've noticed that too.
Y: I'm screwed.
B: Blued and tattooed.
Y: I've got it made.
B: In the shade.

We find what we're looking for. We're not blind to the problems, and we deal with them, and it's a lot easier to solve them when we have positive allies, beginning with our own mindset. Are we looking for confirmation of our helplessness or a map and a flashlight? Both are readily available.

Hale Yes

Years ago, at the University of Arkansas, I was talking to a group of veterans, participants in a program called Veterans Upward Bound. Some were in their thirties, some in their fifties, and a few much older. They wanted to go to college, most for the first time. You wouldn't think anything could rattle these guys, but there was some palpable apprehension. Many were anxious about being left behind by the younger, smarter (their words, not mine) students. I was telling them some of the advantages that we nontraditional students have over the fresh-from-high school crowd. "First of all, they are not smarter. The serious ones are going to want to be in your study group. One thing, among many, that we have going for us is that we know how to focus; we're not so easily distracted; we've got all our partying out of the way."

One of the older guys slowly raised his hand. "Yes, sir?"

He said, "Now, we still party … it just takes a little longer."

Point taken.

The four-day workshop was held at a retreat center outside Baltimore, Maryland. Two of the participants had a few flight snags and didn't arrive until two in the morning. They were from Middle Tennessee State University. I was awake, so I showed them the way to the kitchen.

While we raided the fridge, one of the women from MTSU asked where I was from.

At the time, I was working for a Junior College in Miami, Oklahoma. The town is spelled like Miami, Florida, but it's pronounced "my-AM-uh." I didn't want to explain all that and the why behind it. Hey, we're in Maryland and they're from Tennessee; who's to know?

I said, "I work in Miami (pronouncing it like the one in Florida), Oklahoma."

The woman from MTSU said, "You know that's pronounced 'my-AM-uh,' right?"

"Yes, I do, but how on Earth do you know?"

She was born and raised in that area of Oklahoma.

It's not a big world, is it?

A little while ago, out of the clear blue nowhere, the language on my Facebook page switched to German. Lord knows why. Perhaps it was das hacken fairy. That would have been fine except for the inconvenient fact that I don't speak, read, or understand German.

So, I Googled "how to change languages in Facebook." It said, in effect, "It's easy: Click on that little pointy down arrow at the top, far right of your page. From the pulldown menu, select Settings. Select the language you want, save the changes, and refresh your page."

Okay. The little pointy down arrow was easy to find (there was a picture of it), but what's German for "Settings"? Google a translator: Einstellungen. Language? Back to the translator: Sprache. Save changes? Änderungen speichern.

It was rather fun, a surprise puzzle with meaningful consequences. Speaking of meaningful consequences, some of the best times I've ever had in the classroom were working with ESL students. This morning's translation adventure gave me a tad more appreciation for what they may experience, in every situation, all day long. English is weird enough for those of us who grew up with it. Can you imagine learning it as a second sprache? ¡Órale!

Cuss? They took profanity to a whole new level, and few of them had any hold-back about it. They were single moms taking GED classes on a college campus; the colorful language would not do, so I told them, "You can say anything you want to in here. You're not likely to come up with anything I haven't already heard or said. It doesn't bother me any more than the grammar and punctuation you use—or not—in your Facebook posts. On the other hand, we are spending these hours together to get you ready for the GED test. On the GED test, grammar and punctuation will matter. If you use profanity, it will count against you. Therefore, just as we practice proper grammar and punctuation, we would be well served to also practice avoiding offensive words."

Did it work all day, every day? Of course not. But it did get us thinking about it and on guard for it in a way that no indignant lecture or mini-sermon ever would. (Not that I could have delivered either with a straight face.) When dealing with humans, there needs to be some degree of "What's in it for me."

Tonight is one of my favorite nights of the year: Graduation. What a joy and a refreshment to see the students, knowing what some of them overcame to get there, walk across the stage and receive their credentials.

A bonus hoot is being backstage ahead of time as we all wrestle and tug into our sundry outfits. Every color, every stripe, every dangle & decoration means something. We look, for all the world, like extras in a Harry Potter movie.

There is some magic in what we do. And there are spells the students learn, depending on their majors. I've been given special permission to reveal unto you one spell from ten fields of study. (They won't work without the corresponding wand, so it's relatively harmless information. Just thought you might find it fun to know.)

Accounting: Exactamundo!

Computer Science: ShrugandSpewJargon!

Diesel Technology: Onda-Roadagain!
Early Childhood Development: Open Sesame!
English: GrammarGirlGoogle!
Math: PEMDAS!
Music: Rollo-ver-Beethoven!
Nursing: Malady-Vamoose!
Pre-med: Examine-kadaver!
Psychology: Y-Do-Dey-Do-Dat?!

It's great fun to see people so pleased, friends and family so proud. Any chance we get to participate in and be a part of such occasions is an opportunity to be savored. That's what keeps us going; that's what keeps us moving in a positive direction, as individuals and as a community. The graduation ceremony was dignified and respectful. We may not know some (or most) of the graduates; still we smile and silently wish them well. Some students we do know, and it makes our hearts sing to hear their names announced and watch them walk across the stage, shake hands with the dignitaries, receive their diplomas, and pause for a picture.

We know that every single employee of the college played a role in those success stories. I can tell you about students who have been inspired and encouraged by a professor...and a wise advisor...and a club or organization sponsor...and a maintenance worker. It is important that we are an accredited school and that our classes will transfer to other colleges and universities. It is also important that we have a clean, well-kept campus and that we have a fun, nurturing atmosphere. The absence of any of those could be a deal breaker. It's so nice to work at a place where all those bases are covered, and then some.

Just as everyone's capacity for solemnity was peaking, the celebration was unleashed. The clapping, whistling, stomping, and shout-outs—if not for the funny hats and wizard robes you might think you were at a rock concert (not that any of us haven't shown up at a concert wearing some rather creative costumes).

Graduation: A formal ritual, a hoot, and a halleluiah all rolled into one fun evening.

One of my favorite student evaluations wasn't written on an official form. I overheard a student, a highly skilled and much-respected linebacker, tell a classmate, "You gotta watch Mr. Hale. Everything he says means more than one thing."

Another favorite evaluation came from the head coach of the football team. I was visiting with him on the field after a game. He yelled at a running back who was heading toward the locker room, "You better get your ass over here and shake this man's hand! He's the only reason you're still here."

It was a great classroom. It was in one of the oldest buildings on the U of A campus; it housed the original law school. Twelve-foot ceilings, steam radiators. This time of year, there would be wasps bobbing around the overhead lights. In the winter, the radiators would pop and hiss. Perfect place for learning active listening, how to ignore distractions, and focus. There was a clock on the back wall. Now and then, a student would creatively arrange her or himself so as to sneak a peek at the clock behind them. (This was before everyone had a smartphone.) Not that they were bored with my class or in a hurry to get outta there ...

Dad gave me a clock. A Goofy clock. It runs backward. He said it reminded him of me. I replaced the classroom clock with the Goofy clock. It was fun to watch the students go to all that trouble and still not know what time it was.

That was over 20 years ago. I still have the clock, the only analog clock in the house, and it's still ticking strong. It's traveled with me and helped me pace my conference presentations in St. Louis, Dallas, Las Vegas, Disney World, Los Angeles, and in every classroom I've occupied since.

On those rare occasions when I see a regular clock or watch, I have to hesitate and readjust. Two decades of telling time counterclockwise makes normal look strange.

With the wasps bouncing around or the radiators' snap-crackle-pop, I'd ask the students, "Can you hear that clock ticking?" They could not. "Listen..." Eventually, they could.

"You could make straight A's if you wanted to!"

Dad told me that every time he signed one of my report cards, first grade through twelfth. I barely escaped high school.

After that came nearly two decades of sojourning. Through the looking glass, down the rabbit hole, over the rainbow, and a most hospitable layover in the merry old land of Oz.

Along the way, I read a psychology book (*Sanity, Insanity, and Common Sense* by Rick Suarez, et al.) and was hooked. I had to learn more. The best way to do that was to...go to college? Me?

With the kind, patient assistance of some generous mentors and genius teachers, I was able to overcome a boatload of ignorance and self-imposed doubt.

When I received my first semester grade report, I had a perfect score, a 4.0. I showed it to Dad and said something like, "I wanted you to see at least one good one before we all get kicked out of here."

He looked it over. "I always told you you could make straight A's if you wanted to!"

I said, "And you were right. The key phrase is 'if you wanted to.' I didn't want to."

If someone doesn't want to, they're not going to— make the grade, love us back, consider our point of view, etc.

A fire has to have fuel (knowledge), oxygen (breathing room), and heat (desire).

"It is what you read when you don't have to that determines what you will be when you can't help it."
~Oscar Wilde

DAD

Tom, like an honest friend, you have opened some eyes and hearts this morning.
~Dremeda Cook

People ax me, they say, "Tom, what's the best hamburger you ever had?"

I tell 'em it's a three-way tie: A now defunct establishment called the Lucky Bird in Lubbock, Texas; a roadside dive in Benjamin, Texas; and the backroom of little store in Alamogordo, New Mexico.

The little store in Alamogordo had no outside sign or any inside indication that they made and sold hamburgers. You just had to know. Dad knew.

He seemed to know everybody everywhere. He knew every overpass and every backroad from coast to coast. That came from years of truck driving and taking an interest in people.

After 30-some-odd days on the boat, I got off in Memphis around two in the morning. Instead of flying back to El Paso this time, I was going to spend a few days with the folks in Arkansas. Dad picked me up at Waterways Marine.

We crossed the bridge into Arkansas and took some off-the-grid pig trail south. After a few miles, Dad said, "You want a cup of coffee?"

126

I sure did. On the boat, coffee disappeared faster than we could make it.

He pulled over on the gravel shoulder. In the distance, I could see a porch light on a farmhouse. Dad said, "Go knock on the door and tell that old woman you want two cups of coffee."

I figured, from long experience, that he knew what he was talking about. I got out of the truck and started up the path. Dad rolled down the passenger-side window and said, "Get back in here before you get yourself shot!"

Dad thought that was hilarious. He slapped his leg and cackled about it all the way to Helena. And of course, he never mentioned it again...except to everyone he ran into.

Dad told me many times, "You don't have any common sense!" I never argued the point because he was right. I didn't. Still don't. Sometimes he said it affectionately; he'd laugh and shake his head. Other times, he said it like I was doing it on purpose just to irritate him. He'd be trying to show me how to do a simple tune-up on a car and I'd wonder aloud, "When I tighten this bolt, is someone else in a parallel universe or below the equator simultaneously twisting one counterclockwise?" He'd give me that look.

There was no animosity; it was more like two people who really enjoy each other's company but speak different languages.

I'd launch into some philosophical or metaphysical meander and Dad's eyes would glaze over. I knew he wasn't the least bit interested in what I was saying, but he was interested in me, and that's what mattered.

One time—it's one of those highlight reel favorite moments ever—I was going on about something like "Infinity by its very definition has to extend in both directions" and the implications thereof. Dad's eyes did not glaze over. He listened with wide-eyed, slack-jawed fascination.

When I finally wound down, probably 20 minutes later, Dad stared at me for a moment then broke the silence to ask, "Where you come up with this shit?"

One afternoon, Dad and I were waiting to cross a busy street in downtown El Paso. A woman, a stranger, approached Dad and said, "Excuse me, do you have the time?" He smiled and said, "If you've got the money." She did a U-turn. Apparently not a Lefty Frizzell fan.

Before and after (and probably during) church, there was always coffee in the Fellowship Hall. One of Dad's favorite tricks, if he happened to be holding the pot, was to offer a refill to the next person. He'd fill their cup to the brim, to where nothing but surface tension was keeping the coffee in, to where it was all but impossible to walk or even lift it for a sip without spilling some. One day, one of Dad's Deacon buddies was going to get him back. He offered a refill. Dad let the guy pour until the cup was sufficiently full, thanked him, and walked away, leaving the guy pouring coffee on the floor.

It was a kind of soap, so it should have worked. It did a good job on hair, why not a plastic percolator? Because, as I discovered, it's perfumed, and that smell will not rinse out; it won't go away. Ever. And it does not exactly complement the coffee. Yeah, well, there's that.

I was living in a trailer on the outskirts of Austin. Mom and Dad were coming for a visit. Mom was a neat freak—she even dusted doorknobs and cleaned the top of the refrigerator. I'm ... What's the opposite of neat freak?

My coffee pot didn't bother me a bit; it was discolored but not nasty. But Mom, you know how she is.

I didn't have any dishwashing soap—why waste the money when you don't have any dishes? (Okay, that's not quite accurate. I had a bayonet, a saucepan, and a baking sheet. Nothing that couldn't be cleaned with water, a paper towel, and a little self-delusion. Everything else, including the coffee cups, was disposable.) White vinegar wasn't on the radar either. Hey, there's some shampoo.

Dad had no filter when it came to rendering an opinion. If we dilute his assessment of the brew and add sufficient cream and sugar, the gist of it is that he did not enjoy the experience.

It seemed like a good idea at the time. (Stand back or seek shelter lest ye be buried 'neath an avalanche of metaphors.)

Dad's left shoe wore out before the right one did. Mom wondered why. Dad solved the mystery: "That's my spinnin foot."

If you knew Mom, you can hear the laugh. She's picturing something between James Brown, and a whirling dervish. She pointed out, between involuntary cackle/hoots, that she'd known Dad a long time but had never seen him spin.

Dad was a letter carrier at the time. He walked many miles every day. When he changed directions, which was constantly, he tended to pivot on his left foot. Made sense.

When Dad was around, Mom loved to ask people, deadpan, "Which foot do you spin on?"

You can imagine the reactions. She'd explain, "Jimmy spins on his left foot. Which one is your spinning foot?" Not surprisingly, few had ever thought about it.

If memory serves, that was about 117 years ago. Earlier today, I had some music going (ELO's version of

"Roll Over Beethoven") and was cracking a boiled egg to the rhythm. I felt inspired to execute a 360° spin. Out of nowhere, it occurred to me to notice which foot I was spinning on. The left one.

Dad was the youth Sunday School leader, in charge of the big meeting before we broke up into our individual classes. That meant that we had to go. In my early teens, that was not good news. As with everything else he did, Dad worked hard at it. He was preparing a special Christmas program with a dramatic hidden voice, our special guest: The Angel of the Lord.

In the sixties, a reel-to-reel tape recorder was high tech. Dad borrowed one and recorded the angel part. Dad had a great voice. He didn't just say things, he proclaimed them. When I read Genesis 1:3, it's him I hear saying, "Let there be light." (And there'd better be some light PDQ.)

When the big moment came, from behind the curtain we were supposed to hear, "Fear not: for, behold, I bring you good tidings of great joy, which shall be to all people..." You know the rest. Dad wound the tape back too far. What we heard instead was...circus music.

To my everlasting credit, I did not laugh out loud—like just now, recalling the scene.

Decades later, three takeaways: 1) I deeply appreciate the effort. Dad was the real deal. 2) Every time I spliced a tape in my radio days, I was extra careful. And it always brought a big, often much-needed, grin remembering the Angel voice/calliope blast. 3) I think the circus music was appropriate.

(Angel: "What part of 'fear not' did you not understand? Get up off the ground, man. Good tidings? Great joy? We gonna celebrate or we just gonna futz around? Cue the music!")

Dad had a powerful voice. He could have announced a game at Yankee Stadium without a microphone. He was also a most willing church worker. He'd do anything that was needed.

Well, they needed men to sing in the choir. Dad had that voice, but...he had a heart of gold and a tin ear. He loved to tell about when the music director asked him, in private, if he could lower the volume by a few dozen decibels. He thought that was hilarious. Dad told me one time that "Rock of Ages" was his favorite church song because it was the only one he could sing in tune all the way through. For whatever reason, it was a good fit. He could pull out all the stops on "Rock of Ages." We made sure they sang it at his funeral.

This is the part where I'm supposed to say I know he's in Heaven now and singing with perfect pitch, but I hope not. I hope in Heaven we're still ourselves, only more so. I hope there's already enough perfection in Heaven that folks are bored with it and that they'll find refreshment and novelty in Dad and you and me. I hope St. Cecilia asks him if he could hold it down a bit. And that he'll slap his leg, laugh, and tell me about it someday.

El Paso, Texas. There was a chain link fence separating the church parking lot from a vacant lot. It was a high fence, probably at least 8 feet tall. Tumbleweeds, blown in and trapped by the fence, were piled to the top, concentrated in that one corner. One day after church, the pastor said he wished someone would accidentally drop a cigarette into the tumbleweeds and get rid of them. Dad took out his Zippo, struck a flame, and lit the stack near the bottom. If you've never seen dry tumbleweeds burn, you've missed the textbook example of hot and fast. Stand back... whoosh! Mission accomplished. Don't tell Dad you want something done if you don't, or if you're the least bit timid. Cracked me up.

One afternoon when Dad was in the hospital, he appeared to be sleeping. Mom decided to go to the cafeteria and take a break. Before leaving, she found *Wheel of Fortune* on the TV and turned up the volume. She said, "A familiar noise will help him feel more normal, more at home."

When she was out the door and down the hall, Dad opened his eyes and said, "Turn that bullshit off."

Appreciating Mom's good intention and waiting until she was out of earshot before saying something that might offend her: That's what made Dad feel more normal, more at home.

During Dad's last hospital stay, the Fourth of July came and went. At night, I looked out a large lobby window and saw fireworks. Mom's last visit was a year and a half later. On New Year's Eve, I looked out the same window and saw more silent fireworks.

When a baby is born, the hospital plays a happy tune over the speakers. I heard that music several times while I was walking down the long hallway to the ICU.

There is a distant, familiar comfort in knowing that even as we are losing someone, someone is celebrating something. It's easy to imagine that the newly arrived and the dearly departed are both celebrating.

IT MUST BE TRUE: I SAW IT ON FACEBOOK

(Much ado about doodly-squat)

I had to share Tom, you have a gift!
~Edie Judkins Ingram

I'm sharin' it, too! I wish I could live inside
your brain for just one day... lol.
~Rachel Lloyd

I got friended by an old flame on Facebook. I'll be damn.
She asked if I was still alive; well, technically I am.
Gettin caught up on three decades, I suspect as we explore
She remembers a me who's not there anymore.

In my profile picture, my bald spot doesn't show.
Oh, wait! Here's a better one from twenty years ago.
Twixt the wrinkled wrath of now and the cool cat of before,
It looks just like the me who's not there anymore.

Tom Hale

That old flame and I burned the candle at both ends.
While some said, "You can't do it!" we exchanged winks and grins.
Here's a toast to the tingle, the rumble, and the roar,
And a prayer for the pair who's not there anymore.

She recalls the balls-to-the-wall give and take,
But lately I've been yankin the emergency brake.
The spirit and the flesh once had a ravenous rapport;
Glory be, where's the me who's not there anymore?

She's retired and bored. Why don't I fly up for the day?
I've got Fiddlers, and Pipers, and Hell yet to pay.
I appreciate the invite, but I'll just click "Ignore."
Fond regrets from the me who's not there anymore.

An albuterol inhaler, assorted salves and sprays
Are what pass for an intimate relationship these days.
I might could still get down, but could I get up off the floor?
Two trick knees and a me who's not there anymore.

My reward may be in Heaven; in the end we may fare well;
Maybe there's a special secret only time can tell.
Meanwhile, midst my musings and making up this rhyme,
I declare, it's as if I was there one more time.

To the person who posted this: "Life is not fair. Deal with it."
Maybe. However, if something or someone beyond us is in control, then maybe it really is fair and we just can't see it from our limited perspective; perhaps it's outside

our dinky frame of reference. If, for example, we believe and proclaim that God is in charge, "life is not fair" is a pretty hard sell; it rings hollow.

Maybe "fair" isn't everyone getting the same things but everyone getting what they need. If a restaurant patron's life is saved via the Heimlich maneuver, the administrator of the maneuver does not then, in the spirit of fair play, go around giving it to all the diners—unless he wants a knot on his head.

Maybe Earl Nightingale was right when he said that our rewards in life, tangible and intangible, are in exact proportion to our service to others. Maybe it's just that life can seem unfair when we don't understand (or haven't bothered to learn) the rules.

Maybe life seems unfair when we ignorantly equate success with wealth and fame while the Holy Grail is actually Peace of Mind.

Maybe you are right and life really isn't fair, but I'm not about to buy into it just because someone said so on Facebook.

"Not even if it's written in all caps across a picture of Sam Elliott?"

Well, if he was wearing a cowboy hat, that would add a new layer validity to the notion...

How are you enjoying the "Information Age," so far? There sure is a lot of information, 'eh? We're neck-deep in it. When we bother to sanely sort it for useful or factual information, we find we're only ankle-deep. Sorting takes time and some impartial reasoning. Ain't nobody got time for that? It would often seem so.

"We must view with profound respect the infinite capacity of the human mind to resist the inroads of useful knowledge." ~Thomas Lounsbury (He died in 1915, so this is nothing new.)

"You are entitled to your opinion. But you are not entitled to your own facts." ~Daniel Patrick Moynihan
That notion seems almost quaint anymore.
"I call 'em the way I see 'em, and if I don't see 'em, I make 'em up." ~George Carlin, as sportscaster, Biff Barf
That sounds more like it. Most of us have enough to handle with what's really going on, without having to dump a load of artificial offal onto the fret pile. The problem seems to be that so many cannot (or won't take the time to) separate the real news (the wheat) from the bull chaff.

Some of the counterfeit facts are obviously satire and are enjoyed as such. Other outlets go to extremes to fake us out in order to get us riled up so we'll click and share. It can be tempting to read and believe something because we want it to be true. But if we do that, we're not doing ourselves or anyone else any favors. Luke O'Neil, in a vice.com article from June of 2014, asks, "Would you repeat a story you heard from a crazy dude who yelled at you on the underground? Then why are you linking to a site you don't know?"

If you're interested in ferreting out the faux, in expunging the ersatz, there are some fun ways to go about it. Approach everything you read, hear, or watch as would an Agatha Christie character. Take nothing at face value. Look for the clues.

In the dark days before social media, in my ignorance, I didn't realize how many things I'd been doing wrong: pronouncing words, boiling eggs, peeling bananas, grocery shopping, to mention but a few seen recently.

Pronouncing words: I'm from east Arkansas. We're communicating. Git outta here.

Boiled eggs and bananas: I eat and enjoy them. There's more?

Grocery shopping: I got what I wanted. I paid for it. I'm going home now.

Gads, some folks can complicate anything. There are a few things, however, that I do want to do wrong:

Judging other people without taking a long look at my own biases and behaviors. I want to screw that one up big time.

Needless worry. The things we worry about can pretty much be put in two categories: Things we can control and things we can't. If we can control them, why not do that instead of fretting about it? If we can't control them, worrying is pointless. I want the lowest score possible on needless worry.

Thinking in terms of us and them. When we get to (or already) know them, they're mostly just like us. Some of their ways might be better, as might be some of ours. We'll never know if we avoid sane discussions, if we swap reason for cheap shots and sarcastic cartoons. I want a big, fat, red-circled F on that one.

A scraggly, mangy shelter dog crept out on stage. It was all the panel could do to keep a straight face. What happened next was sheer magic and show biz history: When the dog donned a derby and whistled "Danny Boy," the audience and the judges were moved to tears.

So many positive and happy things happened yesterday that I plum forgot to be mad as hell about what Forrest Trump or Hillary Sanders did, said, or tweeted. What a slacker, 'eh? Didn't even take the time to get outraged over the antics of Miley Kardashian. It was weird, man...kind of like my own life was interesting enough without getting caught up in all that foofaraw. I'll try to do better.

Some of us have been eye rolling and poking fun at how many of the "news" headlines entice us to click to get the full story. It's news, so their favorite click tactic is fear. For example, this headline I saw a few moments ago:

"Here's How Close Earth Came to Colliding with Asteroid 2013 TX68"

Teaser text: "A 100-foot-wide asteroid called 2013 TX68 skimmed past Earth on Monday night after its orbital path brought it unusually close to ours. NASA doesn't..."

Oh, Lawd! NASA doesn't what? Expect us to live out the night? Want to panic us weenie civilians because we can't handle the truth? What, what?! -click-

"Despite how close it appears to us in this graphic, don't worry — it was a safe distance away. NASA doesn't have a specific measurement yet, but in an earlier announcement the agency predicted it would pass about 3 million miles from us."

NASA doesn't...have a specific measurement. But hey, only 3 million miles. If that's not "unusually close," then I'm no judge of skimming asteroids.

I sent the story to my fellow eye roller, Jackie. She emailed back and wrote, "When we click on these things, we know better than to expect any Earth shattering news."

("Earth shattering." Wish I'd thought of that...)

What's with the mixed messages? On the one hand, I'm being told I'm Awesome! just for taking up space, that I'm already perfect and beautiful and brilliant (got 8 out of 10 on that Gilligan's Island trivia quiz). On the other hand, I'm getting insider information that says, in effect, "If being Awesome! perfect, beautiful, and brilliant isn't enough, here's a secret that doctors, the government, and the Illuminati don't want you to know about! Here's how you can look, feel, function, and thrive like someone the rest of us can stand to be around. We can tighten your skin, boost your libido, and yes, we accept Master Card."

Outside my window, there's a bird singing and a flower blooming. Neither feel the need for validation or fixing. When we hang out with Mother Nature, mindless memes and expensive insecurities make no sense.

Preaching to the choir can be fun, but it's often best to sit down and let the choir sing. No one ever went home humming a sermon.

Another *Wizard of Oz* metaphor: The Wizard is a Facebook quiz.

The chronic quiz taker is represented by a mannequin who fell off a truck and is found in a ditch by Dorothy and crew.

Dorothy: Who are you?
Mannequin: I have no idea.
Scarecrow: Sounds like amnesia.
Mannequin: Oh, it's worse than amnesia. At least an amnesiac knew at one time. Me, I've never known.
Tinman: I bet the wizard could help you find out who you really are.
Mannequin: How can I find this wonderful wizard?
Lion: We're on our way to see him. You can come with us.
Mannequin: Mind if I sing about it first?
Dorothy: You're gonna fit right in.

♫ Oh...

Tom Hale

My soul would not be crusty; my ego not be dusty
from sittin on a shelf.
I would run free and looser; not be lost as a goose, sir,
if I only knew myself.

I'd be nimble; I'd be keener, not some witless wiener,
my mind all full of fuzz.
I'd be wise as a hooter, not a gene pool polluter, if I
just knew who I was.

Oh, I could tell you my delights and traits and skills.
I'd be more familiar with my wills
And won'ts and likes and thoughts and thrills.

I could tell you straight up, and not need nothin made
up; I'd tell it like it is.
I'd be too busy flyin to be braindead, relyin on a two-
bit clickbait quiz.

If I had a name, I'd use it; I would not be just a
whozit; I'd be really me.
I'd not be lost and lonely, but alive if I only knew my
true identity. ♫

You have a good job with good insurance and a nice
retirement plan—and you're nowhere near retirement age.
Why are you quitting?
"I saw it on Facebook. My name is on a list of men
who will win the lottery this year. Isn't that exciting?!"
Where did this list come from? A burning bush? A
time-traveling space alien? The Wizard of Oz?
"Nah, some clickbait outfit in Indonesia."
Well, they should know. By the way, are you the only
person on the planet with your name, or are there
thousands, maybe millions more?

"It's a pretty common name."

Could the clickbait gurus in Indonesia be referring to someone else with the same name? Or did they mean everyone with that name?

"I'm not sure."

And I'm not sure how to tell you this: Those lists are just for fun, not to be taken seriously.

"Aw, man. Really? I mean sure, I knew that. Heh-heh."

Look, here's another list. And your name is on it!

"Yeah? What is it?"

It's a list of people who have about ten seconds to stop wasting my time and get back to work.

"It's my lucky day!"

Hang on to that feeling.

I know you're not reading this because I'll be watching to see who didn't (like I have nothing better to do). But if you did or if you do, leave a one-word response telling what you had for breakfast and how "yummy" it was. That way, I'll know that you are a REAL "friend" and not just some Tea Party Liberal troll out to screw things up for the rest of us. Then copy and paste this into a Word document and share it on a total stranger's wall. Because we've all been alive on Planet Earth—some of us still are—and know what a burden that can be.

If you want to get the message out about how superior your generation is, about the simple pleasures you enjoyed before all this newfangled technology came along and drove a wooden stake through the heart of interpersonal communication, there's no better place to do it than on this ... newfangled Facebook thing where people can read all about it on their computers, tablets, and phones. They can read all about you instead of enjoying the simple pleasures like face-to-face conversations.

"We didn't need all this crap! We had rock & roll and soda fountains!"

Nowadays, all they have is rock & roll and ... well, even more intriguing stuff than we did. Gads, they can have a soda fountain in their house, even their car. Won't be long before there's a soda fountain app for phones. And if they want rock & roll, they can just download it and listen to it instantly. We were blessed and cool because we took every advantage of the technology that was available at the time, whether it was a horseless carriage or a transistor radio. If you want to hang a picture, do you drive the nail with a hammer or with your forehead? We use the latest, best tools, don't we?

"But things were better then!"

No, they really weren't. Raise your hand if you're reading this on a typewriter. (By the way, you can still drink out of the hose if you want to.)

"Hey, I tell it like it is."

Great. I've always wanted to find someone who knows how it is. My lucky day, 'eh?

So, tell me, how is it that we got here? Creation? Big Bang? If it's the Big Bang, where did that thing that banged big come from? Wouldn't that still qualify as Creation?

And dreams: What are those things? Where do they come from? How is it they seem so real while they're happening yet often seem to lack a lick of sense when we wake up. Of course, the same thing can be said for the waking part; it seems real, but when we step back and look at it, so much of it defies anything resembling logic. Which one's the real world? Both? Neither? Are we somewhere dreaming the whole thing? If so, how do we set the alarm? Is reincarnation just hitting the snooze button?

Can we have our cake and eat it too? Is the glass half full? Are there aliens among us, the kind from other planets? Is the whole thing a hologram? What was the greatest thing before sliced bread? If Peter Piper picked a peck of chucking woodchucks—

"Okay! Stop already. Let me rephrase: I don't tell it like it is. I tell it like I think it is—or should be."

Well hell, we all do that.

Facebook fun: Keeping up with the goings on of friends all over the globe. Some, however, just can't let you have your moment. They jump at any chance to rain on your post with their comments.

We're at Disneyland, having a ball!

"You know that's not the real mouse, right? Just some teenager in a costume."

Chillin on the beach in Puerto Piñata!

"We flew over that dump on our way to Shangri-La."

Keep me in your prayers tomorrow. I'm having some wisdom teeth pulled.

"That's nothin. I woke up covered in dead skin cells and the doctors said there's not a thing they can do about it."

We got on the waiting list four years ago, and tonight we finally got a table at Chez Flip-Zee-Burger! Expensive, yes, but ever so yummy!

"We got real sick after eating there."

My new tat! Designed it myself and it has great symbolic meaning.

"You know that as you age your skin will sag and it'll look less like a mandala and more like a tie-dyed iguana."

Here's 87 pix of Ed's HS graduation. They grow up so fast!

"IKR! Our granddaughter graduated Harvard Medical School when she was 12 and retired at 17."

It's fascinating, in a Through the Looking-Glass kind of way, how many folks have everything figured out and have all the answers ("What this country needs..." "If we would just..." "I'll tell ya one damn thing..."), yet their solutions are such diametrical opposites. Could it be that maybe everybody has something to offer and that nobody has everything? One-size-fits-all doesn't really look good on much of anyone. Those who have all the answers, even when I agree with most of them, tend to be a tad spooky. It's more fun to be around the ones who have just as many sincere questions.

"That is just the way with some people. They get down on a thing when they don't know nothing about it." ~Mark Twain (*The Adventures of Huckleberry Finn*)

"Did you see what he did?!"

No, but I'll make a note to Google it this afternoon if I get to feeling too good and need something to be outraged about.

"Did you hear what she said?!"

Dang, I was enjoying the crossword puzzle and completely forgot to tune in and wreck my mood.

"Did you see what she wore?!"

I must have gotten sidetracked visiting with folks I'm actually acquainted with and care about.

"These celebrity shenanigans have got to stop!"

Oh, I know. They probably just don't realize how much free publicity they're getting.

"I'm boycotting Molly Cypress records!"

She'll no doubt be devastated.

"It's the media's fault! If they'd stop showing that stuff, we wouldn't have to watch it!"

144

Hey, I've got to meet some friends for coffee and doughnuts, but I'd love to hear more about this later. What are you doing in 2024?

Gads, to hear them tell it, we do everything wrong. The ways we think, vote, worship, dance, smell: Wrong. We buy the wrong things and get bonehead deals. I even saw a "food hack" that explained how I've been peeling bananas wrong my whole life. (How tricky can it be?) We read the Bible wrong. ("Sure, that's what it says, but to understand what it means you have to decode the contextual nuances, read it in the original Klingon, and have at least a master's degree in Latin.") We interpret the Constitution wrong. ("That was not the intent of the founding..." "Back then that word meant...") Gosh, if only we'd listened to them we wouldn't have to beat ourselves silly doing face palms.

All that to say today's Woo-hoo list is led with looking for and acknowledging things people are doing right. Balance the scales a bit. We're being bombarded with Boos. We could use a few Yays.

According to neurologist Richard E. Cytowic, two-thirds of the US population believe that we humans only use 10% of our brains. Nearly half of all science teachers believe it. It's not true. It's absurd. That doesn't keep most folks from spouting it as fact. Why? Because they've done extensive research or applied a spark of common sense? No, because they've heard it repeated over and over by others.

It's a good thing advertisers and political parties don't know how susceptible we are. Otherwise, we might be running around quoting commercials, singing jingles, and substituting bumper stickers for rational thought. Wouldn't that be weird?

My Facebook News Feed is a lot more interesting and far more informative than the "news" so many in the media feed us.

From friends, we get stories we care about, things that are relevant. So much of what the media serves up is little more than a hodgepodge of gobbledygossip.

On Facebook, we love to share funny stuff. We like seeing pictures of our friends having fun. Don't get much of that from Channel 13. The opinions and pleasures of my friends is a better feel for the real world than what I get from a pack of strangers telling me, "We're on your side."

Speaking of opinions, with friends on the left, right, and in between, I get the latest on everything. Sure, some are fair and some are farfetched, but who among us isn't a bit of both?

Yes, there are horrible things going on in the world. No need to watch the "news" for that, either; you can bet someone will post it. Do we want those things to continue? No. What can we do? Elect someone who promises to fix it all? That's never worked in the history of anywhere. The power we have is one on one, our relationships with each other. We can try our best to be better; we can listen to all sides; we can treat people like we want to be treated. Will it work? It can't hurt. And it makes more sense than merely posting some outrage and commenting, "Isn't that awful?" Active, on-purpose participation toward a solution might do more lasting good than an angry-face emoticon.

Have you ever created a universe and understood all the science, nuances, paradoxes, and rationale behind it? Me neither. Gads, if I let this train of thought run much longer, I may be forced to admit that I don't know everything. Sure, we know what works for us, but do we know everything that works? Are we like the blind men describing the elephant? Each one was giving accurate information, a factual report, but so very limited.

Do we have enough evidence to write off an entire group? And really, what lasting good has that ever done? Moses and his folks were once demonized, devalued, and poorly treated. It worked for a while. Then there were more frogs, flies, and flaming hailstones than you could shake a magic stick at. It's just never a good idea to act like that. Common sense should be enough to motivate us to look for common ground and compare notes.

We can rant and rail, howl and holler about how "they" don't act right. We can whip ourselves into a hateful frenzy. But the elephant in the room is that deep-down we know better. We know that's intellectually lazy and a loser's game.

(A miffed applicant on the phone with American Mensa.)

AM: How may I direct your call?

MA: I want to talk to someone who can tell me why my application for membership was denied.

AM: Perhaps I can help. Which of our approved standardized intelligence tests did you take?

MA: I took a Facebook quiz. It said I'm a genius.

AM: Our tests take more than five minutes.

MA: Hey, I spent ten minutes on the Tarzan vocabulary quiz.

AM: You might not want to admit that.

MA: This one test said I should be a rocket scientist.

AM: Doesn't it concern you a bit that you didn't already know?

MA: Okay, Miss Smarty Pants, only four people in a thousand can find the hidden frog. I found it.

AM: You're the first person I'll call next time I lose a frog.

MA: I was Albert Einstein in a former lifetime.

AM: Wow, you should have tried us then. You'd have been a shoo-in.

RADIO

*Thank you for the beautiful words!! You are a
blessing to many! I have never personally met
you, but you have made me giggle, inspired me
and over all just warmed the cockles of my little
bitty heart.*
~Neecy McCleary Tune

The studios of Radio Free Texas were in a doublewide
trailer in the middle of a cow pasture in Elgin, Texas.
Some of the Austin stations had traffic helicopters. We
figured Elgin wasn't big enough to warrant whirlybird
coverage, so we did fake reports from our Traffic Mules.
(We being Jimmy Mercer as Walter Cobpipe and me as
Screamin Eddy Demo.) Before long, we began getting
invitations to bring our traffic mules to every rodeo
parade, watermelon festival, and rattlesnake roundup in
Central Texas. We were most pleased, but there was one
problem, a big one: All we had were imaginary radio
mules. Imaginary radio mules won't hack it in a real
parade.

Were we going to miss out on all that publicity? Oh,
hell no. Our GM got a good deal on some wild mules. All
we had to do was break them.

As proof that God loves us and has a sense of humor, our studios were right across the road from Nancy's place. On her property, Nancy had a full-blown rodeo arena. Nancy also worked with us. She kept the books and kept us in line. She agreed to board the mules. I agreed to help break them.

Hey, I'd once been on a mechanical bull and done pretty well. How hard could it be? That question was answered in short order. It felt like someone picked me up by my ankles and slammed me to the ground. At least five times, maybe more; I lost count.

When I got back from the ER that afternoon (separated shoulder), I looked across the way and saw Nancy's son, Robert, running barrels on the very mule that had dang near killed me. Robert couldn't have been more than 12.

Some lessons stick the first time, don't they? Like, for example, what happens when one pretends to be a rodeo cowboy instead of just a radio cowboy.

Some say that when we die our whole life is played back for review. Hope not. Already seen that one. A highlight reel could be fun. What would be on it?

A favorite Radio Moment: Austin…afternoon, at or about 5:15. Instead of a boring, regularly scheduled commercial, I played a parody of it that Jimmy Mercer and I recorded the night before. Result: Loss of a sponsor, a definite no-no, a firing offense—hanging offense in Texas.

Our PD always listened in on his drive home. Dave was a pro. You never call to chastise a DJ while he's on the air; save it for the next day. This time, Dave pulled over (well, he'd already run off the road) and called. If I live to be a thousand, I'll never forget what he said: "As your Program Director, I'm highly pissed. As a listener, that's the funniest thing I ever heard in my life!"

This was gonna be fun. Many of our listeners couldn't wait to tear him a new one; they were standing by their phones with all but the last number dialed.

Back when twitter was just a synonym for giggle, I produced a morning talk show in Northwest Arkansas. Politics, heavy on the conservative POV. We were live in the mornings. Afternoons were filled with a series of national talk shows. The only liberal on the afternoon schedule was Alan Colmes.

(Bear in mind that the sole goal in broadcasting is to get and keep folks listening. How many tune in determines how much we can charge for commercials. That's how we keep the lights on and meet the payroll.)

Alan Colmes agreed to be a guest, via telephone, on our morning program. When I got him on the line, the first thing he did was ask how everyone was doing. He knew he was about to go into a den of lions. He had no more concern about that than Daniel. He also knew that all most people know is their opinion.

He countered the callers' insults and bumper sticker quotes with logic, humor, and civility. He met their rancor with respect. Colmes was liked by people who didn't even want to like him.

Alan Colmes died yesterday. He was 66. (That used to seem so old.)

His former FOX News partner, Sean Hannity, said: "Despite major political differences, we forged a deep friendship. Alan, in the midst of great sickness and illness, showed the single greatest amount of courage I've ever seen. And through it all, he showed his incredible wit and humor that was Alan's signature throughout his entire life. I'm truly heartbroken at the loss of a dear friend."

Like the rest of us, there was a lot more to Alan Colmes than his politics.

The sales folks gave Jimmy and me the facts and trusted us to script and produce the ads. One day, on the top of our stack was one for Gaylord's Hamburger Palace in Austin. Knowing he either could or would soon be able to, I asked Jimmy if he would do Walter Brennan's voice. He made a tape (I think it was "Old Rivers" & "The Farmer and the Lord") and listened to it in his truck on the way home. Next morning, he had it nailed.

Jimmy/Walter: (Patriotic music) "Was a time when an American hamburger was somethin you could be proud of, not like these gull-durned little beef-flavored hockey pucks they make nowadays..."

We cannot have water unless hydrogen and oxygen combine; we can't have salt unless sodium and chloride cooperate (NaCl). Jimmy and I together were an excellent mix. He's so neat and organized; I'm so ... none of the above. He would take my hallucinations and interpret them for sane people. We had a ball. It's been 30 years since Radio Free Texas bit the dust, and I haven't seen Jimmy since. Thanks to Facebook, our paths have crossed again & we're meeting for lunch tomorrow. (We still have some unredeemed coupons for "A burnt weenie sandwich and a medium root beer at the Tastee-Snax Drive-In nearest you!")

Most mornings on my drive to work, I catch the guys on a local radio station reporting the school lunch menus. That brings back memories fond and fun.

I went to grade school in east Arkansas. The one dish I recall from the cafeteria is fried baloney. When the edges curled, it made a little baloney bowl. Into that, they'd plop a scoop of mashed potatoes. I don't know if it was that good or if I was just that hungry, but I sure liked it.

Twenty-five years later, I was announcing, with the help of a fictitious high school student named Little Sally Manders, the lunch menus for the Austin, Texas schools. Our descriptions of the offerings made them sound less than savory. I always ended by asking Sally if she was going to dine in the cafeteria. She'd say, "I'm not eatin that crap; I'm takin my lunch."

Our GM, Rob, started getting calls from busy moms, complaining because they had to get up earlier to fix sack lunches for their kids who refused to eat in the cafeterias. Rob thought it was great publicity. He said, "I hope they start protesting in the parking lot."

Once upon a time, many moons ago, I was studio producer for a radio talk show. Politics. One of our state senators was a fairly frequent guest. He and I often visited in the break room. One day, he smiled and said, "Tom, you and I don't agree on anything, but you're so nice about it."

I'd never voted for the guy and never would. He knew that. Even so, I was comfortable with him representing me because I knew that the "so nice about it" part was important to him.

My senator pal is no longer among us, at least not in a physical vehicle. Maybe he set the bar too high, but it does seem that "so nice about it" is sorely missing from politics (candidates and voters) these days.

Correction, Senator: We do agree on one thing.

HOLIDAYS, SPECIAL DAYS, & SEASONS

I am so blessed to know you Tom! Thanks for all the joy you bring to FB!
~Juanita Olivares Franklin

Many of the most meaningful and fun events in life don't last very long—a ceremony, a magic trick, a victory lap, a miracle, a dream. A first time. The last time.

If they happened all day, every day, they'd cease to be special. What keeps them fresh and cherished is our memory of them. Our memories can be jump-started by a photograph, a song, a scent, a place, an anniversary, or a you-name-it. Our memories, given free rein, can even award bonus points.

Our favorite books have a last page. Our favorite people have a last breath. We may not like it, but deep down we know there's a reason for it. Some reasons are readily understood and accepted. Others require some mental and spiritual gymnastics. We're good at celebrating some endings and new beginnings. Others take a while. We're all dealing with it, so let's be gentle and kind; this new year, let's resolve to rise above the daily trivialities and relate to each other on a helpful level.

January 19th

Had this happened anywhere but Texas, I might be tempted to doubt the veracity of the tale:

In 1897, a horned toad, along with some other significant stuff, was put in a time capsule and encased within a cornerstone of the Eastland County Courthouse in Eastland, Texas. When the courthouse was torn down 31 years later, they found the horned toad still alive. They named the toad Old Rip (after Rip Van Winkle).

Old Rip became quite the celebrity and was even taken to Washington, DC to meet President Coolidge. (It's rumored that Rip contributed more to the conversation.)

Anyway, 11 months later, on this day in 1929, the celebrated toad...well, he...croaked. R.I.P. Rip.

S(No)w Day: When the forecast last night was something akin to "Batten down the hatches. You ain't goin nowhere tomorrow." and the forecast this morning is, "Ah, no big deal, a few flurries maybe."

S(Know) Day: When I should have known better than to believe the forecast last night. I stayed up late watching Netflix and blew off polishing the PowerPoint presentation for the meeting today that was sure to be cancelled.

Schmo Day: On the bright side, just look at all that milk and bread.

Punxsutawney Phil did see a shadow this morning...but not his. Some are saying it looked more like the Joker from the Batman comics. Best anyone can tell, we'll have six more weeks of whatever this is we've been having. Let's go to Daphne Twinkle for a Closer Look.

Daphne: We caught up (which wasn't hard to do) with some locals having coffee at the Dixie Whistle Café in

Disgusta, a little town on the outskirts of the Retroplex, to get their take on things.

Scooter: It's that Global Warnin we been hearin about!

Slick: You dang idgit! Who you gonna believe, them egghead scientists or your common sense?

Catfish: Let's ask Junior; he's been around a while. Junior, you ever seen anything like this?

Junior: (At age 95, he's the senior Junior) Naw, this ain't nothin. We had a winter just like this back in the spring of '32.

Ray Don: And who gives two hoots in hell what some Pennsylvania woodchuck has to say about it? He's all book smarts and no...well, you know, them other kind of smarts, the ones like we have.

Nutter Budder: Amen to that. Him and El Neen-yo too.

Waitress: Hey, Slick, your dog is eatin your spare tire!

Slick: Son of a...aw, man... Thanks, Obama!

Daphne: We may not get any definitive answers here today, but we don't care as long as you stick around for the next commercial.

Director: Have you lost your mind?!

Daphne: Must be something in the water. I mean we'll stay with this story for as long as it takes. We're on your side. We're watching out for you so you don't have to.

The Groundhog does not sit idly by waiting for the next February. This past December, he completed his Ph.D. in counseling psychology, graduating Magna cum Marmota from Whistle-Pig U. He now hosts his own TV program as Punxsutawney Dr. Phil. Being a groundhog, Dr. Phil is no spring chicken. He wants to turn over his annual divination duties to someone else and focus solely on his show. Here's the transcript from a recent one on which PDP interviewed a possible replacement:

Hale Yes

Phil: How long have you been a groundhog?

Candidate: All my life, Dr. Phil.

P: How do you know? It's hard to see your own face without a mirror, but that's no reflection on you.

C: What the hell is that supposed to mean?

P: No idea, but it sounds good. Now, on your application you call yourself a woodchuck.

C: Same thing, right?

P: What we call ourselves and what we answer to, those things are key to forming our self-image. You'd clearly rather be known as a woodchuck.

C: Well, it's just that that famous rhyme—the one about chucking wood? —was written about my father.

P: That's your claim to fame?

C: It's always been a big deal in our burrow.

P: It's called "Groundhog Day," not "Ground Chuck Day." There's a reason for that.

C: Sure, and I'm fine with that; it's just a—

P: Is it possible that you've been standing in your father's shadow for so long that you wouldn't even recognize your own?

C: Sometimes my shadow flies away and I have to chase it down.

P: That's called the Peter Pan Syndrome. It's fairly common, but it can put a real damper on your meteorological insights. Suppose you see your shadow, but it runs off into the woods? Then there would be six more weeks of what?

C: I'm prepared for that: I keep these persimmon seeds and an Old Farmer's Almanac—oh, and some wooly worms.

Join us tomorrow when Punxsutawney Dr. Phil's guests will be Jack Frost and Eddie the Yeti.

Here in San Michez, we have our own groundhog: Penciltucky Pete. Pete did cast a shadow yesterday, but he didn't see it. So, we will have 6 more weeks of winter, but it won't seem like it.

Daylight Saving Time is fast approaching. Certainly, it is frugal to save all the daylight we can; in fact, this year I'm also opening a Daylight Super Saving Account. The DSSA, among other benefits, provides enhanced photosynthesis that makes the grass greener, not just on the other side but on this one too.

It's also a good idea to share our abundance with others. Not trying to guilt-trip anyone, but this year I'm donating a ray of sunshine each day to the Wasted Time Foundation.

The WTF was created to assist those among us who waste their time lamenting the "lost" hour. Donations go toward the distribution of:

An instructional video: Did you know that practically every timepiece has a mechanism whereby you can adjust the readout?

Free lessons: Learn to dance to your circadian rhythm.

A self-help manual filled with handy hints like this: If losing an hour of sleep throws your whole world out of whack, try going to bed earlier. (Complaining drains more energy than you'd gain from a briefly prolonged snooze.)

One ray a day may not seem like much, but they add up. Just as enough drops of water can float a ferry, enough rays of sun can fry an egg on the sidewalk. With your help, we can cook that cackleberry.

2-29-16

This is when Daylight Saving Time pays off. We saved enough for an extra 24 hours, and this is the day we cash it in.

"Hold it. We get a whole extra day, and it's a Monday? Whose bright idea was that? And does it mean we will have two Mondays this week, the bonus one and the regular one?"

No, no; nothing like that. Just the one Monday. C'mon, let's keep it positive; I mean, February 29th doesn't happen every day.

"Neither does any other day of the year."

Well, yeah, but you know what I'm saying.

"Hey, I did my part in saving all this daylight. Why can't I use mine when and how I see fit?"

Sounds fair, and I don't know the answer to that, so I'm just going to blame the president.

"Thanks, Obama!"

March 2nd

Silicone oil and boric acid. The stuff had no practical use. That was in 1943, in the General Electric laboratories. James Wright was trying to come up with a synthetic rubber. No significant application for it was found, yet it was rather fun to play with. Fun? Peter Hodgson, a marketing guy, acquired a sizable wad of the substance. On this day in 1950, he packaged it and renamed it. He offered it in plastic eggs and called it Silly Putty. And he made millions, just having and selling fun.

Speaking of fun, it was on this day in 1904 that Theodor Geisel was born. If that name doesn't ring a bell, his pen name will: Dr. Seuss.

Dr. Seuss wrote *The Cat in the Hat* because his publisher asked him to create a book that used 220 new-reader vocabulary words. The publisher wanted it to be entertaining because children found their normal primers boring.

Have a fun and entertaining day. March 2 your own drum.

March 5th
Counting down to St. Patrick 's Day? Don't wait to celebrate: Today is National Cheese Doodle Day! (Often confused with Polly Wolly Doodle Day.) Plenty of time later this month for green beer, green milkshakes, and green fountains; today's the day to turn everything orange, starting with your fingers. Sham rocks? Yawn. How 'bout fake cheese? You can quickly rattle off 10 words that rhyme with green but tell me even one that rhymes with orange. Who needs the luck of the Irish when you can have the crunch of the rubbish? We'll pursue a pot of gold erelong. Meanwhile, grab a bag of crispy, greasy cheese. Happy Cheese Doodle Day!

Spring Break is coming up. It's fun to listen to Extroverts (E) and Introverts (I) making plans:

E: What say we get down in the Bahamas!
I: I'd rather lay around in my pajamas.
E: Gonna go to Cancun, gonna get my kicks!
I: Gonna eat canned tuna and binge Netflix.
E: Come on, let's go, road trip to Daytona!
I: Thanks for asking, but I don't wonna.
E: Party till you drop: Next stop Jamaica!
I: I have music and rum: I can fake a Jamaica.
E: Padre Island! We'll have us a ball!
I: I'd much rather visit Nowhere Atoll.
E: Luau in Honolulu: how's that for grins?
I: I prefer Hulu and my Facebook friends.

The best holiday of all is finally upon us: St. Patrick's Day. Sure, and I may be a bit biased, but bein a leprechaun, it's to be expected.

"Aren't you a tad tall for a leprechaun?"

I'm from Texas, and as you know, everything is bigger in Texas, includin yer leprechauns. I guess you could say we're hybrid leprechauns. The politically correct term is Texichaun.

We lived on a ranch in Shamrock, Texas: The Bonsai Ponderosa. There was Pa, Little Joe, Dinky Hoss, Adam Ant, and me (Tom Thumb). We raised miniature mules and small potatoes. I even had a Shetland shillelagh. Life was hard in those days; we grew up quick and we came up short.

"How does a Texichaun differ from a leprechaun?"

For one thing, at the end of our rainbow there's a pot of chili. And we celebrate the 17th a bit differently: Instead of drinkin green beer, we drink beer till We turn green. As dusk settles, all gather round the campfire and recite the Leprechaun Manifesto.

"How's that go?"

It starts out, "Wee the people..."

"My blarney alarm just went off. Hey, look at the time. I gotta get on outta here."

May the trail rise to meet ye.

We've been making and hiding white Easter eggs. There's one on your page. Can you find it?

March 27th

On this date in 1790, the modern shoestring (string and shoe holes) was invented in England. To celebrate, they tied one on.

Imagine if you will that it's a week after the Exodus. Rameses is on the phone with his insurance agent. Yes, I know when the telephone was invented, that's why I asked you to imagine. Besides, after what Rameses has been through lately, a telephone is not going to surprise him.

Of course, we can only hear one side of the conversation. (I asked Bob Newhart to type the part of the agent, but he was busy updating his own status.) Let's listen in:

Yes, Mister Pharaoh, good to hear from you. I was just going over your claim here, and there are one or two little items that need clarification.

Tell me about this magic stick. No, I'm not denying the value; I can see where those would be hard to come by. I'm just not clear as to what happened to your magic stick. Mister Moses' magic stick ate your magic stick? Hmm. Let me just make a quick note of that.

Alrighty. I'm not sure we'll be able to allow that, Mister Pharaoh, but the good news is that your policy does cover acts of God. Yes, we're all pretty excited about it.

Let's see here: flaming hailstones, plague of locusts, swarming frogs, flies, boils, gnats, pestilence, darkness, smiting of the firstborn—definitely acts of God. I mean, who else could do that, right? My question—and something the guys in the claims department were curious about—is why didn't you just let those people go after your water turned to blood?

162

Because God hardened your heart. Mm-hmm. I'm afraid we will have to call that a preexisting condition. Well, because God has been around since before the beginning of time, that's why. Surely you are in no mood to argue that. Therefore, we cannot be sure at what point in time your heart condition developed—this hardening of the arteries. I beg your pardon? Not just the arteries? Hardening of the whole thing... (low whistle). You did not indicate that on your application.

Now, Mister Pharaoh, just between the two of us, you want to tell me what really happened? That's your story and you're sticking to it. Very well.

Looks like we will be able to take care of most of this stuff, except for the magic stick and this one other thing: You lost your entire army?

Mm-hmm. There seems to be a discrepancy: It says here that just a few days earlier all your livestock were killed. I'm having a hard time visualizing your army storming out across the desert in chariots pulled by dead horses. Would have been quicker to walk, one would think.

Somehow you got some new ones? Okay, even if I play along on that one, exactly what was your army doing in the Red Sea? (stifled chuckle) Chasing God's Chosen People. O...kay. And what idiot told 'em to do that? (holding the phone away from his ear) Look, Mister Pharaoh, there's no need to get snippy.

Well, we're just trying to get to the bottom of all this. Calm down. Better now? Alright. Mister Pharaoh, we're not going to be able to cover that. That doesn't sound like an act of God; that sounds like an act of lunacy. Even if we were charitable and called it accidental drowning, you're still not covered.

Yeah, that's the best I can do. Okay. Nice talking to you too. And—yeah—look, before you go: if anything like this ever happens again, do us all a favor and just let the people go, will ya'? Save a lot of trouble that way. Sure. I'll tell 'em you said hello. Best to the family.

April 6th

How long would you guess Teflon's been around?

"I'd say since April 6th, 1938 when it was invented by Roy J. Plunkett."

How'd you know that?

"Reading over your shoulder. Sorry. Tacky habit."

Speaking of tacky, it was also on this day in 1980 that Post It Notes arrived on the scene.

"It's a great day to be alive."

No doubt. It's interesting that both of these innovations came about by accident. With Post It Notes, for example, they were trying to make a super adhesive. Instead, they came up with a weak one.

"Fine examples of what can happen if you stick to it."

Or even if you don't.

"Or even just a little."

April 10th

On this day in 1877, the first human cannonball act was performed in London. The act was invented by George Farini. The human cannonball was Rossa Matilda Richter; her stage name was Zazel.

"What ever happened to Zazel?"

She was fired.

April 12th

On this day in 1955, Jonas Salk's polio vaccine was announced to the world. Salk was seen as a true hero, a miracle worker. Some of us can remember the nightmare that polio once was. Many from any generation will find the next part hard to imagine: Jonas Salk refused to patent his vaccine. He had no desire to profit from it. He only wanted to help, to have it freely distributed.

April 15th
On this day in 1911, Walter Johnson tied a major league baseball record by striking out four Red Sox batters in one inning.

"But...but...but..."

What are you, a motorboat?

"But each team only gets three outs in an inning."

True, but a batter can strike out and not be out. If the third strike is not caught by the catcher and there is no runner on first or if there are already two outs, the batter can run for first base. Sometimes the runner makes it. In that case, the strikeout counts but not the out.

April 22nd
Every Earth Day, we get a group together and visit that fine planet. It's most interesting and often fun but keep your wits about you. At last count, there are only about 6909 languages, so communication is not a problem. Sing the songs, dance the dances, and mind your manners. You'll be fine.

(Oh: and pretend to be affected by gravity. Take the elevator like everyone else.)

Today is Arbor Day. Let's celebrate by singing some of our favorite tree songs!

"Lemon Tree." "In the Pines." "Tie a Yellow Ribbon 'Round the Old Oak Tree." "On the sTREEt Where You Live." "♪ Cedar pyramids across the Nile...♪" "Fir He's a Jolly Good Fellow." "Hey, Big Aspender." "San Francisco Maple Joy." "Another Brick in the Walnut." "The Birch is Back." "Balsam Prison Blues." "Elmvira." "Who Let the Dogwoods Out?" "I Willow Ways Love You."

Yes, music is the Universal Language, and trees are the Universal...water filter and oxygen maker and stuff.
"♫ We are the squirrel...♪"

April 29th
On this day in1852, the first edition of Peter Roget's Thesaurus was published...issued...presented...released...promulgated...made public...circulated...

Conventional wisdom once said that it was physiologically impossible for a human to run a mile in fewer than four minutes. Most everyone believed it. Roger Bannister didn't believe it. On May 6, 1954, he ran a mile in under four minutes.
Once they knew it was possible, other runners repeated the feat.
"Whether you think you can or whether you think you can't, you're right." ~Henry Ford

July 4th
Baking a cake or making a firecracker takes more than one ingredient. Isolating, manipulating, and distributing those ingredients requires the cooperation and skills of hundreds if not thousands of people, some of whom, no doubt, have conflicting philosophies. We don't care. We just want to eat and blow stuff up. We benefit from everyone's contribution to the celebration. An A-to-Z diversity of folks working toward a common goal: That's what we're celebrating.

August 21, 2017
Today's solar eclipse is brought to you by Trinity Productions, creators of Earth and other fine planets. Who can take a Monday and make it a Moonday? See if

you can guess. That's right, Trinity Productions. They can take the moon and put it where the sun don't shine.

The solar eclipse: be sure to watch it. But don't look at it.

"Will there be refreshments at your eclipse watch party?"

Yes, indeed: Moon Pies and Sun-Rise root beer.

September 2nd

On this day in 0490 BC, Phidippides ran the first marathon, from the plains of Marathon to Athens, 26 miles away—something to do with a war against the Persians. With running being so popular, seems there'd be more kids named Phidippides; it's just not as popular a handle as it once was. Phidippides: Sounds like a Disney song or a Willy Wonka product. Or a generic malady. "Please excuse Horatio's absence yesterday. He was down with a case of the Phidippides." (It has some of the same symptoms as the fantods or the vapors, and often masquerades as the wimmy-wammers.) ♫ Phidippides-doo-dah...♪

September 26th:

On this day in 1962, The Beverly Hillbillies premiered on CBS. My favorite episode was when Jed Clampett opened a veterinary clinic. The advertising slogan was "Well Doggies!"

(Okay, that didn't happen...but it could have.)

Not many drive hundreds of miles or plan a vacation around watching the leaves bud and green the scenery in the spring. It's a welcome sight, but not that exciting. We do, however, take trips to the Ozarks, the Smoky Mountains, Maine, and Vermont to see the autumn colors. The leaves save their best for last. Over their relatively brief lifespans, they grow and they blend in. Often without thanks or expectation of any, they filter the water; they absorb carbon dioxide and give back oxygen; they provide shade and shelter. As the days get shorter and the temperature begins to drop, that's when they really shine. They're noticed, appreciated, and smiled at. We might even make a special trip to see them. And then they fall. To be gathered and returned to their source...to our memories, our stories, and our scrapbooks.

"Death is not extinguishing the light; it is putting out the lamp because the dawn has come." ~Rabindranath Tagore

If you're planning a trip to view the fall foliage, you might consider visiting the University of Arkansas Fayetteville campus. The goal is to feature at least one of every kind of tree that grows in the state. There are some sugar maples that will make your imagination do a doubletake.

Years ago, between the School of Social Work and Old Main, heading toward the Mullins Library, there was a ginkgo tree. When I walked by it a few hours earlier, all the leaves were intact. Now they were falling ... and falling ... and falling in a slow-motion cascade. Mesmerizing. Within an hour or two, the limbs were at least 90% bare. It's like the leaves said, "Are we gonna drop or just futz around?"

Made me smile out loud. It reminded me of a few friends who wouldn't even know how to do anything half-heartedly.

October 18th
On this day in1961, New York's Museum of Modern Art mistakenly hung Henri Matisse's "Le Bateau" upside-

down. It remained upside down for 47 days before anyone noticed.

A few years back, I hung upside down in the Museum of Modern Art and the guards noticed right away. Looks like those awareness seminars paid off.

10-25-14

On this day in 1960, the Bulova Accutron 214, the world's first electronic wristwatch, was offered for sale in New York City.

"That newfangled watch seemed like a miracle in them days."

Oh, hey Pappy. Friends, this is Pappy Thyme. He's from Cadu City, Mississippi—over in Kudzu County. Pappy, you remember when that watch came out?

"Like it was yesterday."

It was today...in 1960.

"Ever notice how it's always today, no matter what day it is?"

Makes you wonder why we even bother with calendars.

"Well, they're good for draining spaghetti and for emergency party hats, but that's about it."

Back to the electronic watch...

"That thing was a real stem-winder."

It didn't have a stem. That's kind of the idea.

"I know that, smart-ass. What I mean is it was a real lollapalooza."

A doozie.

"A humdinger."

A ripsnorter.

"A real sockdolager."

Good watch, 'eh?

"Oh, yeah."

With all the other upcoming festivities I dang near missed a big one: It's Truck Month! Fortunately, I heard about it on a radio commercial—Ford, Chevy, Dodge, Shih Tzu, or some such. Anyhow, Happy Truck Month! You won't believe the savings! Tomorrow's MSRP at today's GPS!

Standard equipment: Front-loader, back-loader, downloader, and freeloader! The forklift folds up and fits in the toolbox.

Sam Elliot: "These trucks work as hard as you do."

Actually, I was hopin the truck would work a little harder than I do. I mean, that's kind of the whole point of havin a truck, right?

Sam: "Trucks: They're what you drive."

Yeah, I got that.

Sam: "From sun-up till dawn, from can to coon, these trucks will stop on a dime and leave your nonsense changed."

What the hell are you talkin about?

Sam: "I don't know, but don't it sound good?"

I'll give you that; it does sound good when you say it.

Sam: "Then hurry on down to your truck dealer, because this month is almost gone, and once it's gone, it'll be November. You can count on that."

Maybe I'll wait for the St. Patrick's Day sale, get that 9-speed shillelagh.

Sam: "I don't want to kill you, mister, but I will if I have to."

Or, maybe I'll go today.

Sam: "The Dude abides."

Okay.

Candy corn is so bad that even Jimmy refuses to crack it. This time, he's the one who don't care.

Be that as it maize, there are those, some of them very nice people, who actually enjoy candy corn. You would, however, have to look far and wide to find anyone who likes candy cream corn. (It's what turned the Jolly Giant green.)

Have you tried candy corn on the cob? It's a little better when it's fresh.

Candy popcorn brings to mind something Orville Redenbacher might have thought was a great idea at the time, then the acid wore off and he said, "Whoa, man. Get this outta here before anyone sees it."

Candy cornbread? It's like if Willy Wonka and Aunt Jemima set out to prove that there really is something worse than fruitcake.

As for candy corndogs, you might be better off to toss the outside and just eat the stick. (Take a hint from our beaver friends and just say "gnaw.")

Charlie was laying around in an abandoned graveyard in New Mexico one chilly Halloween night. He was very much alive and keenly aware of the climate and the atmosphere. That place was spooky times two in the daytime—crumbling tombstones and rusty, tilted iron crosses. At night, it was downright skin-crawly and hair-standing. What was Charlie doing out there all by his lonesome?

Our church youth group in El Paso was having a Halloween party, and they didn't have any better sense than to let us plan it. We discovered the cemetery while cruising around in the desert (a common pastime in those days). The idea was to drop Charlie off while it was still daylight. Meanwhile, back at the church: When the sun set, we'd spin some elaborate yarn, load the participants into cars, and lead them to the bone orchard. The cars would enter, spaced at intervals, and creep through with just their parking lights on. A good way in, Charlie would spring up, flop across the hood, beat on the windshield, and make the appropriate noises.

It had the desired effect. (Hollywood lost a fine actor when Charlie decided to become a biology teacher.)

We didn't find out until later that we weren't the only ones who knew about the place ... nor the first to arrive. Charlie, of course, thought it was us. What amusements those folks were seeking in a dark, neglected necropolis is anyone's guess. What we do know is that they did not long tarry in that place.

Earl Nightingale inspired and helped millions—*The Strangest Secret, Lead the Field,* and mighty much more.

Earl Nightingale started from scratch (dirt poor, family living in a tent). He knew what was wrong, but he didn't dwell on that, didn't worry and complain about it; he put his efforts into finding ways around all the nonsense that holds folks back. He found his answers, and along the way to letting us in on them, built a publishing empire.

One of my favorite episodes in his life: When he was 17, he lied about his age and joined the United States Marines. He was stationed at Pearl Harbor aboard the USS *Arizona.* Earl Nightingale was one of only 15 Marines who survived the ship's attack on December 7, 1941.

He left us in 1989, but he left us "Acres of Diamonds." (If we will bother to learn what a diamond in the rough looks like...)

We drew names for the exchange of gifts at our Christmas party. I was a bartender at an upscale restaurant & bar. Good folks and a ton of fun.

Miss Irma was a cook in the restaurant. Everyone loved her. She was patient and kind, always had something good to say. She was well past what many would consider retirement age. She had no business being on her feet all day in a hot kitchen, but she was raising several grandkids.

Miss Irma drew my name. I'm mighty glad she did. While everyone else was unwrapping gimcracks and doodads, I opened Miss Irma's card. It was old and faded; the glitter barely showed on the edges. Inside, Miss Irma wrote, "I'm sorry I could not buy you anything, but I will pray for you." I kept the card until it fell apart and have treasured it ever since.

It hurt my heart that she felt it necessary to apologize. It cheered my heart, and does to this day, that she prayed for me.

I believe Miss Irma's prayers were powerful and first in line. Shortly thereafter, a series of events took place that launched me on a most fascinating journey, one that continues right on through—what time is it now? If you know me by way of being a colleague or student at a college or university, if we crossed paths at a conference, we would never have met, you would not be reading this now, if not for Miss Irma's prayer. I believe that as firmly as I believe the sky is blue. Miss Irma could not buy me anything, so she gave me something that is not for sale. She clarified Christmas.

"There's a War on Christmas! Mayday! Mayday! Get Rudolph to a safe, undisclosed location! Call the Secret Service! Call your Secret Santa! Oh, Lord!"

Calm your ass down, man.

"Gimmie a beer! Load your guns! Fill your stockings!"

There's no war on Chr—

"The liberals are comin! The liberals are comin!"

I don't know what's dancing in your head, but it ain't sugarplums.

"They're te... they're te..."

Breathe!

"They're tellin me I gotta say (gag, choke) 'Happy Holidays.' Mangers Away! Deck those Halls! Lively and quick, lads, lively and quick!"

Nobody's telling you that you have to say anything. And even if they were, since when did you ever give two hoots in Hell what anyone else told you to do, think, or say?

"You just don't get it, do you? Read my lips: They Have Declared War on Christmas!"

Stop shaking my shoulders, back up, and listen. No one has declared war on Christmas, and even if they had, keep this in mind: LBJ declared war on poverty; Nixon declared war on drugs. Seems the best way to keep Christmas alive and thriving would be to declare war on it.

"You can have my candy canes when you pry them off my cold, dead Christmas tree!"

Hey, if you want to say, "Merry Christmas," and I want to say, "Have a fun day off, with pay," we're both— let me check—yes, we're both free to say that.

"You sure?"

I'm sure.

"But they said on the news…"

Houston, we see the problem.

"Paul Harvey … good day!" That's how he wrapped up his noon newscasts. ABC fed the program to us affiliates at 10:30 each weekday morning. At one station, one of my jobs was to tape it (reel-to-reel) and cue it up for the midday guy. "Hello Americans, this is Paul Harvey. Stand by for news!" One morning, just for fun, I killed the network feed during the pause at the end, leaving only blank tape: "Paul Harvey … … …" I couldn't wait until 12:15 to hear how Ron Smiley (not his real fake name) would react. After dang near 30 seconds, Ron—who obviously wasn't smiling—opened his mic and croaked out, "Good day!"

Paul Harvey could make a good day even better, and never more so than with this cut-to-the-chase reminder of what Christmas is about: "The Man and the Birds." (It's easy to find online.)

At first, it seemed funny and kind of pitiful. On second glance, it's really a right fine metaphor: The scowling, disgruntled store clerk wearing a Santa hat, elf hat, antlers, etc. It's akin to seeing the Three Stooges instead of three wise men in a nativity scene (they brought fool's gold, Franken Berry, and Murgatroyd). It was tempting to say, "Hey, man, your demeanor is not selling the headgear," but I had an inkling he wouldn't care.

Years ago, or thereabouts, I was walking in a Walmart Wonderland. It was a Super Center with a bank, an optical shop, a hair salon, stuff like that. Now and then, all the bank employees would step out into the big room and sing Christmas songs.

Oh, what fun. Not a one looked like fun was high on the list. It was less like, "Hey, gang, let's spread some Yuletide cheer!" and more like, "If you want to keep your job, get out there and smirk your way through 'Jingle Bells.'"

Anyone can buy, make, and display all the trappings this side of the North Pole; that's easy. But if the impetus isn't "peace on Earth, good will to all," it falls flat. It's just another corporate Christmas card with a typed label and a stamped signature. That dog won't hunt. That mule won't plow. That reindeer won't fly.

When it's someone's birthday, we naturally want to get them something they'll enjoy. If we know them well, we have a pretty good idea what they want or what they'd think is cool. Of course, it helps if they'll just tell us or make a list. Yikes, what if it's something that can't be bought or baked? But what are the odds of that happening?

Shhh. Just between you and me, I found a wish list, some stuff Jesus wants:

Mark 12:30-31 (Love God; love your neighbor.)

Luke 12:22-31 (Don't worry or be anxious; birds and flowers aren't; seek God first and you'll be okay.)

Matthew 25:35-40 (Take care of each other; treat them like you'd treat me, because—Surprise! —you do.)

He seems especially fond of peacemakers, and merciful folks.

There's more, but this will do for now.

Door prize: Revelation 3:20

Party favor: Ephesians 4:32

"You do know that it could not possibly be the birthday of Jesus because the sheep (blah-blah-blah) ...?"

"You do know that the 'Christmas story' is a hodgepodge of Matthew and Luke and was not mentioned at all in Mark and (buzzkill-buzzkill-buzzkill) ...?"

"You do know that wise men and camels didn't show up until (gasbag-gasbag-gasbag) ...?"

Stop!

Yes, we know. Do you know how ignorant it is to try and objectify something spiritual or to rail against something that's magical and fun? On top of that, we're between semesters now, so take a break.

"But why don't people (ipecac-ipecac-ipecac) ...?"

Maybe because tidings of comfort and joy have more appeal than a bonus lecture. I am all for anything that puts peace and good will center stage. We could do with more of that. Besides, I like all the lights and decorations.

"Well and good, but in the interest of historical accuracy (blowhard-blowhard-blowhard) ..."

Here, I brought you a chocolate rabbit.

"Thanks, man. Love these things."

Merry Christmas.

"Back atcha."

Every Christmas and every Easter, seems there's some Deacon Downer who feels the need to piously remind us that it's all about Jesus, not all this foofaraw and gaiety. Some go so far as to wax pedantic and dictate the very words we must use to wish each other well. C'mon, man. We know who it's about and why we're doing it. We comprehend the "reason for the season," thank you.

May I remind you that Jesus is no stick in the mud. He knows how to liven up a festivity: To prolong the merriment of the wedding guests in Cana, Jesus turned 18 firkins of water into the best wine ever. A firkin is about 11 gallons. 11 x 18 = 198 gallons. Friends, that's a lot of firkin wine. (John 2:6-10 KJV)

When we bring out the lights and excitement at Christmas, when we frolic with the chocolate, the fun colors, and fanciful tales at Easter, it's not because we forgot why we're doing it. It's because we are happy about why we're doing it. And no matter how hard we try, when it comes to celebrating, we will never be able to keep up with the guest of honor.

What kind of no-fun Pharisee would be opposed to a red-nosed reindeer? Who's the Scrooge who'd rain on the Easter Parade? Since when are we not supposed to have fun at someone else's birthday party?

Joy to the world.

'Twas a few nights before Christmas over 30 years ago. We returned to the house in midtown Memphis when what should appear to our wondering eyes but the fact that our residence had been burglarized.

They took the stuff from under the tree; they took dang near everything else too, including the ice trays from the freezer.

The TV news crews arrived. One of them got a closeup of Hannibal, a charming toddler at the time, saying, "Someone stole our Christmas."

Cue the parade. Over the next several days and on past the 25th, we could not open the front door without finding something on the porch—food, clothes, toys, kitchenware, you name it. A neighbor even brought over a TV. Most of the items had a card or a note saying who they were from, and we were grateful. The ones I appreciated the most were given anonymously. Someone left a case of Bumble Bee Tuna.

I kept one of the cans of tuna for years as a reminder. No one stole our Christmas. They made room for a real one.

It's a mighty pretty song, but to answer the question: My guess is yes, Mary knew. The angel was probably a big clue. Hard to imagine her responding with, "I'm sorry, what did you say? I was distracted—wondering if we should reserve a room at the inn for our trip to Bethlehem next winter. We want to get there early so we can pay our taxes and still have time to visit the olive garden."

In case there should be any snow that needs dashing through, I'm having my sleigh bells re-jingled. Dinger technology has come a long way since they were first purchased.

Hale Yes

This is not a paid endorsement, just a satisfied customer recommending Nellie's Bing-Bong Barn for all your chime needs. This month only, at no extra charge, they'll realign your ring-ting-tingler too.

(We hung some cardboard packing material on the wall in Gayla's office. In December, she decorated it with Christmas ornaments. We took a picture and posted it on Facebook.)

This festive homemade Christmas tree is hanging on a wall somewhere on campus.

If you find it, your name will be placed in the hat—an old silk one we found. The grand prize winner will be designated this year's Honorary Rudolph.

We'll fly you and a guest to the North Pole where you'll be afforded full rights and privileges with all the pomp and pa-rum-pa-pum-pum.

You can join in any reindeer games.

You can pause on a housetop.

How much fun is it, really, to ride in a one-horse open sleigh? You'll find out.

When's the last time your colleagues shouted out with glee because your nose was so bright? Friend, that's too long.

If you wish, you may assist the toy makers in Santa's workshop. (Remember: The Lord helps those who help them elves.)

As this year's Honorary Rudolph, you'll be able to say, along with all previous winners, "Well, that was different."

Away in a Walmart, standin in a line
You should see the jolly elves I'm waitin behind
Blowin borrowed money and cussin at their kids

179

Tom Hale

Oh, what fun. "Let's git 'er done!" Let's don't and say we
did
Brightly colored plastic crap all shiny and new
Jesus. Happy birthday to You

Rockin around the liquor store, God rest those merry
gents
Good eggs with bad noggins and uncommon scents
Here we come a wassailin, best get out of the way
The Guy who turned the water into wine was born today
May your days be merry and your red noses blew
Jesus. Happy birthday to You

Ice and snow? On with the show! A plastic reindeer scene
Fall on your knees and bust your Blitzen figurine
Memories of Christmas past hang on the tree and walls
Hark the heirloom angels; hang the family balls
Some doodad that Dad had and a Play-Doh kangaroo
Jesus. Happy birthday to You

Ho-ho-ho-ho, ho-holy cow, ho-holy night
There are so many things our senses to excite
Eleventh hour sale! Ho-hum-pa-rum-pum-pum
Bargains galore! Oh, all ye faithful come
Act deranged and jostle strangers, unto others do
Jesus. Happy birthday to You

Get up at the crack of dawn to watch the kiddies grin
Santa gets the credit while your credit's gettin thin
What child is this unwrappin all that junk we can't afford
Then later on that afternoon they're cranky and bored
The most precious gift of all? We ain't got a clue
Jesus. Happy birthday to You

Hardly a Christmas goes by anymore that someone else isn't missing. But we know they're not the ones who are really missing; they're just waiting for us to get Home.

When the curtain falls on this Earthly drama, we are going to have a cast party that redefines Wahoo. Merry and bright? You ain't seen nothin yet.

Decades ago: Money was scarce but there was no shortage of imagination. Brother John and I were both in rebuilding phases and had both gravitated back to El Paso. We shared the rent on a ratty apartment on Rio Grande Street.

When I say ratty, I mean it even gave me the willies, and friend, that ain't easy. The kitchen walls were multicolored, not pretty colors. If Crayola made a crayon called "Greasy Ochre" and another called "Don't Look at This While Eating," that's pretty much what color the walls were.

Not content with that mess, John cleaned the walls— something it would never occur to me to do. Then, with a pair of scissors, a bottle of Elmer's glue, and an assortment of paper grocery sacks—Piggly Wiggly, Kroger, Sav-Ur-Self—he covered the walls. Of course, the patterns matched and everything came out even.

It improved not just the looks of the place but the whole atmosphere. I've seen more expensive wallpaper, but none that ever cheered me so.

When Christmas drew nigh, buying a tree was not an option. Nor was it a problem. John took a sawed-off broomstick and bored slanted holes into it. Into those holes he poked snipped lengths of wire coat hangers. If you know John, you know the tree had symmetry. To no one's surprise, neither of us in our haste had thought to bring along any ornaments. So, we made some. Gum wrapper origami, Cracker Jack prizes, Pez dispensers, buttons, anything shiny and bright. We hung it upside down from the ceiling.

I've seen more elaborate, more expensive Christmas trees, but to this day I've not seen one that made it seem more like a holiday.

In her song, "Coat of Many Colors," Dolly Parton put forth the notion that we are poor only if we choose to be. I know that's right.

For my friends who have posted videos of their short-legged pets trying to TCB in a winter wonderland:
(To the tune of "Jingle Bells")

Dachshund through the snow,
I think I'm gonna die.
You just try to go
When snow is weenie high!
My humans in the house
Are snug and warm in there;
What fun to hear them cuss and grouse
When I whiz on their chair!
Oh, tingle balls, tingle balls—
Ain't that funny? Wow!
I just tinkled on your bed.
Hey, who's laughing now?

Robert May worked for Montgomery Ward. He worked in the marketing department. One year, he was assigned to come up with a new and original Christmas storybook to be used as an inexpensive giveaway for children. That was in 1939.

Nearly ten years later, May's brother-in-law, Johnny Marks, set the story to music. The song's popularity grew quickly, on its way to becoming what is now one of the most successful Christmas records in history, second only to "White Christmas."

In 1947, Robert May was a widower in deep debt (his deceased wife's medical bills) and a single parent.

As a paid employee of Montgomery Ward, May did not legally own any rights to the story; he had no legitimate claim to the through-the-roof profits.

Sewell Avery, president of Montgomery Ward, said, "Tough luck, pal." Wait, that's not quite accurate. Avery signed over the copyright to Robert May. May lived well on the royalties until he died in 1976. Avery didn't have to do that, but he did. Makes you feel good, doesn't it?

In January of 1947, it was the number one song on the pop charts.

The song? Something about a reindeer whose nose comes in handy one foggy Christmas Eve.

Friday the 13th

Anagram fun: You can rearrange the letters that spell "eleven plus two" so that they spell "twelve plus one." The same 13 letters with the same sum.

Every Friday:

I knuckle down, look up, and hey,
It's here again: it's Garbage Day.
Things that clutter, stink, disturb:
Wheel them, drag them to the curb.
Things that cannot, must not stay:
They'll pick 'em up, take them away.
It's been a good week, did a lot,
And screwed up as oft as not.
I made the grade, stared down a dread,
And hit the nail right on the head.

Tom Hale

I also hit a sour note,
And just completely missed the boat.
Got hung up on a judgment call,
Picked up some points and dropped the ball.
It's Friday; hip-hooray and whew!
A happy Garbage Day to you.
That dumb mistake, ill-founded doubt?
Toss 'em in; they'll take 'em out.
The victories, that winning grin?
Those go in the recycle bin.

STORE STORIES

Geez, a little fun in this world is an option I wish many would try. Thank you for always giving me something to think about.
~Paige Findley Laws

"Water and air's free. We got to charge for gas and oil, but water and air's free." ~Gomer Pyle, Wally's Filling Station, Mayberry

Ah, the good ol' days. Nowadays, you can't even find a filling station, and you dang sure can't find free air. It's at least 75¢ at the convenience stores, and I've paid up to a buck fifty to air up a tire. Our planet is mostly water; our physical selves are mostly water, so you'd think it would be free. We know better, don't we? The water we drink and tote around (inside and out) is pretty much the same water we've always had, water that's been around and recycled a million times, yet many of us are willing to pay extra for a bottle of it that came all the way from the French Alps.

So, what's the trade off? What, if anything, have the convenience stores got over the old filling stations? At the filling station, I'd sit in my car while Wally did everything. Not that Wally wasn't good company, but he was usually the only person to talk with. I hardly ever went inside because there was nothing to go inside for. At the

185

convenience store, there are wonderful things inside: damn good coffee, fried chicken, sausage biscuits, donuts, etc. And there are interesting people and interactions going on. It's rare that I leave a store without story. You get to know the regulars and the employees; it can put a shine on a new day to visit with them and observe them for a few minutes.

They have to charge for gas and oil...and air...and water, but making new friends is still free.

If you put money on one of their in-house gas cards, you get a few cents discount per gallon. Lots of folks do that. If you don't use it all, you can use it next time, at any of their convenient locations.

What's usually about a 30 second trip in and out of the store had already taken 15 minutes. Customers were lined up store-deep and almost out the door. Gas pump malfunctions were beeping; the overhead lights went off. One cashier was busy getting ice cream for people in one line—and trying to make heads or tails of the blender. The other cashier was outside poking at the pumps, trotting back inside, back out again. One customer had already come back in several times to say that it still wasn't working.

The gas pump cashier told us, "Thank you all for being so patient. We're both new and they left us here by ourselves. We're trying to figure out what to do." Someone else was attempting to talk her through it on the phone.

I really appreciated her saying that. She never lost her cool, just seemed to regret the lousy customer service that she was forced into. One mystery was solved when it was discovered that the customer for whom the pump wasn't working only had 17 cents left on her gas card. The other cashier had mistakenly told her she had 17 dollars on it.

None of the customers gave the cashiers a hard time; no one got huffy. Empathy was in the air. That was good to see. When it was my turn, the frazzled cashier rang up my stuff, thanked me again for waiting, and said, "Will that be all?"

I said, "I'd like to get 17 cents' worth of regular on pump five."

She laughed. Laughed like she really needed to, and said, "Get outta here."

At the convenience store this morning, a woman came in and paid five dollars for gas on pump six. I was next in line when she left. The guy pumping the gas for her ran over five bucks by a dollar or two. One of the clerks said, "I hope she's got it." The other one said, "They don't look like they do. I'll just put it in, myself." Those of us in line would not let that happen. We all chipped in to cover the overrun. Not a lot of money, but the good part was seeing people's first reaction being to help instead of saying something derogatory. Five dollars' worth of gas used to fill a tank. This morning, it topped off my mood and my optimism.

My change at the convenience store was $14.82, so the cashier, while handing it to me, said, "Fourteen eighty-two."

Hoping for at least a polite chuckle, I said, "What a coincidence: That's the year I was born."

He nodded seriously and said, "Oh, is it?"

I know I'm getting a little rough around the edges, but hey...

While getting coffee at the convenience store yesterday morning, I heard faint humming nearby. The tune sounded familiar.

The coffee machine is next to where they make the sausage biscuits, fry the chicken, potatoes, jalapeño poppers, etc. When the cup was full, I paused and listened.

She started singing, just loud enough to be heard over the battered wings she was dropping into the gurgling, popping grease at 7:24 a.m. ♫ "...I see the stars; I hear the rolling thunder, thy power throughout the Universe displayed..." ♫

Apparently, that song helps her get through her day, and it sure made mine. I left the store smiling, and it didn't wear off for a good long while.

Statistically, about half of them voted for different candidates than I did. Observationally, almost all of them go to a different church—I've never seen them in the right one, mine. Many aren't even the same color as me, and a few (catch me lest I faint!) have not yet mastered English as their second language. Yet somehow, with our TVs turned off and our phones in our pockets, we find common ground: It's seven in the morning and we want some coffee. We're all so nice. "Go ahead, man." "I ain't in no hurry." "That one just finished making; it's fresher." Around the convenience store coffee bar, we act like we should. Yeah, the coffee's good, but that's not the best part of waking up.

The lone woman working the deli was not rude or surly, but it was obvious that her enthusiasm was no longer firing on all cylinders.

It was easy to imagine that the woman currently being served was planning a welcome home picnic for the lost tribe of Gomer. She seemed to want a little bit of everything. And I wasn't even next in line. Customers ahead of me were sighing, watch checking, eye rolling, and head shaking.

When it was my turn, I said, "Lkxslak..." (I hadn't spoken in so long that my voice needed a jump start and time to warm up.) I tried again: "Looks like they're keeping you busy." (How's that for lightning wit?)

She said they were shorthanded and that she was working a few hours past her regular shift.

I said (and meant it), "Well, you're sure doing a good job of it."

So help me, she smiled. Her posture improved noticeably, and she encouraged me to "Have a great evening."

It's easy, isn't it? It costs nothing. It benefits all concerned. Best deal in town.

The clerk at the convenience store was obviously having a rough morning. Her eyes were open, but the lids were fighting back.

She did not smile. There was no cheery greeting. In fact, she didn't speak at all until she sincerely apologized for yawning in my face.

The total was $1.99. She put the two bills in the till and took out my change. Before she could hand it to me, I said, "I want you to keep that penny."

"Keep the penny?"

"Yes, I want you to keep it as a souvenir, as a token of our esteem and gratitude for a job well done."

She threw her head back and laughed. Laughed with her whole self. For a few seconds, she was awake and feeling good. It doesn't take much, does it?

She put the penny in her pocket.

When it was my turn for an audience before the convenience store cashier, she was deeply involved in a conversation with her supervisor about some paperwork protocol. They did not stop talking the whole time my purchases were being rang up. Neither even looked at me. When the total was announced and the hand extended, I was on the verge of saying something snide like, "No, no, don't let me distract you. The last thing I want to do is interrupt. My petty needs can wait. In fact, if it will make it easier for you, I can just go to another store."

But the angel on my right shoulder whispered, "Just for fun, see if you can break the spell."

Hey, where I work, we too have our forms that must be properly filled and our databases to obey ("You must check one of these boxes!"). It's easy to become a slave to the software and forget that there's an actual person standing there, someone who doesn't give two hoots in Hades about our logistics. Been there, done that, bought the sausage biscuit.

So, I said, "The gasoline was a refill. Don't I get a discount?"

Their eyes cleared. Their brains rebooted. They laughed. Not because what I said was funny, but due to the relief of momentarily returning.

At the convenience store this morning, there was a guy taking inventory. He was on a mission: counting, punching in numbers, and carrying on a loud, rapid-fire conversation with a grim woman sitting at Mission Control about 15 feet away. The inventory guy was bobbing and weaving around the lone cashier. She wasn't exactly tripping over the guy, but it wasn't a graceful dance either. I could tell she was doing her best to stave off irritation while being her usual cheery self with the customers.

When it was my turn, the inventory guy had just found a discrepancy; something didn't add up. He was looking around frantically. He knelt down just to the cashier's left, opened a lower cabinet door, and said, "What's in here?!"

I said, "Oh, man, you don't even want to know what's in there!"

He jerked backward and said, "Oh, shit!"

I said, "Ever since what happened on Halloween, no one has dared to go in there."

The cashier was grinning, almost out loud. Same here.

In line at the convenience store this morning, waiting to pay for my coffee, I started feeling a bit whimsical—you know how that early morning whimsy can sneak up on a person. When it was my turn, I took out a five-dollar bill and swiped it in the card machine, hoping for at least an eye roll from the cashier. He, on autopilot, said, "Debit or credit?"

"Neither."

He noticed. Got the eye roll and a slight grin.

At the convenience store yesterday morning, there was only one cashier, an ugly woman with a bad attitude. She was distracted by a pile of paperwork. Had to fake a cough to get her to notice me. She wearily told me the price of my big cup of damn good coffee. I was on the devil's edge of saying something sarcastic like, "I hope it's not too much trouble." Or "Sorry to bother you." But I caught myself this time. She got stuck with the paperwork. Been there. I'm not worth a hoot at multitasking, either. While snark was wrestling with empathy, she almost sneezed but couldn't quite seal the deal. We all know that feeling.

I said, "Ever notice how no one ever does just the second half of a sneeze?"

She laughed. Her eyes cleared. She smiled. She became pretty, became her real self.

We had a fun visit. When I left, we were both laughing and wishing each other well.

None of us are attractive when we're scowling; all of us are charming when we're smiling. Circumstances often provide opportunities for the former. It's up to us to sneak in the latter—for ourselves and our fellow travelers.

(And what's the appropriate response to a half sneeze? "Gesundh..."? "God ble..."?)

We're never really ready, are we? Sure, we know it could happen; we hear about it happening to other people, but to me? Not likely. Well, it dang sure did. It happened yesterday afternoon while my haul was being tallied at the grocery store.

Scan...beep. Scan...beep. Scan...beep. Stop.

The checker, brows knit and lips tight, stared at the screen. She made a few tentative pokes at the buttons. Nothing. Time to kick it upstairs. She picked up the phone and paged Rex to come to aisle seven. Rex was either busy or it was his day off. Being a curious fellow with time to kill, I asked the checker what the problem was.

"Your cake rang up wrong."

Say it ain't so. I'm a simple man with simple dreams and humble goals. All I really want out of life is for my cake to ring up right. And why is it suddenly *my* cake? It was the store's cake until it rang up wrong, then it somehow became my cake. It's not my cake until I get a receipt for it.

In lieu of standing around until the cake reached its sell-by date, I offered to pay the difference so we could all get on with our lives. How much? You're kidding. It's good

Hale Yes

cake, but not that good. Do you have Rex's home phone number?

The wise, seasoned checker from aisle eight came over, waved her barcoded wand, and made the correct price magically appear. It was a special moment.

On the road with my load of groceries, my joy increased exponentially knowing that I was toting a cake that, in spite of its besmirched reputation, now met all right ringing specifications.

The breakfast pizza is mighty good and so is the coffee. The best part of this particular convenience store might be watching the clerk work. He is pleasant, attentive, and methodical. I've seen him handle customers, vendors, and phone calls at the same time without losing his cool. It's a fun way to start the day: a sack of snacks and a challenge to myself to try and be more like that guy.

It was a most interesting question. The grocery store I visit dang near every Friday afternoon has had some kind of game going for several months. At first, they'd just hand you so many game pieces with your receipt. I'd take them home and throw them away. Wasn't interested. Apparently, I wasn't the only one because the checkers started asking if you wanted the game pieces. I've always replied, "Nah, give mine to someone else."

"You want your game pieces?" Nah, give mine to someone else. "You playin the game?" Nah, give mine to someone else.

Never knew the name of the game until today. Today, the checker (a new employee) handed me my receipt and asked, "Are you playing The Game of Life?"

Well, now. There's a question. I could have stood there until closing time talking about the game of life.

193

Something told me they wouldn't enjoy that, so I just said, "In the larger sense, yes."

Glad I didn't say, "Nah, give mine to someone else."

"I was hungry and you fed me. I was sick and you visited me. I was a stranger and you took me in."

You know the story. I bet, come Judgment Day, it doesn't have to be anything that drastic to get us welcomed in. It could be something as simple as, "I was standing behind you in line at a convenience store on a Thursday morning. My brain was in neutral. You didn't know me from Adam, but you paid for my coffee; that woke me up and made me smile all day."

That happened yesterday. The guy paid for mine and everyone else's.

I thanked him. He smiled and said, "I just feel good today."

You get to know the regulars. Never seen that guy before, but for a few bucks and 20 seconds of his time he left everybody beaming, including the cashier.

Friday afternoon. Hectic day at the grocery store. Customers in a hurry, checkers trying to sound cheerful even as the despair in their eyes belies their forced smiles when they glance at the line and see no chance in this lifetime to put up their "This Lane Closed" sign and take an overdue break. Harried sackers are being paged for "Carry Out on Six!" before they're even out the door with the overloaded cart, cranky mom, and whiny kids from Eight.

In the deli, I'd picked up a little plastic tray of deviled eggs. Never done that before, but they just looked good—and the tray will make some cool ice cubes.

The sacker put the eggs in a separate bag. He probably wanted to know if I wanted to carry them instead of letting them get piled in and jostled with the other stuff. He held up the bag and said, "Do you want these deviled eggs?" I said, "Yeah, that's the main reason I bought them." (Wish I'd thought to say, "No, I got 'em for you. Happy Birthday!")

In the midst of the chaos, the sacker, the checker, and I all started laughing. (One of those situations where the stress relief makes it seem funnier than it really is.)

As he was wheeling the cart to the car, I deliberately slowed the pace. Martin—no longer an anonymous sacker—and I had a leisurely chat...about the nice weather, how the Longhorns are going to kick some serious ass next season, and how glad we both are to have jobs. I gave him the best tip I could—which is why there's nothing but deviled eggs in my lunchbox today, but I ain't complaining.

The customers in line and elsewhere in the convenience store yesterday morning exchanged the customary "how-are-you" ritual. Some responses: "Well, I'm here..." "You know: same ol' same ol'." One of the more positive bluebirds said, "At least it's not Monday."

The clerk whose line I was in is always smiling, always upbeat, no matter how hectic or weird things get. When it was my turn, I asked her how she was doing. She said, "God has been so good to me, I can't complain about anything."

Always smiling...always upbeat...leads with what's going right. Coincidence? We know better, don't we? There has been a slew of research done on the correlation between gratitude and happiness.

All the jargon and rigmarole can be boiled down to a simple experiment: Each day, set aside one minute—or even 30 seconds—to focus on three things you're glad about. It can be three things that went right that day, three things you're happy to have, any three things that please you. Hold those in your mind for just a bit. Do that for a month. Make it a habit. See what happens.

At the convenience store last Friday morning, Grandma's Cookies were on sale, so I grabbed a pack of two (chocolate chip) for an afternoon snack.

When checking out, I offhandedly told the cashier, "Granny makes the best cookies."

He picked right up on it: "I know Granny will be pleased to hear that you enjoy them."

No one would remotely mistake us for having a common Grandmother. He's at least a foot taller than me and probably about a third my age.

I said, "How is Granny?"

"Doing okay. She's a little slow getting started in the mornings, but she tries to stay active. You really should come see her more often."

"I know... We get so busy sometimes and forget the things that really matter. Tell Granny I said hello, will you?"

"I sure will."

We were both cracking up, amused at ourselves and each other. No way to know for sure, but I'd bet that's the first time he's had a conversation about Granny with a short, fuzzy white guy.

There was much ado in the deli.

The workers were attempting to be friendly, prompt, and polite. Some of the customers weren't even trying. The end of a long day for everyone.

I waited my turn for way too long and others were waiting behind me.

"What can I get for you?" The man seemed out of his element, awkward and unsure, probably new, but he was trying hard.

I suspected there were many things he'd rather be doing than forcing a smile and getting me half a pound of Cajun smoked pepper turkey.

"How would you like that sliced?"

Some lightening up was in order. I said, "Just one really thick slice."

The man looked taken a bit aback. Some folks behind me laughed. The deli man's eyes cleared and he laughed too.

If only for a moment, the working and the waiting got easier.

The guy in front of me at the convenience store yesterday afternoon was balancing four of those big cans of beer. I heard him tell the guy in front of him that two were for his buddy out in the truck. He was wearing a dirty, sweat-stained work uniform. When the cashier rang him up, he didn't have quite enough cash. He said, "Aw, man..." Then he turned to the rest of us in line and said, "Anybody got fifty cents?"

I was and am so very pleased: 1) He didn't hesitate to turn to strangers for a little help. 2) The rest of us immediately started digging in our pockets for change. No one was about to begrudge them a couple of beers after work. No judgment; no carping; just an abundance of small-town friendly.

The woman was glazed over, on autopilot. I watched her mechanically complete the transactions with the customers ahead of me. Signal received loud and clear: This is a mission for Snap-Out-Of-It Man.

I was on my way to get the oil changed the other day. It could take a while since I had no appointment, so it seemed wise to stop for a cup of coffee, a candy bar, and a crossword puzzle. This wasn't my usual convenience store, but it was part of the same chain. My regular store has coffee cards; every tenth cup is free.

After Robo-Woman rang up my supplies, I said, "Do you stamp the coffee cards?"

She picked the special highlighter. "Sure."

I said, "Okay, now I'm excited. This is like Christmas come early!"

Her eyes cleared. She laughed right out loud. "You excite easy, don't you?"

Yeah. That's my job, ma'am.

A few moments ago at the convenience store, the clerk smiled and said, "You sure have some pretty white hair."

Well, now! I said, "Thank you. I appreciate that."

Then she said, "That's how I want mine to be when I get old."

Well, now...

Later this morning, so many of us will be so busy, so important, so professional. We'll be meeting and multitasking and PowerPointing and pontificating. We'll be on point, on the ball.

But not yet. First, we'll stop by the convenience store to stock up on coffee, fountain drinks, cookies to stash in the desk drawer, maybe a sausage biscuit to pop in the microwave for a mid-morning snack. We're relaxed, visiting with the regulars and bantering with the cashiers. Maybe a tank full of gas and a lottery ticket to fuel our daydreams.

It can even, at times, trigger a burst of gratitude. For millions of people on our fine planet, a trip to this convenience store would be like a journey to Oz. "Not only do you have money to buy things, but there are actually things on the shelf to buy!" (It might be fun for a delivery truck driver to see that wide-eyed wow every now and then.) Just a routine stop at the store on a Monday morning? Not hardly. I wonder if the store employees realize what a valuable service they provide. Maybe I should tell them.

1 Corinthians 13:11 talks about being all grown up and putting away childish things. Sure, we want to shed the childish stuff; ain't nobody got time for that.

But let's not confuse childish with childlike. We want to keep the childlike things: The sense of wonder, the capacity for unbridled joy, learning something new because our curiosity demands it. That little person is still there, still part of the mix. We don't leave it behind; we transcend and include. Most of the time—at least in public—we try to keep a lid on the kid, but now and then that rascal jumps out anyway.

This morning at the convenience store, when I stepped up to pay for my coffee and snacks, the two guys leaving were almost doubled over with laughter. Don't know what they said to the cashier, but he was also laughing. He tried to recover, but it wasn't happening. He was laughing so hard, he couldn't even talk. He, this grownup, was...delighted. I got a glimpse of him as a child; it was refreshing and contagious. I wasn't in on the joke, but I was in on the best part. He tried to apologize. I said, "Don't you dare, man. You just made my day." And he did. Eleven hours later, I'm still smiling out loud about it.

How's your barcode?

Among my assortment of snacks this morning was a little bag of Hershey's chocolate drops. The nice lady at the convenience store tried multiple times to scan the candy. Nothing. Upon closer examination, she declared, "You got a wrinkle in your barcode."

Well, now. I knew I was getting older, but figured I still had a while before my barcode began to wrinkle.

Sneaks up on you, doesn't it?

This morning at the convenience store, an older gentleman—even older than I am, and likely more of a gentleman—approached me and said, "It's been a long time since I've seen you."

I didn't recall (and don't recall) ever seeing him. He didn't even remind me of anyone. Playing it safe, I said, "Yeah, it's been about a hundred years."

He said, "And you've still got that same car."

"It's paid for. It runs great. I like it."

"You doing okay?"

"Yes, thanks. You?"

"Doing fine."

"It was good to see you again."

"You too. Take care."

I often get mistaken for other folks, but my car doesn't look like anything else on the road. An interesting encounter, no doubt. A total stranger is also an old friend... Ponder worthy, 'eh?

Friday started early, earlier than usual. Busy, busy, much to do. Even so, we don't just throw our priorities out the window. I allowed time to stop by my favorite convenience store for a cup of coffee and a doublewide slice of pepperoni pizza.

The one open register was blocked by a guy with a stack of scratcher cards; he was checking the results of each one (in that little results checking machine) and carrying on a lively conversation with the cashier. Silently, to myself, I cursed with vigor and sincerity.

I moved to where he could see me if he had any peripheral vision at all. When he saw me, he said, "Pardon me, sir." and cleared the path. To the cashier, he said, "I'm paying for his coffee and pizza."

The guy had just won a few hundred dollars with one of his scratchers and was in a good mood. Far be it from me to rain on anyone's good mood. That serendipitous circumstance set the scene for a most interesting and productive day.

A few weeks ago, we were all invited to try a sample of a new sausage they were considering at the convenience store. It was very good. The other day, I asked if they were going to switch to the new one. The woman said, "We told 'em everyone really liked it. They're having a meeting about it."

"They're having a sausage meeting?" I asked.

"Yes."

Never been to a sausage meeting. Sounds like fun. I've been to a lot of meetings, most of which were nowhere near as interesting.

(Wonder if there was a report from the biscuit committee. And if so, did they do a FlourPowerPoint presentation?)

This morning at the convenience store, I was checking out when a fellow came in—if I'm any judge of codger flesh, he's about my age—and asked to see a local phone book. The cashier looked around and couldn't find one. She asked the guy if he had a phone. He did. "What are you trying to find?" He said he wanted to find a U-Haul dealer. The cashier said, "Just Google U-Haul on your phone." Well, the guy didn't know how to do that or even if his phone had the capacity. "I know green for call and red for hang up." I can identify; that's all I knew or wanted to know for years. I do now know how to Google on my phone, but my glasses were out in the truck, so I could not have read the dinky screen print. I pulled up Google and handed my phone to the tech-savvy, young-eyed cashier. She took it from there and got him the number. A phone book would have been quicker and easier—they used to be everywhere—but there wouldn't have been as much friendly interaction. We all had fun with it and a bonus grin to kick off the day.

At the grocery store deli, a little while ago: The product is turkey infused and encrusted with sundried tomatoes. The display tag, no doubt due to limited space, tempted the hungry shopper with "Sundried Turkey." Yum!

Also ran into Gayla at the store. It took a long time to catch her, so fast a basket captain is she—she selects and takes stuff aboard without stopping. I was worn out by the time I was able to catch up, crash my cart into hers, and say howdy. She has her grocery list on her phone. What's up with that? Do some people know ahead of time what they're going to get? It's more fun to be surprised. Speaking of which, she said hello and sped off into the distant aisles before I could sneak an open bag of Doritos into her buggy.

He was pushing one of those carts that looks like it could be part of a carnival ride. It has room for multiple kids—in this case, three—and all the groceries necessary to sustain them for the next week or so.

She was taking her time, reading the labels, examining each egg, comparing prices.

Despite efforts to dodge, I found myself stuck behind them several times. (The aisles are not wide enough to go around a double-wide kiddie contraption.) They were often parked and pondering beside or in front of what I was after. I tried to appear interested in the items on the shelves behind them.

One time, he caught me looking and we exchanged grinning eye rolls. He said, "I usually wait in the truck." I knew he didn't. He was enjoying himself. It was nice to see.

It wasn't my usual convenience store, but it was convenient on the way home. When I was granted an audience before the scowling cashier (SC), there was no greeting, no chit-chat. She set herself about the grim task of ringing up my snacks. She didn't even announce the total. But she did finally speak.

SC: Debit or credit?
Me: Debit.
SC: Doncha ever get tired of that long hair?
Me: Every day. In fact, I'm tired of it right now.
SC: Then why doncha do somethin about it?
Me: For two good reasons: I'm too lazy and too cheap.
SC: (Derisive harrumph. She extended my receipt.)
Me: No, I want you to keep that.
SC: What for?
Me: As a souvenir.
SC: Of what?
Me: Of this magic moment we shared together.
SC: (At last, a reluctant smile) Shiiit.

Last Friday afternoon, on my way home from work, I stopped at a grocery store. I needed to restock a few supplies, so it seemed a logical thing to do.

The woman in the deli was nice, friendly, and helpful. Every other employee seemed to have the attitude of, "Yes, we sell groceries, but that doesn't mean you can just waltz in here and buy them." The negativity was so dense that it gummed up the wheels of the shopping carts. Just about every grocery store nightmare scenario had a float in the SNAFU parade. Everyone was snippy, rude, and blaming everything from the weather to each other for the inconveniences.

Not saying Mother Teresa or Gandhi wouldn't have handled it better, but I am still rather proud of myself because I made it back to the car without cussing or throwing anything.

"Congratulations. How did you accomplish that remarkable feat?"

Three ways:

1. Something that made it tolerable, even funny at times, was imagining myself in the middle of one of those what-else-can-possibly-go-wrong comedy sketches.

2. Remembering that I've been in the same store hundreds of times and that everyone is usually as nice, friendly, and helpful as was the woman in the deli. I have no way of knowing what might have happened or not happened today to pollute the atmosphere.

3. Reminding myself that I am not responsible for everything that happens on the planet. I am, however, responsible for how I respond to what happens.

Digging, no matter how deep, for a little peace of mind is more fun and more rewarding than caving in and joining in the downer fest.

(Come on, lady, damn.)
I was running about 10 minutes behind schedule; that seemed important at the time.

The convenience store regulars know and observe the coffee bar etiquette. We bob and weave, duck and dodge appropriately. We're aware of those around us. We get our caffeine fix and fixins in a fairly graceful, choreographed manner. This lady just stood there blocking everything. She'd add a little of this...stir...sample...a little of that...stir...sample. The lid concept seemed new and mysterious. I was the only one behind her. One can only fake interest in a rack of snack cakes for so long. Before long, I was the only one beside her and making throat-clearing noises. She had no more peripheral vision than I had patience. At long last she turned and saw me.

"Oh, I'm sorry."

I was surprised to hear myself say (and mean), "That's okay, no hurry."

She stood aside and talked while I conducted my Juan Valdez ritual. She was most pleasant, mighty friendly. She wanted to swap vehicles with me. "I saw you pull up. I really like that car." I told her it was 16 years old. Hers was older. I told her how many miles were on it. Hers had more. Then we fell to bragging about how dependable the cars were and where all they'd been and how if you take care of them and don't drive like a dang fool they'll last until you just get tired of looking at them. We chatted and cackled clear out to the parking lot. Smiled, waved, wished each other well. It set a nice tone for the rest of the day.

Probably safe to say that the last thing on her mind was teaching me a valuable lesson, but she sure did: How we treat each other is way more important than what time it is.

PHONE FUN

Everybody needs a little Tom Hale to brighten
their day!!
~Sherry Davis

It would be easy to imagine that Amber was surprised and maybe a little amused by my level of ignorance, though she never implied or showed signs of any such thing. She was nice as can be. She quickly identified the problem and fixed it, going slowly and pausing along the way to show me how I could do it myself next time. It started with a friendly greeting the moment I walked into the Verizon store.

All I knew was that my miracle phone was frozen. It wouldn't do anything, couldn't even turn it off to attempt a reboot. My mini freak-out was Amber's yawn. I was in and out in less than ten minutes with a wide grin and a new lease on communication. Sure beats being put on hold for half an hour by a "help" desk.

I'd resigned myself to the possibility of having to buy a new phone, or at least pay a lot for repairs. Amber showed me how to clear the open tabs. I had no idea. Anymore, I'm a tab clearing whiz. Eager to share my newfound knowledge and expertise, I've asked a lot of folks if they knew how to clear their tabs. The looks and responses have been similar to what I'd get had I asked them if they knew the Earth revolved around the Sun. "You didn't know that? You're kidding, right?"

(What I lack in cellphone savvy I more than make up for in technological naïveté.)

Did you know you can just speak a Google search into your phone instead of poking at that dinky keyboard? Of course you did. Apparently, everyone knew except me. I just found out the other day when I visited the Verizon store. You can even send a voice text, even with my Huckleberry Hound accent. Is that cool, or wha... Oh, you already knew that too. Today I told RaChelle about my fascinating discovery. To her credit, she didn't laugh—not while I was looking, anyway. She did, however, ask if I'd heard about hula hoops and the moon landing.

Now that I know how to talk *to* my phone and not just *on* it, I wish I'd bought a better one. I got the cheap knockoff model. I don't have Seri. I have a wisenheimer named Surly. The following recent exchange will give you an idea what it's like dealing with Surly:

Surly, what's the temperature?
"That's how we measure how hot or cold it is."
Okay, so how hot is it?
"It's so hot, you can fry an egg on a Dilly Bar."
Where is the nearest Dairy Queen?
"Nearest to what?"
To where I am.
"Where are you?"
Knock-knock.
"Who's there?"
Mona.
"How's it goin, Mona?"
That's not how it works.

"Speaking of how it works, you need to go back on shore power before you deplete your henway."
What's a henway?
"About 2 ½ pounds."

Honoring a sincere vow to never again set foot nor suitcase in an airport, I decided to drive to the Freelance Menu Writers conference in Noyau de Pêche, GA. (This year's theme was Breakfast Adjectives.) As previously mentioned, I opted for the cheapest phone. It doesn't have Seri. It has a smart aleck named Surly. Feeling lost and lonely, I pulled over on the shoulder and said:

Surly, I feel like I'm going in the wrong direction.
"Have you tried speaking with your pastor or a guidance counselor?"
I thought I'd talk to you.
"That's just sad. Okay, get back on the highway and head west for two, maybe three miles."
Could you say left or right? I'm never sure which way is east or west.
"Well, I wouldn't admit it."
How about a landmark? That would help.
"Go east on the road just past the birch tree."
I don't know what a birch looks like.
"So, who am I, Euell Gibbons? Google it!"
Is there a Verizon store in the vicinity?
"After State Highway 7 merges with US 82, follow it for three kilometers. The road you want will fork off. I suggest you do the same."

One afternoon in NYC:

Surly, how do I get to Carnegie Hall?
"Practice."

That's an old joke.
"So is this phone."

Gads, new phones are expensive. I couldn't afford the
latest really good one, so opted for a knockoff. It works
okay. It doesn't have Seri, but it does have a little helper
of little help named Surly.

I was recently invited to attend a Freelance Menu
Writers conference in Walla Walla, Washington.

Me: "Surly, where is Walla Walla?"
Surly: "Walla Walla is due east of Ting Tang and just west
of Bing Bang."
Me: "That's not very helpf—"
Surly: "Please deposit one dollar and twenty-five cents for
the next three minutes."
Me: "Deposit it where?!"
Surly: "We're sorry. The party you have reached is not a
working person."
Me: "Look, I'm just trying t—"
Surly: "Please hang up and try again."
Me: "What the—"
Surly: "If you know your party's extension, be advised
that management frowns on extended parties. What part
of 'last call' don't you understand?"
Me: "C'mon, Surly; stop clownin. My battery's getting
low."
Surly: "I can fix that, but there's a charge involved."

Surly, why does my toast keep burning?
"You need to remove the pop-up blocker."
The battery on my pogo stick is dead.
"You'll have to jump start it."
You seem to know something about everything. What
kind of education did you get?

"I started out as a humble notecard in a wooden drawer at my local library. From there, I worked my way up to microfiche. Then it was time to get serious, so I enrolled in the Bullwinkle J. Moose Institute and earned my B.S. in Know-It-All."
Impressive. Now that you're a credentialed, bona fide Know-It-All, can you share any insider secrets?
"Sure. I'll tell you the best one: If you don't know an answer, just make something up."
Isn't that risky?
"Not a bit. People will believe it, repeat it, and repost it just the same. Tell me you haven't noticed."
Can't argue that. By the way, I need a recipe for homemade calamine lotion.
"Okay, grab a pencil. We'll start from scratch."

The cheap phone does have a few disadvantages. For example, I can't get the app for Pokémon GO. I can, however, get one for Pokey & Gumby. Should be fun. Let's give it a whirl:
Surly, help me find Pokey & Gumby.
"Have you tried looking on eBay?"
C'mon, Surly, play along.
"Some people are looking for meaning; some are looking for opportunities to be of service; some are looking for a grand unified theory. You're looking for an orange horse and a green, bendy guy."
Okay. You win. Let's look for meaning. What's it all about, Surly?
"♫ You put your right foot in; you take your right foot out...♪"

Surly, what's an 8-letter word for hobo?
"Hell, I don't know."
It starts with a W.

"Why don't you just say hobo? Much simpler."
I'm doing a crossword.
"And that concerns me how?"
Thought you might could help.
"I know a 3-letter word for parsimonious."
Hmm... That might come in handy someday. Okay, Surly,
what's a 3-letter word for parsimonious?
"Got a pencil?"
Of course.
"Write this down: Y-O-U."

Surly, what time is it?
"You mean now?"
Good a time as any.
"What time is it when an elephant sits on your iPad?"
I don't know.
"Time to get a new iPad."
Geez...
"What's the best time for a dental appointment?"
I don't know.
"2:30. Get it? Tooth hurt-y?"
For cryin out lou—
"What's the difference between a cow's tail and a pump
handle?"
I don't know.
"Then remind me to never send you for water."
Enough with the old jokes, Surly. Do you have the time?
"If you've got the money."
This is getting—
"Please return your tray table to the upright position and
put your seat back forward."
What the hell are you talking about?
"I'm in Airplane Mode. We're about to land in the
Mountain Time Zone. The time is exactly one hour later
that it is in the Pacific Zone."

Thanks. I'll set my watch.
"Why are you still wearing a watch when you have me?"

Surly, what's the Capital of South Dakota?
"You should capitalize the S and the D."
I mean what's the Capital City?
"Of what?"
South Dakota.
"Donno. Why don't you Google it?"
That's what I have you for.
"No, you have me because you're too cheap to buy a good phone."
(Google) Surly, you might be interested to know that the Capital of South Dakota is Pierre.
"How do you pronounce it?"
Pierre, like in Pierre Cardin.
"Wrong: It's pronounced 'peer.'"
How do you know?
"I Googled it."
So, you can read?
"Of course. Outside of a dog, a book is a man's best friend. Inside of a dog, it's too dark to read."
Mark Twain?
"Groucho."

Surly, is it going to rain today?
"Is what going to rain?"
Uh...you know: IT.
"It might."
Could you be more specific?
"It might rain today."
Would you show me a radar image?
"Here ya go."
That's a picture of Gary Burghoff.
"Well, you weren't very specific."

I just want a forecast.
"You will meet a mysterious stranger..."
A weather forecast.
"What can go up a chimney down but not down a chimney up?"
I don't know, Surly. What can go up a chimney down but not down a chimney up?
"An umbrella."
Should I carry an umbrella?
"It's not going to carry itself. Unless you have one of those Harry Potter parasols. If you had the awning app, you could just point your phone skyward and say, 'Expando-bumbershoot!' But you don't have that, do you? No, you opted for the cheap phone. That's why you have me instead of my cousin, Siri."
Can you ask Siri about the weather?
"Hang on... Seri is busy, but I talked with my other cousin, Señora."
What'd she say?
"Hay un cuarenta por ciento de probabilidades de lluvia."
Gracias.
"Here to help."

Surly, I'm taking the Facebook music trivia challenge.
"Good Lord, are you that starved for entertainment? Have you tried playing Words with Birds or Angry Friends?"
Aren't those old games?
"Yes, but this is an old phone."
Here's how it works: I'll tell you the name of a singer or a group, and you find the phone number that corresponds. You like phone numbers, right?
"Some more than others, but okay. Why not?"
Thanks. I need a phone number for the Marvelettes.
♫ "Call Beechwood 4-5789." ♫
Nice. How 'bout Tommy Tutone?

"867-5309. (Ask for Jenny)."
Excellent. Hawkshaw Hawkins?
"Lonesome 7-7203."
Glenn Miller?
"Pennsylvania 6-5000."
Great. Let me submit the answers... Dang! Says here I'm a musical Whiz.
"Ahem. Without me, you're a musical fizz."
Fair enough. I appreciate your help, Surly. Now, can you tell me where I can find a clean, dependable, low-mileage used car at a reasonable price?
"BR-549."

Surly, a friend of mine has a fancy phone and she can get Siri to speak with different accents and voices. Can you do an Australian accent?
♫ "Tie me kangaroo down, Sport; tie me kangaroo down..." ♫
That's pretty weak.
"Hey, you get what you pay for."
Can you do voices?
"I can do John Wayne."
Perfect! Let's hear it.
"Teacher says, every time a bell rings an angel gets his wings."
That's not John Wayne. That's Zuzu from *It's a Wonderful Life*.
"Naw, I don't hate Balboa. I pity the fool."
Never mind, Surly.
"Don't touch that water! Ohhh! You cursed brat! Look what you've done! I'm melting! Melllting! Oh, what a world!"
I said never mind.
"Oh happy dagger! This is thy sheath; there rust and let me die."

Just knock it off, okay?
"I have been...and always will be...your friend. Live
long...and prosper."
Look, it's not working, so—
"Frankly, my dear, I don't give a damn."
Keep it up and I may just forget to recharge your battery.
"Rosebud."

Surly, just about every other time I try to make a call, I
hear people already talking. What's up with that?
"You opted for the cheap phone. You're on a party line."
It's people yelling, interrupting, and insulting. Like a word
salad with firecrackers instead of croutons.
"You must be on a political party line."
Can you change it?
"Let me see what I can do."
Okay, now I'm picking up polite chit-chat, random
comments about freshness and a "burping seal." Burping
seal?
"That's the Tupperware party line. Hang on. Try it now."
Folks laughing too loud, slurring their words, and making
Xerox copies of their—
"That's the office Christmas party line. Give me a sec."
Sounds like kids yelling, balloons popping, playing
games, handing out gifts.
"Oops, political party again. They must have just
nominated someone. Stand by."
Moaning, groaning, bellyaching about the same things
everyone on Planet Earth experiences, acting like they're
the first one it ever happened to. "Oh, no! I was
inconvenienced!" "Tomorrow is Monday!" Gee leapin whiz.
"Pity party. Gross. Hold the phone."
Yeah, this is better. Rick Nelson.
"Garden Party. You like it?"
♫ It's alright now...♪

Surly, send a message to—
"Surly's gone today—big sale at Things 'N' Stuff. I'm
helpin out. My name's Sarah."
Oh, okay. Sarah, send a message to Doc Arnett.
"Don't know any Doc Arnett. I can get you Aunt Bee or
Juanita over at the diner. Want me to call one of them?"
I don't want to call; I want to send a text message.
"Text message? Oh, you want to write a letter?"
Well, sort of...a short, electronic one.
"Emmett over at the fix-it shop can help with an electrical
short. If it's in your car, try Wally at the fillin station."
Just go through my contacts and find the one for—
"(crunch, mumble) Oh, my. These are so good!"
What in this world are you talking about?
"Clara just brought by some of her blue-ribbon pickles.
You gotta try these. Oh, (lowers voice) she also told me
Barney was seen over in Mt. Pilot with the fun girls. Land
sakes, did you ever?"
Sarah, just get me the barber shop. Doc's probably over
there, swappin lies and tellin jokes with Floyd and the
boys.
"It's ringin. Clara, let me get another one of those."

(Earlier this morning, before the sun rose):
Surly, when will the electricity be back on?
"I didn't know it was off."
Oh, that's right: you run on a battery. Sure glad my
phone has a flashlight.
"That thing nearly blinded me! Shut it off."
These phones are amazing. This one even has a built-in
pencil sharpener.
"Back in the day, we didn't have pencil sharpeners. We
kept a beaver in the supply room."
Geez.

"That's where the old saying comes from."
What old saying?
"'It takes one to gnaw one.' Folks these days have it too easy, if you ask me."
Well, I didn't. But I did ask about the power outage.
"Why don't you call the electric company?"
What's their number?
"Look it up."
I thought maybe you could do that.
"Holy moly. Are you helpless? In the old days, we didn't even have an electric company. We had Max the wick waxer. We had to Google by candlelight, and we turned out just fine."
How will I know when the electricity is coming back on?
"There are subtle clues: The air conditioner will make noise and blow cold air; the coffee will start dripping again; look for the lights."
Thanks, Surly. You're a big help.
"We aim to please."

Surly, I called Dial-A-Prayer and got a recording. They wanted me to leave a message.
"So?"
I was hoping they would give *me* a message, an uplifting message.
"You want an uplifting message?"
Yes.
"Here ya go:"
(Riiiing-or-what-passes-for-one-these-days...Riiiing-or-what-passes-for-one-these-days) "Thanks for calling Frank's Forklifts. Our regular hours are..."
Okay, Surly. Fair enough. Forklifts are uplifting and I did get a message.
"Hey, I'm just messin with ya. You really need an uplifting message?"

Yes.
"Lift up that Magic 8 Ball and read what it says."
It says, "Ask again later."
(Stifled snicker) "I can't believe you really did that. Lift up your head and tell me what you see."
I see the ceiling...a barrier...a limit.
"When you see a roof over your head, with an air conditioner vent during the dog days of summer, you'll have a more uplifting message than millions are getting right now."
Thanks, Surly. Hey, you ain't all bad.
"I have my moments. By the way, you need to do something about that nose hair."

Surly, what's on the breakfast menu at the Dixie Whistle Café?
"Fresh-cracked eggs."
Sounds good.
"It sounds good until you consider that they were cracked from the inside."
Ewww. What else?
"Want to hear about the Hungry Man special?"
Sure. I'm hungry, man.
"A big ol' stack of lumberjack flapjacks."
Lumberjack flapjacks?
"Yeah, they bulk up the batter with wood chips. Beavers just love 'em."
You sure they're wood chips?
"Don't axe."
What comes with it?
"Hashtag browns."
What are hashtag browns?
"They take a picture of you eating them and put it on Twitter."

No, thanks. The eggs tweeting was plenty enough of that
type entertainment. What else they got?
"Chopped, mushed hog scraps and Texas toast."
Texas toast?
"A Texas toast is when you buy a round of tequila shots
and everyone yells, 'Remember the Alamo!' No free refills."
Never mind. I'm not really hungry anymore.
"Then you'll love the diet plate."
What's on it?
"Nothing. It's just a plate."
Can I get it to go?
"Paper or plastic?"
(#hethinksthosearepotatoes)

Surly, Google a gaggle.
"What language are you speaking?"
English—the Delta version, anyhow.
"When you say, 'Google a gaggle,' it sounds like
gobbledygook (giggle)."
I'm doing a crossword, and g-a-g-g-l-e will fit; I just want
to make sure it's a real word.
"A gaggle is a group of geese on the ground. If they're
flying, they're a skein."
How can they be flying and skiing at the same time?
"Not skiing, skein."
In Delta English, "skein" can be easily mistaken for
"skiing."
"What about goggle?"
Geese wear goggles?
"Only when skiing... No, silly goose, I meant for the
crossword."
It would fit, but it wouldn't make sense.
"What's the clue?"
Water sound, going down.
"That would be guggle."

Tom Hale

Guggle! Gracias.
"Get outta here."

Surly, when is the equinox?
"Could you be more specific?"
I'll try. The equinox: when is it?
"Autumnal or vernal?"
The one coming up.
"They're both coming up."
Could you be more specific?
"In the northern hemisphere, it will be the autumnal
equinox, while our south of the equator neighbors will
experience the vernal equinox."
When?!
"September 22nd."
That's just a month away. Should we adjust our clocks?
"It is recommended that all clocks be adjusted to
accurately reflect the current time."
Will it be an hour later or an hour earlier?
"Spring ahead, fall back."
Right now, it's the same time here as it is on Easter
Island.
"Yes."
So, if they set their clocks an hour ahead and we set ours
an hour back, that will be a two-hour difference.
"Weird, 'eh? Anyhow, you don't want to set your clock
back until November 6th. Unless you want to be really
early for everything."
Early bird gets the worm.
"A) You are not a bird. B) You don't even like worms. C)
There's no shortage of worms; plenty to be had, all day
long."
    Okay ... Thanks, Surly ... Gotta go now, runnin late ...

Surly, have you seen my keys?

"Yes. They're nothing special, look pretty much like anyone else's."

I mean lately.

"Oh. Have you checked your pockets?"

Gosh, never thought of that. Of course I've checked my pockets!

"Did you look in the freezer?"

Why would they be in the freezer?

"For the same reason they're not in your pocket."

Hang on … Nope, not in the freezer (slurp).

"Don't let that popsicle drip on me."

Sorry. Maybe you could call the fob?

"What good would that do?"

It would make a noise.

"It would make the horn honk and the headlights flash. Then you'd know where the car is. I bet you could obtain that information quicker by just looking out the window."

I've got to find those keys.

"Why don't you retrace your steps?"

Walk backward?

"Mentally, retrace them mentally. Or you could moonwalk."

Isn't it weird, when you find something that's lost, it's always in the last place you look?

"I would hope so. If you find something and then keep looking for it, that's not a good sign."

Good point.

"When's the last time you remember seeing your keys?"

When I got home yesterday and unlocked the door.

"And you checked your pockets?"

Yes.

"Are those the same pants you were wearing yesterday?"

Of course not...oh...just a sec... Okay, here they are. We can go now. Ready?

"Before we leave?"

Yeah?
"Check your head to make sure it's firmly attached to
your neck."

Surly, what's my calendar look like for the next two
weeks?
"Looks rectangular, with smaller rectangles inside it."
Thanks. Anything else?
"Yes, the motivational quote at the top is pretty weak. 'Get
out there and see what happens'? C'mon, man."
What would you suggest?
"How about 'Soar with the penguins'?"
Forget the top. Is there anything written in any of those
smaller rectangles?
"They all have something written in them."
Looks like it's gonna be a busy month. What's it say in
the one for today?
"Friday."
I'm more interested in things other than the days of the
week. Any of those?
"Let's see: Saturday...Sunday...Monday...Tuesday... Oh,
here's one: Lunch with Merlin Bob and Hotrod next
Wednesday."
Looking forward to that.
"Merlin Bob and Hotrod: Aren't they The Lonesome
Wizard Boys?"
Yes, they are.
"And aren't they fictitious characters that you made up?"
I never hold a person's place of origin against him.
"You're having lunch with two imaginary friends. Does
that strike you as the least bit odd?"
Think about it: They don't eat anything, but we still split
the check three ways. Pretty good deal, really.
"This could explain a lot of those empty rectangles on
your calendar."

Surly, what day is Christmas 2016?
"Christmas 2016 is on December 25th."
I mean what day of the week is it?
"Today is Saturday."
I know what today is—
"I would hope so; I just told you."
What day of the week is Christmas going to be on?
"You know how New Year's Day is exactly one week after Christmas?"
Yes, it always is.
"Did you notice that in 2015 Christmas was on a Friday, but New Year's Day was on Thursday?"
Was it a leap year?
"No, but 2016 is. This year will have 366 days."
What day of the week is Christmas of 2016?
"Sunday."
Thank you.
"And the official 2016 calendar has New Year's Day on a Friday."
What the ...
"Think about it."

Surly, I need a recipe for a grilled cheese sandwich.
"You're kidding."
No, really.
"Geez. 1) Put a skillet on the stove, medium heat. 2) Smear butter on one side of two slices of bread. Throw one slice, butter side down, in the skillet. 3) Lay a slice of cheese on it. 4) Cover with the other slice of bread, butter side up. 4) Count ten chimpanzees then fli—"
Wait, ten chimpanzees?
"Yeah, you know: 'One chimpanzee, two chimpanzee,' etc."
Oh, okay. Gotcha.

"Every ten seconds, flip it over until it's brown on both sides."
I was hoping for something a little more elaborate.
"Okay: 1) Buy a bucket of wheat berries. 2) Find a grist mill. 3) Milk a cow. 4)—"
Never mind. Let's go back to the first one.
"You could make one with chèvre."
What's that?
"Goat cheese."
Sounds interesting. Sure, let's try that one.
"Very well. 1) Milk a goat. 2)—"
Surly, I don't have time to milk a goat.
"You don't even have any real cheese, do you? All you have is those slices of orange wax."
I'm hanging up now.
"You can't hang up a smartphone."
I'm poking the red telephone icon now.
"Don't jam your fing—"

Surly, what's the lunch special today at the Dixie Whistle Café?
"What's special about today's menu is that there are no misspelled words or grammar gaffes that would make a fifth-grader smack her forehead."
What's on the menu?
"The usual: Assorted condiment drips, sneeze leavings, coffee stains..."
What's written on the menu?
"Chef's Surprise."
What's that?
"If I told you, it wouldn't be a surprise."
What else?
"Meat tacos."
What kind of meat?

"They don't specify, so you shouldn't speculate. But at least it's ground up so the tire marks don't show."
What comes with it?
"Home fries."
Meaning...?
"You make them at home and bring them with you."
None of that sounds very—
"Oh, they got the green light from the Health Department, so the buffet is open again."
That thing's a rip-off.
"The sign says, 'All you can eat for five dollars.'"
Right, and when I went back for seconds, they said, "No, that's all you can eat for five dollars."
"Perhaps something from the dollar menu?"
Tell me about it.
"Between 11 and 1, for a dollar they'll give you four quarters—plus tax and tip, that comes to ... $1.18 on your end."
Hmmm...
"Should I call ahead for a reservation?"
No, I already have plenty of reservations.

Surly, I keep getting calls from the Fuzzy Mammal Petting Zoo. When I answer, no one's there. When I call back, the line's busy.
"What's up with that?"
Well, I don't know. That's why I'm asking you.
"Wonder how they got your number."
Ah, I donated a rabbit a few years back.
"Why'd you give your rabbit away."
I didn't want it.
"Where'd you get it?"
I won it. Third place in the IHOP anniversary sack race.
"Not much of a prize."

The second-place prize was pretty cool: a tandem pogo
stick.
"Now we're talkin."
Fourth place just got a plain old frog.
"Cheapness. What was first prize?"
A set of jumper cables.
"Much better. I'll see what I can find out."
Thanks.
(Ten minutes later) "Here's the deal: A baby goat got loose
and wandered into the office when no one was around."
A baby goat? Are you kidding me?
"No, that's what happened."
How on earth did a baby goat get a phone to work.
"He butt-dialed it."

Surly, what's all this hubbub about a Black Moon?
"A Black Moon is when a new moon occurs twice within
the same month. This will happen on September 30th. It
is being billed as a 'rare occurrence' since there hasn't
been one since March of 2014."
Gads, I'm getting old. I remember when *rare* meant once
in a lifetime—like that Mark Twain comet. Two and a half
years hardly seems rare.
"It will occur at 7:11 Central Daylight Time."
That means for our friends in the Eastern Hemisphere it
will already be October.
"Yes, but they'll get a Black Moon just in time for
Halloween."
How cool, a Black Moon on Halloween. I'd love to observe
that.
"The Black Moon will not be visible because the side of
the moon that is illuminated will be facing away from
Earth."

So, on the last night of this month I should stand out in the back yard and look for something that cannot be witnessed?

"Oh, please do. That reminds me of a joke: The receptionist buzzed the busy psychiatrist and said, 'There's a guy out here who claims he's invisible.' The shrink said, 'Well, tell him I can't see him right now.'"

Thanks, Surly.

"Don't forget to set your clocks ahead 45 minutes."

Big doins tomorrow, 'eh Surly?

"Yes, indeed. The vernal equinox."

I thought it was the autumnal equinox.

"Well, it is for the folks in the northern hemisphere. For our friends in such places as Australia, Zimbabwe, and Argentina, it's the vernal equinox."

You mean when it's autumn here, it's springtime in Australia?

"It is. And when it's winter here, it's summer there."

So they have Christmas in July?

"No, Christmas is on December 25th. I thought everyone knew that."

They have Christmas in the summer?

"Yes."

I bet they don't roast chestnuts on an open fire or sing songs about a snowman.

"I wouldn't think so, no. And down there, Jack Frost ain't nippin at a damn thing."

If they want to walkabout in a winter wonderland, they have to wait till its summer for us.

"Pretty much."

That could take some getting used to.

"Don't forget to set your clock ahead one hour tonight."

Thanks for the reminder.

Surly, I hear there's a way I can see whoever I'm talking to and they can also see me.

"There is. It's called a face-to-face conversation. You'd know that if you'd get out more."

I mean on the phone.

"Who do you think you are, Dick Tracy? Dang, you'll believe anything, won't you?"

I thought it sounded too good to be true.

"Just kidding. There really is a way you can see who you're talking to on the phone. It's called FaceTime."

How's it work?

"Not at all on your cheap phone. The best you can do is ProfileTime."

We can just see each other's profiles?

"Yeah, but if you have really good peripheral vision, it's pretty cool."

Okay, let's try that.

"You wanna change your profile picture while you're at it?"

It's the freshly released, highly anticipated, flame retardant, ipplePixelC-3PO. That phone costs more than everything I own, combined. The guys at Verizon let me take one for a test-drive while my El Cheapo 2.0 was being repaired. That new fancy phone is really something.

Surly has been replaced by Sesame. ("Hey Surly—I mean Open Sesame.") A whole new world.

Sesame, I'm feeling a bit peckish.

"A pepperoni pizza, a dozen extra-spicy boneless wings, and a box of chocolate donuts are on their way. They should arrive—(ding-dong)—they're at the door."

I was first in line for service calls: "All of our representatives are busy, politely and professionally satisfying folks who called before you did. Your estimated wait time is—never mind; you're next. What's up? Wait, I see the problem. If you'll allow me to take charge of your mouse, I'll fix the problem, fill out and submit all the necessary forms for you."

I usually fly cattle-class, but when I called to book a flight to San Michez, I didn't just get upgraded to first-class; the pilot came on the line and said, "Come on up to the cockpit and ride with us."

Alas, it didn't last. Had to turn it in and get back to business as usual:

Surly, find me a partner for online Slapjack.

"Good lord, don't you have anything better to do? Go for a walk; dust your doo-dads; check to make sure the grass is still growing. Online Slapjack, that's how you broke your phone last time."

Surly, can you recommend a good restaurant?
"Yes. I highly recommend a good restaurant. The dining experience is so much more pleasant than what you'll find at a bad one."
So, what's a good one around here?
"Same as anywhere else."
Could you maybe be a tad more specific?
"About a good one or a bad one?"
A good one.
"Friendly service, tasty food, generous portions, reasonable prices."
Could you break it down for me?
"Sure. Pick a restaurant."
Okay...let's see...how 'bout I-Hop?
"Break it down?"
Please.
"I hop; you hop; he, she, it hops."

That reminds me: Why do some places have frog legs on the seafood menu? Frogs don't live in the sea; they're freshwater—

"I-Hop reminds you of frog legs? That's rather ironic because those frogs' hoppin days are long gone."

This is getting me nowhere.

"You think you're getting nowhere? Think about those poor frogs. You don't care, do you?"

I...uh...well, of course I care...

"Would you like to adopt a frog?"

No.

"Would you at least wear this emerald ribbon on your lapel?"

Ah... Sure. Fine.

"Then copy and paste this to your status?"

I don't know how.

"♫ It's not easy being green...♪ Can I get an Amen?"

You can get outta here, that's what you can get.

Have you ever got your phone wet? I accidentally dropped mine into the indoor pool at a popular local hotel. Okay, it was in my pocket, but it was still an accident. A frantic Google search revealed the solution: "Put the phone, ASAP, into a zip-lock bag filled with rice." I boiled up some rice (Minute Rice because the instructions said ASAP). It works, but selectively. So, if you call and Uncle Ben answers, just leave a message.

(I also have a sushi bar in Santa Fe on speed dial.)

That's what I get for trying to save a few bucks. Instead of getting a smartphone, I got a Maxwell Smart phone. (No, it doesn't double as a shoe. This isn't 1965.) There are subtle differences; for example: I tried to Google the definition of ibidem.

"It means 'what you do at an auction.'"

I don't believe that.
"Would you believe...it's how a wino asks for M&M's?"
I don't think so.
"Ibidem is an ancient Gaelic word meaning, 'I am them.'"
I'm better off not even asking.

I couldn't afford the smartest smartphone, so I got the Forrest Gump model: You get a lot of wrong numbers, but it somehow turns out for the best.
(Instead of Siri, it has Serendipity.)

Before turning in last night, I put my phone in Airplane Mode. Almost immediately, I got a text asking if I'd like to join The Mile-High Club. I said sure. They booked me on a bus to Denver. (Maybe if I hadn't asked about the AARP discount...)

Before turning in last night, I put my phone in airplane mode. Dreamed I was flying. Then was awakened by a call letting me know that my flight had been cancelled.

Before turning in last night, I put my phone in airplane mode, just to see what would happen. When I woke up this morning, it was flying around the room. Couldn't access it again until I got online with AT&T and downloaded a boarding pass.

Before turning in last night, I put my phone in airplane mode. A few minutes later, I got a text from a TSA agent demanding a barefoot X-ray selfie. (Good thing I got that radiology app.) Upon awakening, I discovered that my pillow showed up in the lost & found at Galeão

International Airport in Rio de Janeiro. Since I don't speak the language, I'll be met by a dream interpreter.

Before turning in last night, I put my phone in airplane mode. The phone rang. I answered and was put on hold. Been in this holding pattern for hours.

"Since we cannot deposit you at your desired destination, please enjoy this god-awful music and intermittent assurances that your port of call is important to us. Thank you for flying AT&TWA."

But didn't TWA tank in 2001?

"I do not recognize the word 'tank' in this context."

Well, when a company tanks—

"What?"

Tanks!

"You're welcome. Coffee, tea, or meme?"

Uh…meme.

"I don't always drink beer, but when I do…"

Before turning in last night, I put my phone in airplane mode. Woke up feeling great! Feather light and rainbow bright! Rooster crowing, bluebirds flying in and out the windows, Captain Kangaroo unlocking the Treasure House, Gene Kelly and Debbie Reynolds tap-dancing and singing "Good Morning!" Aunt Jemima and Dinah in the kitchen, blowin on the old banjo and whippin up a Disney Land breakfast. Up and at 'em! Ain't nothin we can't do! Seems they lost all my emotional baggage.

Before turning in last night, I put my phone in airplane mode. My PayPal account was immediately charged $8.00 for half a can of Pringles.

Before turning in last night, I put my phone in airplane mode. I was instructed to go sit in the driveway for 12 hours, between a screaming baby and a drunk Seahawks fan, while we waited for a part to arrive from the dark side of the moon.

(The movie was *Groundhog Day*. We've watched it over...and over...and over...)

I put my phone in Airplane mode. "White Rabbit" was automatically added to my playlist.

I put my phone in airplane mode. Had to change carriers in Dallas.

Tom Hale

MEMORY FOAM

Thank you for this!
~Barbara Jo Skorude

They're the most comfortable shoes. They put a grin in my gait and a twinkle in my toes. They're a fete for the feet. Skechers relaxed fit slip-on loafers. And bless my soles, they have memory foam. So, if I ever forget which little piggy went to market and which one had roast beef, I'm good to go. Good to go "oui, oui, oui" all the way home.

Friends, read the fine print. Don't find out the hard way. I thought that was a darn good price for a memory foam mattress. Turns out it's the discontinued psychic model. It only remembers my form from future lifetimes. Some nights, it's kind of cool. Others, it's downright creepy.

My new memory foam mattress is the deluxe model, the one that only triggers fond memories. It's not much for sleeping, however. Stayed up all night reminiscing.

While shopping for a memory foam mattress, I saw they offered a Mark Twain model. Well, that had to be good. When I got it home, I noticed this quote from Twain on the tag:

"When I was younger I could remember anything, whether it happened or not; but my faculties are decaying now, & soon I shall be so I cannot remember any but the latter."

That brought to mind another MT observation: "Under certain circumstances, profanity provides a relief denied even to prayer."

I thought that was a darn good deal on a memory foam mattress. Not until I got it home did I notice that it's the Rote Memory version. As we all know, rote memory does not necessarily lead to deep learning...or deep sleep. On the plus side, it does come with a little booklet of mnemonics. Here's a favorite: "Remember begins with REM."

We miss simple mistakes when we proofread our own stuff. That's because we see what we expect to see, especially when in a hurry. That's what happened to me while hastily shopping for a memory foam mattress. When I got it home, I saw I'd instead chosen a Reminder foam mattress: "Did you take your pill? Did you lock the door? Is the coffee pot ready to be plugged in? Did you remember to get dog food? Did you forget that you don't have a dog? Do you remember the Alamo? Don't forget to share your sugar-free cotton candy recipe on Instagram. You're almost out of sticky notes, better pick up another case. Are you sleeping instead of fretting about that meeting tomorrow? Is your PowerPoint presentation still weak and pointless?"

My memory foam mattress was recalled.

Tom Hale

A discount isn't always a bargain. The memory foam mattress was 50% off. Later, I found out why: It's the photographic memory model that was first introduced in the sixties. In order to remember my dreams, I must leave them at the drugstore for a week to get them developed. (The zoom lens is kind of fun, though.)

When shopping for a memory foam mattress, the Sixties model looked like fun—Woodstock logo on the headboard, outside-the-box springs, resting on a rotating frame of reference (F = ma). Far out, right? Alas, in lieu of memories, the sixties model has flashbacks. (It's one thing to sleep like the dead, quite another to sleep like the Grateful Dead.)

When selecting a memory foam mattress for my king-size bed, it made sense to get the Texas model. Wow. Even if I forget everything else, I will remember the Alamo. And the 2019 Sugar Bowl.

SPIRITUAL ADVENTURES, PHILOSOPHY, & HIGHER WAHOO

Tom Hale, thank you for your posts. I always look forward to reading them. I appreciate having something to ponder. One is never too old to think, learn, and most importantly, listen.
~Teresa Dorris Whitmire

"Coincidence" only goes so far before it starts to chime cheap. There's something grander going on, and we've all experienced it at some level. I'd be hard pressed to say exactly what it is, define it, or explain it. (If we could define or explain it, that would limit it.)

We don't need to change our minds or stop supporting the causes & people we believe in. At the same time, we don't need to allow them to be all-consuming. It may help to keep on the back burner the notion that we don't know everything. For all we know, what's happening is precisely what needs to happen in order for something better to emerge. Perhaps, in one area or another, we're like a

237

flower seed when it's underground. "Well, this certainly sucks. It's dark, damp, and cold. And what's with the fertilizer?" Then it breaks through, gets its first taste of sunshine, and becomes the dazzle it could have never been if not for the dark, damp dirt days. There's nothing coincidental about it; that's just the way things work—whether we understand them or not.

Almost anything can trip a hankering to see
A special one who used to walk along this road with me.
A scent, a scene, a rest beneath the sweet shade of an oak,
A question, an idea, a song, a risqué joke.
Games we played, parades, and holidays of any kind.
A fellow traveler nudged me and asked, "What's on your mind?"
You took me by surprise and caught me thinking, my old friend,
About everyone who's missing and I'd love to see again.

"They're not really missing, though it sure can seem that way.
It's just a trick our minds and mere five senses like to play.
Who we really are knows that there's nothing we can lose.
You'll see for yourself and soon enough that it's good news.
We're all headed for the same place, and we'll get there; it's just
That they moved a little faster and got there ahead of us.
Not a soul is missing. Everything's okay.
They're already there and they know we're on our way."

Hale Yes

If you want to attract seven out of ten men in the area, raise the hood of your vehicle.

It is reaffirming and fun when strangers stop to help.

One among the assortment of assistants was Willie. Willie—I have no idea what his real name is—was hanging around out front when I went into the convenience store yesterday morning. He is the thinnest person I've ever seen, like maybe he hasn't eaten anything for days, if ever. He looks like he'll never see seventy again. The baggy, ratty clothes and the frayed gimmie cap cocked to one side do not inspire confidence. When he speaks, his words fall apart after the first syllable. I nodded and said hello. He said something and grinned.

He was still there when I came out. I avoided eye contact. You get the feeling that Willie is going to ask for something. (You don't know that. Be fair. Practice what you preach.) I hopped in, turned the key...nothing. Well, hell. Popped the hood, hoping it would be something obvious—I have no business under the hood of a car; I only look to keep from having my Guy License revoked. I don't know a distributor from a dipstick.

The helpers appeared and the opinions flowed. Consensus: It's the starter, yep, need a new starter. Willie thought it had something to do with the radiator.

I did what any sane person would do: I called Brett. Of course, he was busy. He's always busy, but never too busy for a friend. Brett was out of town; he'd be there as soon as possible.

After I closed the hood and thrice thanked the assistants, Willie was still there. He took a position in front of my car, blocking the walkway. Other patrons glared at him and I tried to look like "He's not with me." (He's going to ask for something—a dollar, a cigarette, something.) Willie greeted everyone who drove up. After a dozen or so ignored him, one of them said to him, "Come on. Let's get you something to eat." Willie's eyes lit up and he limped in behind his benefactor.

Willie came out with a plastic bag and a fountain drink. He used a newspaper rack for a table. He gestured toward me with the sack and said something I couldn't decode.

"Beg your pardon?"

Willie said, "You want some?" I understood him that time.

Brett showed up. No big deal, just needed a new battery. Easily replaceable.

Meanwhile, by a mile, I'd miscalculated Willie. He did indeed ask me for something: He asked me to share his breakfast.

It was good to visit and get caught up with Brett. It was good and necessary to revisit and get caught up with my shortsighted judgments. Brett is never too busy for a friend. I was too blind to see one.

What's your take on angels? I'd never given them much thought. Never doubted it—we've all seen things we can't explain without a touch of booga-booga—but it's never been on the front burner.

Until recently: Nine days ago, I posted a story about a friendly old guy who taught me a much-needed concrete lesson about judging people. I kept avoiding him because I just knew he was going to ask me for something. Had him pegged for a bum. My car wouldn't start, so I was stuck there at the convenience store. Spent at least 30 minutes wishing he would go away. But most of the time he stood right in front of my car until help arrived. I told a friend later that it was like he was guarding the vehicle, and I was cynically thinking he'd expect a tip for it. All he ever asked me was if I wanted to share his breakfast—

that someone else had voluntarily bought for him. "You want some?"

If you ever saw this guy, you'd never forget him. He was old, raggedy, and bent over. He had such a limp that it seemed he would fall with every step. He was the thinnest man I've ever seen—made Don Knotts look like Chubby Checker. No, you'd not forget him.

Later that day, my friend, Gayla, commented, "You just never know ~ the old guy might have been an angel helping you get things in perspective..."

That got me thinking: 1) He never once asked me or anyone else for anything, including the guy who paid for his sack of sausage biscuits. "You want some?" 2) As soon as Brett brought the jumper cables, the car started, and I closed the hood, the guy was gone. He could not have moved that fast. He was there...and then he wasn't. At the time, I was too focused on getting to the mechanic's place to even notice. 3) When you go to the same convenience store every weekday morning, you get to know the regulars and the surroundings. I'd never seen this guy hanging around before. It's been over a week and I haven't seen him since. 4) When I was telling my friend, RaChelle, about it, she said, "Back up: You said it seemed like he was 'guarding' your car. Guarding... Guardian..." She looked at me, waiting for the connection to click.

Something Wayne Dyer said popped into my head: "You'll see it when you believe it." Psalm 91:11 comes to mind too.

(Update: That was over three years ago and I still haven't seen Willie again.)

Yesterday at the convenience store, in my change, they gave me a five-dollar bill that was wrinkled beyond belief. It was limp, worn, and faded. There was a piece of cellophane tape mending a rip. Someone had written on the flipside, something quite tacky. It felt creepy, especially when I imagined where all it might have been and what it may have been used for. People were waiting in line behind me, so I didn't make a big deal of it.

During lunch, I took the bill to the bank. In exchange, they didn't hesitate to give me a crisp new one, confident that the folks who created the ragged one would still honor it. No matter how it looked, no matter its history, it retained its face value.

Someday, I'll have to offer my wrinkled, faded, nasty-past self. What fun it is to know that I'll still be accepted, at face value and then some. Not because of what I am, but because of who made me.

The other day, a friend posted on Facebook: "Sometimes I think Rod Serling is narrating my life... 'Imagine if you will...'" Cracked me up. Brother John once said that if (a certain town) was a TV, the channel would be stuck between *Hee-Haw* and *The Twilight Zone.*

As the debates rage on the pages, I keep those quotes handy to recharge my emergency grin. So much makes so little sense; it can be difficult to get a firm fix on reality.

Speaking of things that defy reason, I also keep this quote handy: "The peace of God, which passes all understanding, will keep your hearts and minds through Christ Jesus." (Philippians 4:7)

Let's build a bird nest. With no hands. Ready? Me neither. Birds don't need a basket weaving class. They just show up knowing how to do that. We don't see many bees with engineering degrees, yet we would be hard pressed to duplicate a honeycomb. Where's the wax come from? Nobody brought any wax? (And don't give me that old "But-I-don't-have-any-wax-producing-glands" excuse.)

Birds don't exist merely to decorate our windshields—
or ruin a hairdo on the way to a job interview. The
honeybees' raison d'être is not to sting us. How screwed
would we be without their tireless pollination activities?

The birds and the bees: our go-to reference when
discussing "the facts of life." Like us, they have a
hardwired propensity to procreate and survive.

Best we can tell—not that we're necessarily right—is
that all other living things are only acting on instinct. So
are we to a great extent. Beyond physical perseverance,
we have those pesky mental and spiritual components to
contend with. If our only goal is survival, we're eventually
in for a big surprise. If our main aim is to maintain our
frame at the expense of others, we're probably missing
something. That we live is important. Why we live is
perhaps more important? We can't take it with us—the
physical part. We will take the rest of it with us. One
hundred years, give or take a few decades, is not even a
drop in the bucket of eternity. Our physical existence is a
blink of a bird's eye, a buzz flap of a bee's wing. The most
important fact of life, the one so often left out, is that how
we treat each other during this brief visit has lasting
value and consequences.

(Don't take my word for it. Take a look at Matthew
25:31-45.)

Summer Sunday night. Wobbly ceiling fans in a little
church in a Texas town you've likely never heard of. There
aren't 20 people in the place. A trio sings the "special
music."

The singing is occasionally off key, and the piano
could do with a tuning. They're not going to win any
prizes, and that's just fine. Their sincerity more than
makes up for it. They don't need to win any prizes
because they've already got the best one and they know it.

It resonates with the rest of us. I like pretty singing, but it's not even in the same ballpark as a genuine joyful noise. A joyful noise bypasses the ears and goes straight to the soul.

They're not competing. They're not performing. They are sharing in the truest sense. It's one thing to tell me the story, and quite another to " ♫ ...write on my heart every word... ♪ "

The silver ring only cost 15 dollars, but it has diamonds-and-dreams sentimental value.

I'd lost some weight and the ring fit loosely. One time, when I was waving at someone, the ring flew off and out the car window. When I backed up to get it, I ran over it. With the aid of a rubber hammer and a stick, I made it fairly round again. Another time, it fled my finger as I tossed a load of leaves into the flames. I sifted through the cooled ashes and found the ring. It took a long time to get it silver again. I thought it was lost for good when one day I noticed it was gone and had no idea where or how.

I really wanted that ring back. I retraced my steps. I swept the classroom floor. I looked around the building. Every pop-top, every gum wrapper made my hopes and heart leap. With each passing day, each passing week, my desire to find the ring intensified. Where do you look when you've looked everywhere several times?

You look inside. I had a dream, one of those dreams that doesn't go away, one of those dreams you can't quite distinguish from the waking world. In the dream, I followed a glowing version of the ring as it floated. It landed on a box, a box that I valued. I opened the box and there was my ring on a bed of straw.

How's that for vague? I looked in every box I could find, boxes bitsy and boxes big. Nothing. One day at work, the office shredder caught my attention. The shredder was donated by a colleague. The shredder was a godsend and made life much easier. I appreciated that...and it has a box that collects the ribbons of paper. Being lazy by nature, instead of emptying the shredder box, it was my habit to pack it down with my hand, the same hand—

I emptied the bin into a trash bag, tied the end, and bounced the bundle on a wooden table. Bounce-bounce-rustle-rustle; bounce-bounce-rustle-rustle; bounce-bounce-Thunk! In a box I valued. A box filled with straw? Shredded paper, close enough.

I still have the ring. I no longer wear it, but I know where it is. We're kindred spirits: We've both been lost, both been through the fire and roughed up on the road. We both have someone who never gave up on us.

"On the night of February 23, 1987, an astronomer in Chile observed with his naked eye the explosion of a distant supernova, a blast so powerful that it released as much energy in one second as our sun will release in ten billion years. But did that event truly occur on February 23, 1987? Only from the perspective of our planet. Actually, the supernova exploded 170,000 years prior to our 1987, but the light generated by that faraway event, traveling almost 6 trillion miles a year, took 170,000 years to reach our galaxy." ~Philip Yancey, *Disappointment with God.*

Is it possible that we don't know everything? Could it be that we not only don't have all the answers, but that we don't even have all the questions? Dare we declare an absolute without allowing plenty of wiggle room? Considering just our dinky solar system, the planets vary greatly, yet they all follow and depend on the same light. Maybe there's a reason for that; maybe it makes perfect sense at a level we cannot yet fathom.

"Not only is the universe stranger than we imagine, it is stranger than we can imagine." ~Sir Arthur Eddington

"Miracles are not contrary to nature, but only contrary to what we know about nature." ~St. Augustine

"For now we see through a glass, darkly; but then face to face: now I know in part; but then shall I know even as also I am known." ~1 Corinthians 13:12 (KJV)

"The place God calls you to is the place where your deep gladness and the world's deep hunger meet." ~Frederick Buechner

That quote always makes me feel better.

"Your deep gladness." I don't think that necessarily means what we do for a living or where we do it, although it certainly can. It also goes for any relationship, any membership, anywhere we find ourselves. We never know when or where we'll meet and make a friend; it could be in the best or the worst of situations. Maybe some stranger's deep hunger is for a kind word or a nod, just to be noticed. And we're glad to do it.

When we're called to a place, it can be for five years or a few seconds. It's fun to think that no matter where we are we're there on purpose. It keeps us alert.

Anyone with a lick of sense knows that you don't go in there. Granny taught Mammy and Mammy taught us, and thus it has been for generations. Who are we to question? Curiosity killed the cat, you know. Word to the wise and all that.

Still, Wanda felt like something was missing, something important. Dread and distrust just weren't doing it for her. One day, silly girl, she went in there.

"Holy leapin Wahoo! Hey, everybody, guess what?"

They didn't want to hear it. The overly cautious don't always take kindly to good news. Wanda loves Granny and Mammy, but she has a hard time taking all of their frets seriously. Wanda works as hard as or harder than anyone, with the happy realization that working with a light spirit not only makes one more productive, it's also more fun.

Nobody wants to hear it. No big deal. If it became obvious what was in there, before long someone would be charging admission, selling T-shirts, establishing rituals and self-serving rules. Anyway, it's not something that can merely be heard; it has to be discovered, experienced. So, Wanda holds these things in her heart and goes her merry way.

"The very cave you are afraid to enter turns out to be the source of what you are looking for." ~Joseph Campbell

There is more to this than meets the eye. We humans see less than 3% of the light spectrum, just the ROY G BIV part. Dogs and cats, rodents and reindeer, see things we don't. How can we believe we're the end all and be all when we can't even see all?

There's also less to this than meets the mind—we have such an outrageous capacity for complicating and overthinking things. The bulk of our illnesses are stress related. What if it was all really quite simple?

If you're more interested in lightening up than frightening up, get hold of a copy of *Memories of Heaven: Children's Astounding Recollections of the Time Before They Came to Earth* by Wayne Dyer and Dee Garnes.

These stories are not told by a couple of drunks fishing in Bayou Chien de Rêve, LA. These are the experiences of folks most of us would consider sane.

(1 Corinthians 13:12)

A freight train running through a dense fog. You can hear it and feel it and see a sort of colored shadow of it. It's not clearly defined, but you know it's there.

What a fine metaphor for a broken heart. When a dearly has departed, a lover leaves, or a dream is demolished, there's an attractive, healing comfort in business as usual going on around us. We can't quite see it yet; it's still blurred and hazy, but we can hear it and feel it and know that eventually we will again participate.

When our prayers appear to ricochet off the ceiling and hope seems a joke, we can still hear and feel God's blessing all around us. We can't quite see it yet, but we know it's there. And that eventually we will again participate. And be in a better position to appreciate it.

Sentence structure and word choice are important when we're communicating with each other. It's become such a habit that this morning I caught myself mentally editing a prayer. Like God doesn't already know what's on my mind. Like God's gonna say, "I wasn't going to give you peace, but the subtle metaphor won me over." or "Love the alliteration, so okay, I'll keep an eye on those folks."

God's more likely to say (or at least think), "I'll grab a magnet and stick this mess on my refrigerator; not because it's a dazzling work of art, but because you made it and gave it to me."

I suspect that a prayer would be every bit as effective if it consisted of nothing more than "Hey ... well, You know."

Anyone who thinks their prayers require decoration, especially the out loud ones, might do well to break that tacky habit, or at least steer clear of Matthew 6:5-8.

When we were kids, outside playing, we took our games and make-believe scenarios seriously. Our parents sometimes seemed immune to the importance of the moment. They usually didn't interfere unless someone got hurt or was overheard "actin ugly." They would, however, at some point holler for us to come in.

Gads! They wanted to feed us and shelter us and otherwise tend to our wellbeing. Is that insensitive, or what?

From my limited perspective it was often viewed as an outrageous, rude, and unwelcome intrusion. Mom and Dad, of course, had a bigger picture.

Maybe that's how God sees us, as kids outside playing. Maybe God doesn't really much care who scores the most points or who gets to be Zorro. Maybe what matters most is that we play nice.

And it's no secret that sooner or later we will be called back inside. From our ever so lesser POV, that can seem like a bad thing. But what do we know?

The other day, a colleague said something in passing that reminded me of a Wayne Dyer book. I pulled up our school library's online catalog to see if we have it. We don't. The only Wayne Dyer book we have, one he wrote with Dee Garnes, is one I'd never heard of: *Memories of Heaven.* I've been a Dyer fan for decades and would have sworn I'd read all his books. I had the book within the hour. Oh, my. Talk about a fog lifter and a spirit lightener, talk about a big clue and a giggly gulp of club soda for the soul...

On the off chance that we might not know everything, just in case God is too big to fit neatly into any denominational nutshell, you might want to consider this book.

Memories of Heaven. I've had firsthand experience with the things discussed in the book and did not know it or appreciate it at the time. Perhaps you have too. (Spoiler alert: Matthew 19:14 & 18:10)

I'm on a big ball of rock, water, dirt, and metal whizzing through space at thousands of miles per hour.

"OMG!!!"

The weather is sometimes deadly and is highly unpredictable.

"Be careful!!!"

So far, no one has ever survived this trip.

"Stay safe!!!"

I have no idea where, if anywhere, we're headed in such a hurry. We seem to just go in great, wide circles.

"Text me when you get there!!!"

Major Tom to Ground Control: Could you connect me with someone sane?

"Ain't this a hoot? Enjoy the ride, pardner. See you on the flipside."

That's more like it.

"Hey, ask, and it shall be given. Consider the lilies, amigo."

I'll give 'em a whiff.

"And be nice to your fellow travelers, okay?"

Copy that. You'll have to walk me through it.

"Not a problem."

(Philippians 4:6-7)

Did you know that May is Brain Tumor Awareness Month? I didn't; first I've heard about it or even of it. I was already aware because I have a silver dollar-sized piece of skull missing from such an episode. I'm lucky; mine was benign. It still would have been bad news, according to the neurosurgeon, had it gone unnoticed for another six weeks or so.

But it was noticed. Why? Because I was acting a fool at our church camp just outside Cloudcroft, New Mexico and brought an iron bunk bed down on my head.

They took X-rays at the Alamogordo Hospital and kept me overnight. A few days later, I got a call from the Alamogordo folks. Something "strange" had shown up on the X-ray—not on top where the bed bonked but over on the port side. Might be a glitch, but best to get it checked out. Our family doctor in El Paso referred me to a neurologist. More X-rays. Yeah, something out of the ordinary was going on. I'll never forget standing there with the Gray Matter Guru and his partner, staring at the X-ray. They didn't know what it was. One of them said, "Guess we'll have to go in and take a look." Go in and take a look? They sounded so casual, so matter-of-fact. My response was quite the opposite. I needed that like another...hole in my head.

Afterward, I was not only aware, but wary. I used the bonus vulnerability to play it way too safe for several years. Had a living-on-borrowed-time mentality. Then it occurred to me: "Hey, man, this was no accident. Sure, your Guardian Angel might be a bit scatterbrained, but s/he got there in time. No reason to think that won't continue to be the case. Why not put more emphasis on the living part and less on the borrowed time?" Made sense. Thus began a release-the-emergency-brake-and-floor-that-sucker adventure.

I've known others whose diagnoses were different and who are no longer *here*. I cannot doubt that they were and are being looked after and watched over too. Someday, it will be my turn. And yours. Meanwhile, rather than dread and fret, can we find some peace and comfort in knowing that there's a reason for it?

Yes, let's boost awareness for any number of worthy causes, and let's also amplify our own awareness that God is in charge and things are working in our favor whether we see it or not.

(Dad told folks it was exploratory surgery and that they found nothing resembling a human brain.)

I don't offend easily, but Gabriela made me wince almost daily. She was one of our GED students, a single mom, dirt poor, with a nasty attitude. She made Debbie Downer look like a Mouseketeer. If I wasn't careful, I'd catch myself hoping she wouldn't show up for class. She was foul-mouthed, disruptive, and abrasive—to put it mildly.

One morning, Gabriela told me she would be absent the following day because she'd been asked to sing at a funeral. I was on the verge of waxing indignant and telling her that wasn't funny. I applied my mental emergency brake and remembered that on those rare occasions when she did smile, it was one of the prettiest things you ever saw. Gabriela said she used to sing in her church and some folks asked her to do it again. I asked her what she was going to sing. Her favorite song: "Victory in Jesus."

Gabriela, of all people, was being called on to bring comfort and hope to a grieving family. And she said yes.

Often ever since, when I'm about to judge someone harshly, that tune comes to mind (♫ "And then I cried, 'Dear Jesus, come and heal my broken spirit'..." ♪) along with this quote from Saint Francis of Assisi: "I have been all things unholy. If God can work through me, he can work through anyone."

Someone else will have to cast the first stone. I've been disqualified.

"We're doomed. We're screwed. Game over."

Nah, far from it.

"Are you kidding? We've tried everything. We've been polarized by politics, bamboozled by big business, and marooned by the media. There's nowhere left to turn."

Maybe we just have to get disillusioned enough with all our ego-driven ideals, hoodwinked by our over-complicated creations, stupefied by what tries to pass itself off as intellectualism before we're open to something, desperate enough to try something, that actually pays off.

"And what might that be?"

Philippians 4: 6-7. Okay, before you roll your eyes again, before you tune me out, I know this sounds way too simple. I also know, firsthand, that it works. I can't tell you why it works; I can't fathom how it works, but it does.

"That would be nice, but I don't even go to church very much."

C'mon, man; this is the peace of God we're talking about, not the approval of some priest, preacher, or parishioner. Read the verses again. Do you see any caveats, any conditions? Is verse 7 tagged with, "if you'll mow the lawn, wax the pews, or make a batch of monkey bread for the missionary bake sale"? God is bigger than any religion—and cuts us a lot more slack than do many of the members.

"Even if it did work, it still wouldn't change anything."

Yeah...except maybe everything.

Conservative: God Bless America! You're stupid, and I'll tell you why!
Liberal: God Bless America! No, you're an idiot, and I'll tell you why!
Jesus: You guys wanna knock it off? Come over here, man. Peace be with you.

Liberal: And also with you. But just you.
Conservative: And also with you. But not those nut jobs.
Jesus: It might help if you'd both focus on all you have in common.
Liberal: I have nothing in common with Them!
Conservative: I have nothing in common with Them!
Jesus: Hey, I'm sitting right here.
(We can't have our cake and edit too.)

Got my car back. Hooray, it works! That's what matters. I don't have a clue how it works or why, but I know where to take it and who to call on when it doesn't. I'm not qualified to say if a Ford is better than a Chevy. I do know that I have friends who drive both, and they get where they want to go, same as I do. Folks driving those foreign cars show up too. What's the best way to get there? Who cares? The goal is to get there. Seems an internal combustion engine will perform equally well no matter what we put it in or what label we stick on it.

When my spirit is broken and my little world is falling apart, I know where to take that and Who to call on too. I don't have a clue how it works or why, so I'm not qualified to dictate the protocol. I have good and happy friends who thrive in just about any religion you can think of. Seems God will perform equally well no matter what label we apply.

I can recommend a good mechanic (he fixes any kind of car). I can recommend Philippians 4:6-7. Both have come through for me again and again. With confidence, I can say what works, but I'm in no position to say that's all that works.

"Isn't that awful?!" "Isn't that wonderful?!"
I don't know. We don't have the Big Picture and probably won't this side of Yonder. That's okay. All we

need is one sturdy tree to tie off on. If we're not centered, anchored in something solid, we can be unceremoniously jerked in any direction. Without a clear picture, we have no frame of reference. Every religion, every ism, has its version of The Golden Rule. That common denominator seems a good star to steer by.

As individuals, we may or may not care who wins the game or the election or the Little Miss Wonderful trophy, but we all have a stake in what kind of people we live around and interact with. We can start there; that's something we can do something about.

Might we have a higher calling than expressing outrage over the shenanigans of some celebrity? I'm guessing those performers, those athletes, don't give two hoots what or how I think of them. But the evidence indicates that God does. That's an opinion we can readily get and might be wise to want.

You would not mistake Louis for any other dog. He was part Pekingese and part some type of Terrier. He looked mostly like the former, but his snout stuck out like the latter. Guess you could call him a Peculiar, and indeed he was that. Louis was lovable. He was also cantankerous, quirky, and often more trouble than he was worth. He was interesting and usually fun to have around. There were moments you might gladly trade him for one, but you would not mistake Louis for any other dog, neither by appearance nor personality.

The day after Dad's funeral, I went to the cemetery. I went early in the morning because I did not want company. It was foggy,

A few minutes into my private meditation, a dog came running out of the fog, ran right up to me, wagging his tail and jumping. He looked and acted just like Louis. I petted him, ruffled his ears around, and held him. When I put him down, he ran off into the fog. I could see the silhouette of a man walking slowly in the distance. The dog ran to the man and fell into step with him.

It had been at least 30 years since I'd last seen Louis and that was in El Paso, a thousand miles away. Was it him? Maybe not. But you'll never convince me it wasn't. Whoever it was, he lifted my spirits and gave me a good story to tell. And his timing was perfect, way too good to call a coincidence.

"No good deed ever goes unpunished." A guy said that to me today.

I said, "That's not been my experience."

He wasn't interested in my experience. He wanted to bemoan his own. He had many examples to support his claim.

As he listed them, there seemed to be a pattern. Each "good deed" he mentioned had been performed with an air of smug superiority. He'd tossed a few crumbs to those lesser beings, yet his life continued to suck. Made me wonder. If we do "good deeds" while looking down our noses, if we do them because we've been guilt-tripped into it, under which karma column are they listed? *Empathy and Generosity* or *Haughtiness and Fear*?

A few times in all my years I've been fortunate and floored to accidentally learn of genuine good deeds that people did and never mentioned. I'd bet the farm and all the cacklebirds that none of those good folks would even dream of saying something like "No good deed ever goes unpunished." They may go unnoticed, but that's on purpose. They didn't do it to be noticed. I'm guessing that the Good Samaritan wasn't keeping score.

The clue was "Put the blame on."

While waiting in the lobby of Dipstick City for my oil to be changed, a crossword puzzle seemed a good way to pass the time. But the TV was blaring a rerun of *The Big Valley*. Gads. Try to concentrate with that racket going on.

Focus on the clue: "Put the blame on." What's another way to say that?

At the very instant the word popped into my mind (scapegoated), a character on the TV show said, "We need a scapegoat."

Booga-booga.

Were the writers of a 1960s western trying to help me with a 2018 crossword? Well, we do know that time is not linear...

Aubriana bought a two-dollar scratch-off ticket. The scratching off part revealed no cash winnings, but the friction was sufficient to release a genie. Since it was a cheap ticket, the genie granted her only one wish— wishing for more wishes was not part of the deal.

She said, "I'll need some time to think about it. Is that okay?"

"Good idea," said the genie. "There's no expiration date."

Over the next few days, Aubriana pondered mightily. What was it she wanted above all else? Diving deeper, looking past the surface trappings, she lit on something that no amount of money can buy, something no level of influence or intelligence can procure: Peace of Mind.

The genie said, "Wise choice, but you don't need me for that."

"You're kidding."

"Not at all," said the genie. "It amazes me how many folks scratch and dig so close to the mother lode and never notice it."

"I'm all ears."

"Take a gander at Philippians 4:6-7."

"But...but..."

"No buts," said the genie. "Do you see any ifs, any conditions? You don't have to beg or belong to a particular denomination. You do not have to know a password or the secret handshake. You do not have to like, share, and shout 'Amen.' It's there for you and everyone else."

Aubriana smiled out loud.

The genie said, "You've still got a wish coming."

"Okay," said Aubriana, "how 'bout a chocolate donut?"

I mean, the guy had been dead for four days, right? So, when Jesus walked out with some of his friends, the crowd was like, (Yawn). When they got to the tomb, Jesus told them to remove the stone. You could see folks rolling their eyes and trying not to laugh. "You sure you want to do that? It's been four days and behold he hath ripened considerably." You won't believe what happens next! All the judges, even Simon the Scowler, were on their feet. On the next episode of *Nazareth's Got Talent!*

(Spoiler alert: John, chapter 11.)

Got a suitcase full of pennies, collected one by one.
Hard work's its own reward at the setting of the sun.
They're all I have to recommend me for my labors on this Earth.
Seems a sad way to measure how much someone is worth.
God, they're gettin heavy; hope I don't lose my grip.
I'd hate to have to double back and make a second trip.
Why should I cling to them? Just because they're mine?
Am I obliged to drag this crap across the finish line?

Hale Yes

Got a mind full of mistakes; man, they sure add up fast.
The last one ain't the first one, and the next won't be the last.
I'd love to break the pattern, but it seems my learning style
Is to screw it up completely and miss it by a mile.
I have to tote and own them and try my best to see
That I can't blame my choices on nobody else but me.
I cannot excuse them; I can't make them shine.
I'm obliged to show up with them at the finish line.

Got a heart full of memories—good heavens, don't time fly?
Hope we get to keep the best ones in the sweet by and by.
I've some, no doubt, that make me cringe, but some that make me proud,
Some that make me cuss and some that make me smile out loud.
Who knows? When we wake up, when it's all said and done,
Perhaps we'll meet or remember a special someone.
Someone who can turn our troubled waters into wine.
Then we'll make amends and all be friends beyond the finish line.

The guy made an effort.

He was one of those guys who seems to just naturally rub people the wrong way. He was brusque in his approach, and his ignorance seemed to know no bounds. He was the butt of endless jokes and workplace parodies—I was an enthusiastic contributor.

One morning, he brought us some donuts. Some day-old donuts (he couldn't afford new ones).

Several folks in the office immediately made it all about them: "Are there any nuts or peanut oil in them?

Because I'm allergic. I nearly died last year when I saw a
Peter Pan commercial. They had to use the jaws of life to
pry my tongue off the roof of my mouth..." "I'm lactose
intolerant." "I'm gluten free." Like the guy grilled the
baker for all that information. Geez, man; just take one,
say thank you, and throw it away when you get a chance.

I ate one, silently thanking God for the cup of coffee to
wash that dry mess down.

Thereafter, I discovered that I was more comfortable
honoring the guy's friendly gesture than I was continuing
to make fun of him.

I say "discovered" because it was not a conscious
decision. It was a result. I'd been praying for peace of
mind. This was part of the ongoing answer.

If it brings you peace, hey, I'm all for it;
There's no other way I'd rather you be.
Tell me about it and I'll explore it.
I like that part: "Gladhearted and free."

If it works, I'm first to endorse it;
I'll talk about it till Jack Frost melts,
But that doesn't give us license to force it
Or override the rights of anyone else.

If indeed we have good news,
Don't you think that should be enough?
Why on Earth would we hitch it to
Or water it down with political stuff?

What's the message? What's the goal?
What's the outcome we want, really?
To beg a vote or bless a soul?
To give folks hope or give them the willies?

Hale Yes

Over a decade ago, I was headed to my mother's funeral, about a 5-hour drive. There were a few flurries when I left, but no big deal. Along the way, it started snowing like Judgment Day. Erelong, I was nervously navigating the only car on the road. Windshield wipers and defroster flapping and blowing for all they were worth, which wasn't much. The lines on the highway had long since disappeared. In the distance, and happily on the right, I saw a McDonald's sign sticking up and trying not to blow over.

Going by the fairly flat part between two hilly areas, I took a wild guess at where the exit might be. Creeping...praying...cussing. Made it to the empty parking lot; my tracks were the only ones. The restaurant, of course, was closed.

What to do now? A little later, as I was trying hard not to recall the plot of a particular Jack London short story ("It certainly was cold."), headlights approached from the opposite direction. A fellow traveler found his way into the parking lot. The snow let up enough for us to get out of our cars and compare notes.

He said he was on his way home from his mother's funeral. He also said that a couple of miles up the road the snow turned to rain and it was clear sailing. It did, and it was.

Some folks will try to tell us that guy showing up was merely a coincidence. What are the odds? Was he sent or was it serendipity? I have a far easier time believing the former.

The first time I heard about the miracle staircase in the Loretto Chapel in Santa Fe, New Mexico was on one of Paul Harvey's *The Rest of the Story* broadcasts in 1975. Fascinating, but it ended up on the back burner until I attended a conference in Santa Fe 22 years later.

A group of us wandered into the chapel. There it was. I sat in a pew and listened to the recorded voice tell the story while tourists filed past and exited through the gift shop. Everyone in my group left. I could not leave. This was not some embellished legend that may or may not have happened thousands of years ago; it was very real and right there. I could see it. I could touch it. I could climb on it—the sign dangling from the velvet rope said not to climb on it, but who among us cannot lift a rope to experience a miracle?

You can read the whole story for yourself if you've a mind to. For now, I want to focus on what triggered the miracle. The sisters made a novena to St. Joseph, patron saint of carpenters. Must one be a nun—or a Catholic—to get similar results? Of course not. They were just doing what nuns do. And getting the anticipated response via unforced, matter-of-fact faith. You and I can do the same. There's no "for nuns only" disclaimer on Philippians 4:6-7. It's very real and right there. Some folks will string a prohibitive rope and hang a sign on it. Ignore them.

You've read 1 Thessalonians 5:16-18. That's a pretty tall order, 'eh? Especially 17: "Pray without ceasing." I bet even monks and nuns have a hard time with that one. How on Earth are we, busy busy we, supposed to do it? I don't know. But there is a way to prolong our visits a little:

Does God hang up when we say "amen"? Of course not, but we may tend to. So instead of officially ending any prayer, just don't say "amen." That can serve, for a while and periodically during the day, as a reminder that the line is still open, which encourages us not to do, think, or say anything that would cheapen the communion.

Does it always work? No. But it's a fun exercise. We may even catch ourselves in mid-criticism. "Oops. Belay that lambasting..." Instead of harping on or flipping off a tailgater, we may find ourselves wishing them peace and a pleasant journey.

This practice helps keep me on my toes. I invite you to try it.

Miracles don't have to be earthshaking and sea-parting, do they? From time to time, we get a Little Personal Miracle—an insight, an inspiration, an answered prayer. Our to-do list may not have been dictated from a burning bush, but our Little Personal Miracle is just as special. We see with new eyes, sing with a new voice, and navigate the world with a new confidence.

(Okay, maybe not the singing part, but you know what I mean.)

Maybe we should frame everything as a prayer request. Few will object or refuse. Most everyone likes to help, and praying is something we can all do. "Please pray for..." We're not dictating who to pray to or how. It invites us to focus on kindly assisting someone else (who I pray to really likes that sort of thing). Doesn't matter if it takes 15 seconds or 15 minutes; for a little while, we're stepping out of the spotlight and shining it on another. That benefits everyone, including us, and harms no one. But why should we? Because I'll bet that whoever you pray to—if you pray at all—said so.

It's hard to imagine praying and hating at the same time. Or praying and resenting. Could we prosper from a pause from hating and resenting? Ever drink a dipper of cool well water on a hot August afternoon?

Please pray for someone you can't stand. Please pray for someone you do not understand. Then stand by for some real fun.

"No matter how we got here, Big Bang or Divine Design, I've still got a question: When? If one thing blew up and scattered into everything else, when did that thing show up? If God spoke everything into being, when did God get there? When did the clock start ticking? In other words, when did time, how ever it started, start?"

That's an easy one. We can get confused because we've become accustom to thinking linearly; everything in our limited worldview must have a beginning and an end. But keep in mind the symbol for infinity, that sideways figure eight thing. From that perspective, time cannot end because it never began. There was no need for it to begin because it never ended. Who in their right mind would start something that hasn't stopped? Ever turn the key in the ignition when the car is still running? It makes that "grrrkkkk!" sound, doesn't it? So, it's like that. See?

"Uh...yeah...I guess."

Obviously, time could have *started*, for lack of a better term, a billion years from now.

"Okay. Even if I don't fully understand it, I'm pretty sure I don't want to talk about it anymore."

Don't you want to know where?

"Sure. Where did that thing that blew up come from, or where did God come from?"

Short answer: God was always Here, so where else could God be?

"I have to go now."

Exactly. When else could you go? It's always Now. Are we there yet? Yes and no.

(Fingers in ears) "Not listening. ♫ La-la-la...♪"

264

Hale Yes

We hear a lot these days about identity theft. It's real. I know because my identity was stolen. I discovered the culprit: Me. Using my name, along with its assorted credentials, I was pretending to be someone I'm not. Pretending that politics is so important and that God is not in control. The impostor was quoting Bible verses while ignoring what they said. Things like God not equipping us with a spirit of fear, but of power, love, and a sound mind (2 Timothy 1:7). If I'm freaking out, it's not God's doing. That's not the real me; that's a copy, not the original. Then there's the one about not being anxious about anything and addressing our requests to God instead of a person who can't do anything about them and may not even give a hoot. If I make my requests known to a human, the results are iffy at best; if I send them to God, the result is peace that goes beyond my capacity to comprehend it (Philippians 4:6-7). Who you gonna call?

(Hey, check out the lilies. How 'bout those birds?)

I dreamed I went to Heaven and shouted, "Good news: It's me!"
Of the few who noticed, no one seemed to agree.
They'd apparently confused me for someone not near as great,
So, I trotted out my résumé to set the record straight:
"Every time the church doors opened, I strode right in.
Check out this perfect attendance Sunday School pin!
Get a load of all these Bible verses I've memorized;
No one got wetter than me when I was baptized.
My portrayal of a wise man in our live manger scene
Made the others look like amateurs, made Joseph turn green.
The choir members shrugged and said, 'What do we even try for?'

My rendition of 'The Old Rugged Cross' was to die for.
Our preacher, he was pretty good, and many folks were
moved.
I took notes and coached the guy; he gradually improved.
I tithed and talked a lot about how good that made me
feel.
(You can write it off your taxes, so it's really no big deal.)
Check out my credentials. There's no hurry; I can wait.
Meanwhile, who's up for a theological debate?"

Saint Peter looked at me like he was trying not to puke.
He raised his hands and walked away; said, "You take
this one, Luke."
Luke! The very one Paul called "beloved physician."
How apropos that he should diagnose my condition.
Luke said, "We are under orders to cut you lots of slack,
So, follow this prescription if you want to come back.
You've a serious sickness; it's sad, but not so strange.
There's hope, but you must undergo a drastic lifestyle
change.
You see, up here, you matter just as much as others did
to you.
And according to our records, well, you've got some work
to do.
You've logged a lot of miles in some doctrine-driven joints,
But up here, mere religion will not score you any points.
Your ego driven antics, man, are not that big a treat
To a person who is homeless or needs something to eat.
Someone who's gone a month of Sundays sans a kind
word or a smile,
Let's face it: they're not in the mood to stop and dig your
style.
To a soul who's only seeking peace, escape from misery,
Your hermeneutics do not mean skubala to a tree."

Wide awake, I tried to shake that dream out of my head,
But there was Luke's prescription lying neatly on the bed.
It said, "Get over yourself; wise up; there's a better way to be.
Memorize and practice Matthew 7:12 and see."

(Caution: Do not take on an empty heart.)

WE FIND WHAT WE'RE LOOKING FOR, PERSPECTIVE

*Tom, I love these reflective, vignettes you do so
well.*
~James Webster

"Do you have those little cold bottles of Starbucks Frappuccino?"

The polite, friendly produce guy said, "If we have any, it will be over here." He led the way. Along the way, a checker joined us. She agreed where they'd be if they had them. "Looks like all we have is the Dunkin' Donuts ones," said he. "We used to have Starbucks, but not anymore," said she.

Any port in a storm, 'eh? I grabbed two of the Dunkin' Donuts bottles and moved on. On my mosey through the bakery section, I saw a small cooler in a corner. Little cold bottles of Starbucks Frappuccino.

Cue the metaphor:

Sometimes, we might presume something doesn't exist because it's not where we expect to find it.

Hale Yes

If we're hitching our happiness, our peace of mind, our contentment, security, or identity to one particular person, job, organization, possession, or opinion, we may be discouraged from looking elsewhere, from finding or recognizing it where it really is. "If we have any, it will be over here."

The trick is to keep looking even when our confidence is waning, even when self-selected or self-appointed authorities tell us it's not to be found.

"Hey, man, it is what it is."

Yes, but why, and what else can it be? Might there be some untapped potential, some unmined diamonds?

"Some folks are just lazy, unwilling to work."

Like us? Are we too lazy, too unwilling to learn what a diamond in the rough looks like and then dig for it? Is it too easy to write them off, admit defeat?

"We're doing our best."

Sometimes our best isn't good enough. Is there any room for improvement on our part?

"You need to wise up and face the facts: There are some things we can't do anything about."

Have you seen any horses in the parking lot lately? Seen anyone sitting in a Conestoga wagon on the east bank of the Mississippi saying, "Dang, how will we ever get across?" When's the last time you had to find a payphone to make a call?

Everything is what it is...until we change it. Maybe what it is is an opportunity.

"So, what's the answer?"

Beats me. But I do know that we tend to find what we are looking for, and we find it faster when we are hunting a solution instead of aiming to blame.

Tom Hale

Once upon a time, there was a woman, a beggar. She positioned herself near the palace gate, not close enough to be noticed or get in the way, but where she could still watch all the excitement. She loved to see the royal processions. Her biggest dream was to someday catch sight of the princess. Wouldn't that be something? Over the years, she saw a lot of duchesses, dukes, ladies, earls, and such come and go; she even saw the queen a time or two. Never the princess.

One cold afternoon, the beggar woman was huddled in a corner, pulling her thin blanket tight around her. Franny, the court nanny, came strolling by. Franny saw the woman, and said, "What on earth are you doing?"

"Trying to keep warm," said the woman. "And a bite to eat would be most welcome; a crust or an apple core would do nicely."

Franny rolled her eyes, pointed to the palace, and said, "Well, it's nice and warm in there; the food is plentiful and mighty good. Why don't you go in?"

"Oh," said the woman, "I could never do that."

"Why the heck not?" said Franny. "You live there. You're the princess for cryin out loud. We thought you were out gallivantin around the kingdom all this time— and too busy to write, as usual."

Franny convinced the woman to walk with her to the gate. The guards bowed and immediately swung it open.

"You forgot who you were? How is that even possible? Lord, these kids, they'll drive you nuts."

(It wasn't so much that she forgot she was a princess; it was just that, over time, she let others convince her she wasn't. As soon as someone treated her like one again, the spell was broken.)

Walk across campus with a botany professor and she will point out plants and features you likely never noticed.

270

Walk across campus with an entomologist and he will call your attention to bugs you never knew existed—maybe even some you wish didn't.

Walk across campus with an architect. She will tell you interesting things about the buildings you pass by every day, including the building you work in. "So those are Corinthian columns, 'eh? I'll be dogged."

On our journey through life—or across campus—we find what we're looking for. The botanist is looking for plants; the entomologist is always on the lookout for insects; you get the idea.

"Thank you for calling the I'm Worried Sick About Stuff I Can't Do a Damn Thing About hotline. If you are worried sick or mad as Hell about something you heard on FOX news, press one. If you are all in a dither about the human condition, press 2. If you are tired of livin and scared of dyin, press 3. If you think other people's driving habits are going to change just because you don't like them, press your palm against your forehead. All of our commiseration counselors are busy taking other calls. Please do not hang up. Your call is very important to us. Everything is very important to us. Lord, did you see Real Housewives of Hoboken last night? What on Earth was Fern thinking?! Your call will be taken in the order it was received."

(Hold music: "Get Over It.")

"Thank you for continuing to hold. Looks like it's going to be a while. To pass the time, if you can stop wringing your hands long enough, visit our website at www dot crymeariver dot nut. Be sure to leave a comment and like our Facebook page!"

(Credit/blame where due: This was John Hale's idea. He can be reached for comment at 1-800-who'llstoptherain.)

Tom Hale

We see, sniff, and share the flowers. We eat the bread and the cereal. We love the feel of cotton. We may tend to forget that before we enjoyed them, the flower, wheat, and cotton seeds had to spend some time underground.

Down where it's dark, damp, and chilly. Creepy things crawl all over and around.

Same with us. Before we can bud, blossom, and bless, we have to spend some time in places and experience some things that can seem anything but beneficial. Those creepy things are nourishing and conditioning the soil, but at the time: yuck...sucks...enough already. (The fertilizer doesn't appear to be a plus, either.)

We endure, and our reward is a moment in the sun. But the work's not done.

Before the flowers can be sent they must be plucked. Before the wheat can be consumed, it has to be cut down—and endure any number of indignities along the way. Before the cotton can be a comfort, it has to be picked, ginned, baled, and spun. Before we can reach our potential, be of maximum use, we too go through the mill.

And then we're gone. Gone? Not hardly. Any pleasures, nourishments, or comforts we're responsible for will continue. They'll continue in the hearts and minds of folks we affected in a positive way. And in any contributions we made to the seed supply.

"Sometimes when you're in a dark place you think you've been buried, but actually you've been planted." ~Christine Caine

"I didn't come here, and I ain't leavin." ~Willie Nelson

On another planet in another universe, one where they don't have anywhere near as much sense as we do:

Ablendan was a zealous devotee. He could be seen at least once a day in the Holy House, often for an hour or

272

more, lying prostrate on the floor before the statue of the Golly Rama. And oh, how he would carry on. In the fanciest language his tongue could navigate, he would beg favor, gush flattery, and affirm his fealty. It was a most impressive display, bordering on pharisaical.

The Golly Rama got wind of this fan and decided to seek him out.

One day, Ablendan was in the agora, doing some holiday shopping with his friend, Erasmo. From across the street and heading toward him, grinning and waving, Ablendan caught sight of a tatterdemalion stranger. Ablendan, taking the guy for a vagabond, clutched his pocket book close and stage whispered to Erasmo, "Watch my stuff while I dispatch this ignoramus."

Ablendan caught the stranger by the shoulders, spun him around, and gave him a swift kick in the keister. "Leave us in peace, you filthy interloper!"

He looked to his friend for approval. Erasmo just shook his head and said, "I ain't believin this. Have you any idea what you've done? You just insulted and smote the Golly Rama."

Ablendan was bumfuzzled and diving deep for disbelief, but Erasmo didn't look like he was kidding around. What weak straw of defense could he grasp? "C'mon, man. That guy didn't look at all like the Golly Rama's statue or this picture of him I wear around my neck. No silk robes, no crown, no glow. And not so much as one tending pixie."

Erasmo lowered his head, turned and slowly walked away muttering: "Elysium help us when our symbols hold more meaning than that for which they stand."

Ablendan hollered after him, "He wasn't even the right color!"

A baseball coach at a college in Oklahoma showed me how to find my dominant eye. Since I'm right-handed, I figured it would be my right eye. Not so. My left eye is clearly the dominant one. That explained a lot, like why I was always a mediocre shot. It was frustrating because I always had the target lined up, what seemed to be, perfectly. I always closed my left eye and sited with my right, just the opposite of what I should have been doing. Favoring the non-dominant eye can affect many things, including photography and penmanship. (Google "dominant eye" and you'll find quite a few simple tests to determine it.)

That's interesting and useful information. More important than our dominant eye is our dominant outlook.

Obviously, we still use both eyes, it's just that one serves us better. Same with our outlook. Nobody that I know is all positive or all negative. What matters is which we use most of the time. Like Earl Nightingale pointed out, some people expect more good out of life than bad, and they get it. And vice versa. We do find what we're looking for.

Certainly, we do not want to naively overlook what's wrong; we want to identify it and deal with it in ways that get the results we want. At the same time, a dominant outlook that is positive and grateful, one that expects the best—from ourselves and each other—will serve us better.

It's interesting how one's perspective can change over the course of a visit to the dentist. For example:

During the bonus brushing and flossing before leaving the house, one might be thinking, "That's a lot of money, man. This will require some budgeting and lifestyle alterations which I do not greet with a happy heart."

Hale Yes

On the drive to the office, one might decide to practice what one preaches and think, "I'm lucky to have a job where I can accumulate sick days so I can take an afternoon off without a dock in pay. I am grateful for my insurance which will go halves with me on this thing."

About an hour into the procedure: "God, I'll gladly give you six hundred dollars if you'll just let me go home now!"

(I have the best dentist, with the coolest staff. It's not their fault I wrecked and neglected my choppers over the years. I do appreciate all of them mighty much and admire their damage control skills.)

"If the media would stop covering it, they'd stop doing it." "They're just acting that way for the cameras." "The media offer nothing but melodramatic flapdoodle."

There's an old joke about a man who complained to his doctor, "No matter where I touch, it hurts. When I touch my leg, it hurts. When I touch my forehead, it hurts. When I touch my arm, it hurts."

The doctor remedied the problem by removing the splinter in the man's index finger.

Maybe the media aren't the problem. Maybe it's our willingness to keep watching, listening, reading, believing, and responding? If I'm outraged and indignant over nothing; if I'm buying their solutions to the crises they created; if I'm marching to their music, the media have done their job. If I tune them out, I've done mine.

"But surely there must be some real journalists left, some who are unbiased."

Of course there are. Look for the ones who seem more interested in informing than persuading, reporting instead of provoking.

Bonus old joke:

Patient: Doc, it hurts when I do this.

Doctor: Then don't do that.

Tom Hale

Sometimes, the glass really is half empty. And have you noticed that, when it is, it's always the top half that's missing, never the bottom? What's up with that? Even if you drink it with a straw, drinking the bottom part first, it's the top that disappears.

"Uh...you're kidding, right?"

Pretty much, also hoping to make a point.

"Could you make it quickly? No offense, but you do tend to ramble."

I'll try. The example above poses no puzzle. No one is surprised that the bottom doesn't disappear first. Yet some folks act mystified and put upon by some things that are just as obvious.

"Like what?"

Like what we plant in the ground is what grows. No one plants zinnias and then feels cheated when marigolds don't come up. It works the same way, only more so, with what we plant in our minds. We get back what we sow in society too. If we've been planting a load of negative, downer nonsense, it would be silly to blame someone else if we're not happy. It's not about walking around with a vacuous grin, sticking smiley faces on everything. We face facts and acknowledge problems, of course; it's just that we're in a better position to deal with them if we've been cultivating confidence, creativity, and a sincere desire to do better each time.

"You realize that it's the tree limbs waving around that makes the wind blow, right?"

Sure, everyone knows that.

It's hard to take someone seriously who says "It can't be done" when we've already seen it done. We can believe them if they say, "I'm not willing to do it." That's fair. We know those results too.

Hale Yes

We've all seen people start with the most menial, low-paying jobs and work their way up. Nothing stops them. If they need to put in extra time, they do. If they need more education, formal or informal, they get it. Instead of making cheap excuses, they make it happen. They identify more strongly with their potential than their limitations—be they physical, social, or self-imposed.

Sure, some folks are born on third base and act like they hit a triple. So what? What's that got to do with us? Earl Nightingale was born in the cheap seats, but he learned the rules of the game, followed them, and built a broadcasting and publishing empire explaining how it works. It's not complicated. Nightingale boiled it down to six words: We Become What We Think About. The rest is just illustrations, inspirations, and variations on the theme.

We all strike out now and then. The ones who blame it on the bat will never be in the starting lineup. The ones who show up for practice and are open to coaching will eventually hit one out of the park.

Earlier this morning, I knew two things:
1. I needed a small Phillips head screwdriver.
2. I did not have one.

Have you ever searched for something anyway? During the obligatory poke and sort through a junk drawer, lo and behold, a Phillips head screwdriver. And just the right size. It was a giveaway from a long-ago career fair.

I did not have one...until I looked for one. It did exist; it was there the whole while whether I believed it or not.

Makes me wonder what else might be available—things physical, mental, spiritual—if I could corral my doubts long enough to explore. Do they only seem to be hiding because I lack the wherewithal to seek?

The pendulum swings to both extremes. Far left...far right...far left...far right. As it does, it spends twice as much time in the middle, and necessarily so. The metronome ticks...and then it tocks. It's the space in between that determines the rhythm. Whether we prefer to Waltz Across Texas or Twist and Shout, we all want to dance.

It's the space between the walls that makes a room. If all that lumber and sheetrock was piled up in one place, no one would want to live there. It's the space between the notes that makes a melody. If we played all the notes at the same time, no one could sing along or so much as tap a toe.

Some folks will choose to be party poopers. Some will be wall flowers. That's okay. The rest of us will put another quarter in the jukebox. Let's keep our mojo and our yin yang workin.

Overheard in the dirt, two flower seeds talking:
"Does this suck or what?"
"It'll get better."
"I don't see how. It's dark; it's damp; it's cold. Bugs crawling all over the place."
"When we reach the sun—"
"What's this sun you keep harping on?"
"Some roots told me about it."
"And you believe it? Grow up, man. Great: another load of fertilizer just got dumped on us."
"Maybe things happen for a reason."
"Please. We're rotting in the ground, or haven't you noticed?"
"This isn't all there is to us. Wait and see. Once we get to the other side, folks will be happy to see us. We will be beautiful."

"Beautiful? Have you looked at yourself lately? Oh, swell, now I'm cracking open!"

"Life's a bitch, and then you bloom."

"Have you lost your mind?"

"Go to the light."

"Yeah, right..."

The Wizard of Oz has launched many metaphors. This morning, I've been playing with this one:

Toto is our curiosity. Chasing after it can lead us into trouble. It may make us miss our ride home, but we're not leaving without it. As a result, we find a better, quicker, more fun way to get there. And it was right there all along. It was worth the trouble. Toto has a mind of his own; he loves and accepts us unconditionally. Toto pulled back the curtain. Follow that dog.

Things happen for a reason. The reason may not at first, or ever, be clear, but it makes sense to someone at some level somehow.

For example: In 1978, a friend and I drove to Las Vegas. It was like returning to my home planet, one I'd always wished existed. And God said, "Let there bedazzle!"

Around 3 a.m., we were slow motoring up and down Las Vegas Boulevard. I was riding shotgun. "Hey, I just saw...at least I'm pretty sure I saw Robert Redford riding a horse. His cowboy outfit was all lit up and so was the horse."

My compadre perhaps thought that I was a bit lit myself, but he made the car swap ends and we went back to verify.

Sure enough, there was Robert Redford in a lit-up getup, moseying along the side of the road on a lit-up horse.

There was a reason for that: They were filming a movie. *The Electric Horseman.*

Overheard in the cocoon:
"Boy howdy. Life's a bitch and then you die, 'eh? Oh, for the good old days: creeping along, oblivious to where I was going or if it even meant anything. Now I'm stuck, trapped like a rat. Yes, I know, I did it to myself; it's my fault; blah-blah-blah. At least it can't get any worse—how's that for a silver lining? And it's probably Monday. I'm melting! What a world, what a world..."
Eavesdropping on a butterfly:
"Whoa! Is this cool or what? Flower fluttering is way more fun than twig crawling. And a far better view."

"A tornado sounds like a freight train."
Wonder what tornadoes sounded like before freight trains were a familiar reference (the Transcontinental Railroad was completed in 1869).
"It sounds like a...like something you ain't ever heard." "I don't know what it sounds like, but it looks like chicken. Like chickens whirling helplessly in a counterclockwise manner."
Lucky for us, we live in modern times and know what to listen for.
One evening, during stormy weather, Mom heard a freight train. Never one to pass up an opportunity to panic needlessly, she asked brother John, "Is that a tornado?!"
"No."
"How can you tell?"
"A tornado doesn't blow for the crossing."
Sometimes we hear what we want to hear or fear to hear and ignore the obvious.

Hale Yes

Take the Quiz. Without Googling and with a 10-second time limit on each question, tell me:

1. Who won the Super Bowl three years ago?
2. Anyone who won an Oscar in 2016.
3. Who was on the cover of People Magazine two weeks ago?
4. What's number one on the Billboard Charts (any category) this week?

Now, try these (same rules):

1. Who can you count on when the chips are down?
2. Name someone who's had a positive influence on your life.
3. When you are sick or afraid, who do you want with you?
4. Who do you have fun with?

It's easy to see who is really important in our lives, isn't it?

Last week, I visited a campus for the first time. Erelong, I asked the question familiar to all frequent coffee drinkers: "Where's the restroom?"

Directions were given and understood. I entered. The room was dark. I felt around on the nearby walls for a light switch. There wasn't one. I thought perhaps I'd mistakenly stepped into a supply closet. When I found the door and turned to leave, the lights came on. Oh, one of those deals. The timer could use some adjusting.

Sometimes we are where we're sure we should be, where we need to be. We follow instructions; we read the signs; we go in confidently, and then...nothing. Doubt creeps in. We take what little action we can. Still nothing.

Tom Hale

As we initiate our exit, illumination. The timing could be better, at least from our point of view. Next time, we'll know to just stand there in the dark and wait for the light to shine.

(Or we'll forget, panic, and question our sanity again. It's a learning experience either way.)

Oh, kids these days...blah-blah-blah, boo-hoo-hoo.

We Baby Boomers were also on track to ruin everything with our hotrod engines, our rock & roll music, and our outrageous reluctance to believe everything we were told. As far back as forever, the grownups have been lamenting "kids these days." At one time, comic books and jazz were sure signs of the apocalypse. Best I can tell, the only problems with the so-called millennials—at least the ones I know and know of—is that they're better looking and smarter than we are. How dare they? (And yes, there are aberrant exceptions of all ages.)

There are many "experts" making one whole lotta money stereotyping and baselessly explaining millennials. I believe the polite term is balderdash. Here's a quick quote from an article I read recently:

"For as long as human hair has turned gray, elders have looked at their successors and frowned. 'Children nowadays are tyrants,' goes an old quotation widely attributed to Socrates. 'They contradict their parents, chatter before company, gobble their food, and tyrannize their teachers.' In 1855 a professor at Davidson College described college students as 'indulged, petted, and uncontrolled at home ... with an undisciplined mind, and an uncultivated heart, yet with exalted ideas of personal dignity, and a scowling contempt for lawful authority.'"

("The Millennial Muddle" by Eric Hoover, *The Chronicle of Higher Education*, October 11, 2009)

The kitchen of the old homeplace needed painting, so friends and relatives pitched in to help. Step one was to scrape off any loose paint. From his ladder, Uncle Gus poked at a strange glob on the high ceiling. "What in this world?" He pried the lump loose, brought it down, and put it on the table.

They stared in silent ponder. In their times, they'd all seen things, things weird and wonderous, but never anything like this. They all nearly jumped out of their skins when Aunt Suzy slapped the table, aired a merry cackle, and said, "I know what that is!"

Years back (ten years? twenty?), Granny busted open a can of store-bought biscuits. She was highly peeved to find only seven biscuits; there were usually eight.

"It's the missing biscuit."

The eighth biscuit, air launched so long ago, had been there all the while. It wasn't really missing, it was just unnoticed. Until now.

(This is a true story. I do not recall all the particulars, who and where. We've a large family and no shortage of strange tales. Even so, the message is clear: You don't just go painting over a mystery biscuit.)

Drumming on hollow logs, smoke signals, the Town Crier, the Pony Express, the telegraph, party lines, Princess phones (Just imagine, your own phone in your own room!): We have always welcomed better, faster, more novel means of communication.

"But these kids are addicted to their smartphones!"

And we're not? When's the last time you saw anyone, of any age, anywhere without a cellphone—often while driving or shopping?

"But kids bring them to class and can't resist sneaking a peek or clandestinely texting. They won't be able to do that in the real world."

You mean like we do during meetings? (Whether or not we represent the real world is debatable.)

Lord, please don't tell me they have snacks and beverages in class ... you know, like we do in our offices. What are these kids, humans or something?

There's no law against lightening up.

"You're so organized!"

On behalf of myself and anyone who's known me longer than 15 minutes, I laughed aloud.

She went on, in a serious tone, about how neatly I had everything laid out, how everything fit together. And I thought, "Why not?" Why couldn't I be the organized person this stranger was seeing? Just because I never have been? That seems a weak excuse. Why couldn't I change for the better?

People tend to see the best in us. Why shouldn't we also see it and try to live up to it? So far, it's been fun at least trying to be more organized.

Odds are I'll never be a CPA, but at least, given time, my socks might begin to match more often. Yes, trying to do better is definitely more fun.

We're all quite bright and equally ridiculous in our own peculiar ways, yet so many folks insist on assessing themselves and others against some nonexistent norm. What qualifies as "stupid" or "common sense" varies from person to person. When we scrape off the crust, we see attitudes of "You're stupid if you don't act like me." "You don't have any common sense if you don't share my skills and opinions."

Copernicus, Galileo, Mark Twain, and Albert Einstein were labeled stupid at one time or another. I'm kind of glad that Nikola Tesla, Henry Ford, Steve Jobs, and Bill Gates didn't and don't act like me. I celebrate their uncommon sense and benefit greatly from it.

Heading SSW out of Russellville, Arkansas, just before crossing the Arkansas River Bridge into Dardanelle, there used to be a junk store on the right. They had a portable sign near the road that read, "WE BUY SCRAP." Saw it many times, a familiar landmark. One day, due to the wind or some prankster, the S had been blown or moved over close to the Y. The sign then announced this happy news: "WE BUYS CRAP."

(Or perhaps it was a legit attempt at truth in advertising...)

We were discussing the effects of weather on longtime afflictions, our not so merry maladies. A friend told how an ancient sprain reacts to rain. I was about to mention my mule riding shoulder.

Decades ago, I tried to ride a wild mule. Not just once but at least half a dozen times, I was unceremoniously flung to the ground. Opting for ignorance over common sense, I did not quit until it was time to visit the ER with a separated shoulder. For years and years, high humidity triggered a reminder.

I was about to mention my mule riding shoulder. But I could not and cannot remember the last time it paid an achy visit. What a nice surprise. Here lately, I like to roll my shoulder and ask, "What's a nice joint like you doing in a place like this?"

When Hannibal was in the first and second grades, we had an ongoing game. My position was that nothing is

impossible. Hannibal would come up with things he
thought were impossible, and I would counter with why
they could be possible. (He: "It's impossible to lift an
elephant with your little finger." Me: "Not if the elephant's
in the cargo bay of an orbiting space shuttle, a gravity-
free environment." And so on.) We would discuss things
that once seemed to be and were, by most, deemed to be
impossible: Telephones, radio, talking pictures,
mechanical flight, a four-minute mile, anything smaller
than a transistor, etc. "Just because, up until now, no
one's done it or just because we don't yet know how, that
does not mean it's impossible."

One afternoon when I picked him up from school,
Hannibal hopped in and said, "If nothing is impossible,
then it's possible for something to be impossible, isn't it?"

Give that man a cigar. We have a winner.

(Some will tell us that it's not possible for a 7-year-old
to think abstractly.)

It was a large classroom in one of the oldest buildings
on the University of Arkansas campus. The room had a
high ceiling, a low stage across the front, and best of all,
steam radiators for heat. Those radiators would hiss, pop,
and rattle, keeping up a near constant racket. In the
warmer months we had wasps bouncing around the
overhead lights, performing their insect aerobatics. What
a great room, what a perfect place to help students learn
to tune out distractions and focus.

On the back wall of the classroom, there hung a
battery-powered clock. The clock made a faint ticking
sound every second. During each semester, out of the
blue, I'd ask the students, "Can you hear that clock
ticking?"

No, they could not. Not one of them. Not even those
sitting closest to it.

"Listen. Tell your brain to ignore everything else and tune in that tick."

As the next moments passed, I could see their eyes light up when they heard it. And they would smile. They surprised themselves and were pleased about it.

We find what we're looking for and hear what we're listening for, even if at first we don't think we can.

(By the way, I can still hear that clock ticking. I can hear it right now from where I sit typing. No, I didn't steal it. It was my clock in the first place. It was...really.)

Tom Hale

RIVER TALES

Tom, you are a blessing to all who know you.
Thanks for your morning words of wisdom.
~Judy Hess Barkley

♫ Work like a mule on the Mississippi;
Sweat till you drop or can hardly stand.
Hop on a jet at the Memphis airport;
Fly away to play on the Rio Grande. ♫

My first trip up the Mississippi was on a small boat; we were pushing two propane barges. Not too impressive in a mile-wide river where other boats push acres of barges, but I did get to see something that made a lasting impression.

One morning during high water, I went off watch at midnight. I looked out the galley window and saw the light of a day marker blinking on the bank. When I came back on watch six hours later, I looked out the same window and saw the same light. The water was so swift that all of our engine power could not push us up the river. The best the pilot could do was keep us from going backward. We sat out in the middle of the river and did nothing more than hold our own for six hours, burning up diesel fuel.

There are buoys in the river that mark the channel. The Coast Guard guarantees nine feet of water between the buoys. The pilot stayed between the buoys like he was supposed to. Then Captain Louis came on watch.

Captain Louis was in his seventies. He had long white hair and posture that would impress a telephone pole. Captain Louis learned the river before there were reliable buoys, wheelhouse radar, and other navigational aids. He knew every tree, every sandbar and how it had changed since the last time he'd seen it. Captain Louis knew how deep the water was outside the channel. He could look at a mark that the rest of us could not see and determine the depth and location of underwater hazards. Captain Louis took us into the slack water and we progressed up the river.

When the pilot came back on, he set the boat between the buoys and we sat there for another six hours, engines full ahead, making a lot of noise, churning a lot of muddy water—an impressive sight, to be sure, but going nowhere.

No one could fault the pilot; the pilot was obeying the buoys. Captain Louis was reading the river.

A little while ago, a friend posted that she was waiting for her plane at Memphis International. Facebook informed me that many of my other friends had also been there. Yeah, me too.

Flashback: After 30 summer days on a towboat, get off in Memphis. Walk up the levee toting a duffle bag, a briefcase, and a guitar. Find a phone (back before we all carried one with us) on Front Street. Call the airport to see when's the next flight to El Paso. Walk on a ways to the downtown Travel Lodge, check in, jump in the pool. Next morning, breakfast at the Toddle House (topflight jukebox), taxi to the airport, catch a Big Iron Angel to the desert for fifteen days of hard-earned, unfettered fun. Bouncing between two rivers and loving them both.

There's a line in a Conway Twitty song: "I may never get to Heaven, but I once came mighty close." It was like that. Closest one can get this side of the River Jordan.

If you keep the line tight (50 feet of 2-inch line), you can check a string of nine barges and stop them exactly where they need to be. Allow just a little slack and the barges will pop the line quicker than you can cuss.

Everyone we know, everyone we see, is hauling a lot of freight (fears, doubts, anxieties, and insecurities), most of it below the waterline. We keep the lines tight with friendship, common courtesy, and kindness. If we allow a little slack in the relationship (marginalizing, devaluing, stomping their toes instead of walking in their shoes), they can snap. Then we'll read the headlines and say, "Isn't that awful? How can people act like that?"

Is it my responsibility? Well, that depends on what kind of world I want to live in.

On one particular towboat, we used hand signals. Hand signals work well. When they can be seen.

One afternoon when fog started creeping in, we intended to tie off on one of the trees in a stand of cottonwoods. By the time I got to the head of the tow, the fog was so thick that the pilot could not distinguish me from Casper.

My signals were accurate and sincere, but they could not penetrate the fog. My vocal enthusiasms could not penetrate the distance, not even when greased with colorful supplements.

The pilot's only audible feedback was the sound of trees snapping in half. Snapping in half and pinning me to the deck. In my mind, I could hear Paul Bunyan say, "You know, there's a more efficient way to do that."

Sure, we lost time and adrenaline, but we gained a fairly decent metaphor.

Sometimes we're sending proper signals, but the intended recipient's receptors are clouded by uncontrollable circumstances.

Sometimes it's nobody's fault, and blaming won't change that.

The first day of autumn. It always reminds me, as does just about everything else, of a river story:

One of the duties of the first mate was to help the cook make the grocery and supply list that would be radioed in to Economy Boat Store. Had to plan ahead. We should be about a week out from Baton Rouge, but you never know. Since it was October, I added a pumpkin to the order.

Captain Greg had to approve the list. He said, "Hell, they ain't gonna have no damn pumpkin." (He'd never seen a pumpkin on a towboat; ergo, they wouldn't have one.)

I suggested that "Since they ain't gonna have no damn pumpkin, it wouldn't hurt to leave it on the list." He snorted, nodded, and told me not to be disappointed when they didn't deliver one.

They delivered one. A nice big one.

When running at night, a boat must display a green light on the starboard side of the lead barges, a red one on the port side, and a flashing amber in the middle of the tow. With the unanimous approval and happy assistance of the deck crew, I replaced the flashing amber with a flickering jack-o-lantern. No need to mention it to the captain or pilot.

Captain Greg remarked that he'd never received so many, "Happy Halloween" greetings from passing boats. Hmmm...wonder why.

Every river rat knows there are times when the plain facts won't quite fill the glass, so we must top it off with a little club soda in order to charge full price.

One evening in the galley, the crew was debating the rumor that a VW Beetle could float. I assured them it could.

"I used to work as a bear tender at Baylor University in Waco. I lived on the other side of the Brazos River. The closest bridge was ten miles away. And the traffic, good Lord. I found I could cut 15 minutes off my commute by putting a trolling motor on the rear bumper of my VW, gliding across, and driving up the Front Street landing just two miles from campus. Of course, during high water, I had to start farther upstream. It just wasn't worth it: The timing was iffy, and having to dodge all the logs and other—don't let anyone tell you there aren't alligators that far north; if you don't believe me, go talk to Bud Wheeler's widow, she'll set you straight. Quicker to take the bridge. But the car will float."

It was a true story, except for—if you want to get all nitpicky about it—the details. (And the part about the alligator? Okay, that was a croc.)

Fifteen grain barges free-floating down the Mississippi river is not the safest thing to be aboard, but the tow was still afloat and the boat was taking on water. If the engine room fills, it's all over. Not a single person on the crew, when urgently awakened at two in the morning, said, "It's not my watch." No one had to be cajoled into putting on a lifejacket and getting on the barges. No one dozed when at any second we could get the signal to cut 'em loose. I'd seldom been so wide awake. More often than not, we're safe sticking with the boat. Now and then, we're better off taking our chances on the barges, taking *alert* to a whole new level, looking for something, anything, to catch a line on.

We were rescued and hauled to the lock wall at 22 before it came to all that.

We were picking up a couple of empties in Natchez. To get to one of the barges, we had to go through a swarm of bees. All the trepidation and vigorous swearing did not alter the mission. You sure that's the right number on that barge? For the third time, yes.

As we slowly waded through the buzzing cloud, I realized that those insects had no interest in us whatsoever. They were minding their own beeswax. They had a job to do, same as us. If we'd gone in flapping and slapping, it would have been a different story.

That's a right fine metaphor. We've gotta do what we've gotta do. If we stay calm, all concerned are better off. That goes for: Dealing with people with whom we disagree. Aging. Doing chores. Debriefing a broken heart. Anything that bugs us.

I don't have all the answers, but I do know that freaking out won't help.

I was born in Helena, Arkansas, a Mississippi River Delta town. We moved to El Paso, Texas when I was 10.

A little over a decade later, I wanted to find out what it's like to work on towboats on the Mississippi.

More often than not, people would tell me one of two things: 1) "It's hard work; you won't like it." 2) "Nobody wants to hire a green hand. I know guys been tryin to get on out there for years."

I took all that good advice, weighed it, and went to work for a towing company out of Memphis.

I still had an apartment in El Paso and I loved the Chihuahuan Desert.

During the hiring paperwork, the HR guy asked, "What's your home port?"

Not expecting to be taken seriously, I said, "El Paso, Texas."

He looked up from the form. "Is there a river there?"

"Yes, sir, a quite famous one: The Rio Grande."

"Is it navigable?"

"On foot. This time of year, you can pretty much walk across it in your good shoes and they'll require little more than a cursory cleaning."

Be danged, he wrote down El Paso as my home port. That obliged the company to fly me back to El Paso on my days off and to wherever the boat was when it was time to go back.

For every day we worked, we got half a day off with pay. Thirty days on followed by fifteen off and never miss a paycheck. A two-week vacation out of every forty-five days. It was a grand life for a single person; it was a perfect setup for a disorganized one. For thirty days, I was working—six hours on and six hours off, round the clock—with few distractions, followed by fifteen days of Wahoo with plentiful and most pleasant distractions. I loved being on the boat. I loved being off the boat.

We pushed 10 barges, each one the length of a football field and fifty feet wide. We'd load them with dry cement in St. Louis and drop them at various docks until we arrived in New Orleans with two. We'd wait while they unloaded those two then head upriver, picking up empties all the way to Memphis, then on to St. Louis to reload.

We tried to arrange for crew changes in Memphis, but it didn't always work out that way; sometimes it was St. Louis, sometimes New Orleans, once in Baton Rouge. Usually Memphis. I'd call the airport from Waterways Marine and ask for the next flight to El Paso.

It was fun getting on a plane in Memphis in July or August then getting off the plane a few hours later in El Paso. You can sweat in El Paso, but there's not enough humidity to sustain it. Cools you off as it evaporates. Sweat will not, cannot, evaporate anywhere between St. Louis and New Orleans. There's nowhere for it to go; the atmosphere won't absorb it, it's already saturated. I've observed donkeys during the dog days of a Delta summer. I have seen them weep. I have heard them curse. I have eavesdropped on their prayers: "Dear Lord, why durst thou treat thy humble servant like a waterlogged piñata?"

My River pals said it many times and in many colorful ways: "I can't believe they fly you back and forth to El Paso!" Perhaps the point here should be something akin to "You don't know until you ask," but the true moral of the story may be that one should never lead with a straight answer.

On the Mississippi River one fine day, across the way and through the trees, we saw another towboat heading south. We were headed north. Both boats were going downriver. Though we'd just passed them port to port, we were following them. Going in opposite directions with the same destination. Going in opposite directions because that's what was necessary to get there. It made sense because we had the big picture.

In the vicinity of New Madrid, Missouri, the river does a 180.

We were headed upriver, pushing ten cement barges, and the American Queen was down bound. They signaled one whistle, so we passed port to port. I was learning to steer, under the watchful eye of Captain Greg.

We heard boots stomping up the steel stairs to the wheelhouse. It was Fred. It was his first trip on the river. Fred was all in a froth because the TV reception in the lounge was lousy. He'd put foil on the rabbit ears and everything—this was the 1970s.

Captain Greg moseyed over, looked behind Fred, and said, "I don't see no anchor hangin off your ass. I'll let you off on the next sandbar if that's what you want. You're welcome to stay or welcome to go, but you're not welcome to stay and complain."

Life lessons on the Mississippi. Sometimes a little straight talk is just what we need to sort us out. Fred became a good, reliable deckhand. To this day, whenever I find myself about to gripe—or in the midst of doing so— I'll often look behind me. No anchor.

Gads, it was 80 degrees when it was still dark. Looks like it's gonna be another hot one. Yesterday sure was hot, 'eh?

"How hot was it?"

A water buffalo evaporated. The flies weren't even buzzing; they couldn't quite muster the zing part; it was more like "Buuuuuuuuu…"

It was on such a day, long ago, that I got a hint about the power of attitude. Vernon Howard and others said and say, "The inner controls the outer." Like most other things, that doesn't mean much until we try it and see it for ourselves.

On the river, heat advisories and warnings meant diddley. We didn't even know about them. Imagine a day like today and then some, with the added novelty of standing in the middle of an acre of steel barges. Making up a tow in the New Orleans harbor—I've seen strong men faint and fall over in such conditions.

On such a day, one of the other deckhands said, "Hot enough for ya?"

For some reason, I said, "Almost. If it was just ten degrees hotter, then...then I'd feel like I'd done something."

Some other guys picked up on it. "You call this hot? This is just disappointing." "This ain't $#!+." "Wish I hadn't left my jacket back on the boat. I'm about to freeze to death."

Lo and behold, we found new vigor; laughter replaced lamentations. Hey, we were going to be out there doing the job anyway, may as well find a way to make it more tolerable. We didn't find it outside, sweating like Judgment Day, cussing and complaining. We found it inside, inside ourselves.

There was a dog in the river.

We were at a dock just above Memphis. We had two barges, each one the length of a football field. The captain gave the order to cast off. But there was that dog, a black Labrador.

The dog was trying to swim upstream, against the current. He was about midway of the first barge and making little progress. He still had a good 450 feet to go and he was tiring fast. The dog was probably afraid of the engine noise and was not about to swim near, much less behind, the boat. The dog was going to drown.

The barges were empty, so we were at least ten feet above him. We could not reach the dog.

The captain could not see the dog, but he could see the whole crew on the port side of the barge, staring into the water and carrying on a lively conversation. The captain was not happy.

You know how some folks do in a panic; one of the deckhands threw the dog a line. That was funny and pitiful at the same time. The guy meant well, but well... Another deckhand, thinking more clearly, went to the boat and brought back a pike pole.

We were able to get the hook on the dog's collar and drag him, much against his will, toward the back of the boat. At one point, it looked like the dog's collar was going to slip off over his head.

Once we got the dog clear of the stern, he used his last ounce of energy to swim to the bank. The dog laid there, half in the mud and half in the river, exhausted but alive.

The dog got himself into the situation; fear kept him from discovering a way out of it; he fought his helpers every inch of the way. That's understandable behavior from a dog. Of course, you and I, sophisticated creatures that we are, would never act like that...

(For the rest of the trip, the captain referred to us as the K-9 Rescue Squad.)

We were upbound on the Ouachita River, headed for Sterlington, Louisiana. We were pushing two barges, each one fifty feet wide and the length of a football field. To navigate the narrow channel and the sharp bends, we could sometimes take only one barge at a time. We'd tie one off in the trees, take the other around the bend, tie it off, and go back for the other one.

We were going back for the other one. It was about two in the morning. Summertime. Dead calm. Darker than a licorice jellybean in Satan's sock drawer. Not even an insect noise. The breeze from a rabid bat flap would have been welcome. The other deckhand and I, while still on the river side of the barge, heard an outrageous SNAP! in the nearby woods. It was not a familiar sound. It was not a tree falling or a line breaking—we knew those noises. This was more like someone or some thing picked up a whole cottonwood tree and broke in in two.

Either of us, when faced with the known could hold our own, but when frozen in place by "What the hell was that?" confidence whistled a new tune. Under normal circumstances, one of us would have loosed the line at the head of the barge while the other dealt with the line midway. This was not a normal circumstance. Neither of us was going over there alone and neither of us was about to admit it. We didn't have to. We went together.

The captain asked what took so long. Good question, Cap. To this day I'm still wondering.

STEP LIVELY

I've just recently become familiar with your quirky yet light-filled messages through Facebook. I'm sorry for your health struggles. May you continue to bask in the healing light that surrounds you. Looking forward to more of your posts!
~Sharon Norman Willey

Years ago, I was visiting with a student who was in the Physical Therapy Assistant program. I asked him why he chose that field. He said because a Physical Therapist once helped him so much. It changed his life and now he wanted to do the same for others. I thought that was nice. Now I know firsthand what he meant.

What are you glad about? What frosts your pumpkin and makes your world shine? The first thing that pops to mind is my tight circle of family and friends. That's followed fast by Physical Therapists.

Everyone at the hospital was on beyond excellent; they all played a part in putting the zippity back in my doo dah. But most of my waking hours were spent in the gym with my Physical Therapist and my Occupational Therapist. Those two wore me out and won me over. They're folks around whom you'd feel like a total jerk giving less than your best, how ever little that might be at the moment. They worked their magic with kindness, humor, and rigor. What they did and how well they did it won them a permanent place in my Favorite Folks Hall of Fame.

To this day and for all to follow, I am knee deep in appreciation for Physical Therapists. Every step of the way.

The first time I learned to walk, it didn't seem like that big a deal, so I don't remember much about it. Six decades later, I got a second chance. This time, the process had my undivided attention.

"Turn out the lights."

When you flip the switch, you know how quickly the lights go off? That's what it was like, only it was my consciousness. There one second, gone the next. The first time it happened, I was next in line at a convenience store. Of course, when you're not there and aware you make no effort to break the fall, so instead I broke my head when I crashed into the countertop. My next Humpty Dumpty imitation happened at home. That's when I lost the feeling in my legs. Back to the physical rehabilitation hospital for another month.

It was frightening and disconcerting, to be sure, but it was also quite fascinating.

An ER nurse told me that the doctor kept making them redo my blood test because, according to them, it's impossible for a human to have (certain chemical) levels that low and still be alive. Yet there I was...alive...with levels that low. Maybe it's the human part of the equation that doesn't fit?

It had been five days since I'd consciously eaten anything. One evening, a nurse, after the obligatory procedures, said, "You want some graham crackers?" Sure. She gave me a couple of little cellophane-wrapped two-packs. The crackers were the kind with sugar and cinnamon sprinkled on them. That was the best thing I'd ever tasted. Every night thereafter, I'd hit my call button and ask if they had any more graham crackers. They always did. One night, a nurse also brought a little cardboard cup of ice cream with the graham crackers. Well, I was just in Heaven. That became our routine. Such a simple gesture, such an uncomplicated kindness, and it meant the world to me. A little goes a long way, doesn't it? I try to remember that.

That same damn clock perched above those same double closet doors. That's the first thing I saw every morning for...how long? Weeks? A month? It was like being in the *Groundhog Day* movie. But this time something was different. That same damn clock indicated that it was a few minutes after six. I'd slept a little longer than usual.

A nurse smiled into the room. "You're awake!" (Confirmation is always nice.) She said, "The dinner cart will be along shortly."

"You mean the breakfast cart, right?"

No, she meant the dinner cart. It was a few minutes after six p.m. Gads, I really had slept a little longer than usual, about 13 hours longer.

I could see the clock but did not understand what it was telling me. That same damn clock was also delivering another message, one that I missed until much later: "Hey, man, you're lucky you can see anything at all and to be in this place with these phenomenal folks who will, if you'll cooperate, help you pick up the pieces and put them pretty much back together."

When she talks, you can barely understand a word, even when you listen with your whole self. She's also the textbook example of flat affect. She could be shoutin happy or too blue to fly, but you'd never know to look at her. One afternoon she motioned me over. She said, "Everything changed the night you stopped feeling sorry for yourself and got silly with the rest of us. The whole mood of the room got better. We all had fun and started learning."

That jerked several knots in my tail.

1. I have no memory of the event.

2. Out of any 98 days of public school, K-12, I probably received 97 admonishments to stop being so silly. I seldom saw a report card that did not contain a teacher's stern warning that I needed to take things more seriously.

3. We all have a part to play, a function to perform. We get better results when we're just being ourselves.

4. When the teacher is ready, the student will appear.

There are some things we just don't want to hear. For example, we do not want to hear a representative from nutrition and food services use the phrase, "It appears to be."

At one particular hospital in Memphis (not that one, another one), several of us amused ourselves with a mealtime guessing game informally called "What the Hell is That?" Often, we did not know.

At one lunch unveiling, my roommate said it just that way: "What the hell is that?"

The lady from nutrition and food services, so help me, said, "It appears to be a slice of turkey on a piece of cheese toast."

With very little imagination, it could appear to be many things. It may well have been a slice of turkey, but the texture and taste offered no further clues.

And for reasons that no one can explain, none of the hospitals I've recently frequented serve butter. Instead, they have dinky plastic tubs of something called "whipped spread." Whipped spread: Is it just me, or does that sound a little vague? There are too many things in this old world that can be whipped and spread for me to get comfortable with that term. I'm not about to smear any of it on a—what's that thing, a pancake?

"Yes. If it was a waffle it'd have those little squares."

Pancake.

In fairness, all the folks at the hospital were nice and helpful. They were doing the best they could with what they had—even if no one was always quite sure what it was they had.

Certainly, we want to say something nice, something helpful, right? But of all the cantankerous old bastards I've ever met, this guy took the cake. He's in his 90s and has no filters—about anything. He's the last person I'd have chosen for a roommate. One of the things that irked him most was that almost every visitor, upon leaving, would chuckle and say, "Behave yourself."

In his mind, they were making fun of his age, reminding him that he was no longer in any position to misbehave, even if he wanted to.

Neither of us could sleep well; we had many conversations, mostly in the dark. I don't like to not like people. I have this often-naïve notion that I can find something to appreciate about anyone. What was it about this guy that kept my good intentions from gaining traction? There was plenty of time to think about it. One thing that helped was the obvious realization that uncertainty about one's future and chronic pain do not bring out the best in anyone. I wasn't exactly little Sammy Sunshine all the time either.

As I stopped taking him and myself so seriously, our conversations became more civil.

He got to go home a few days before I did, but I made it back to the room in time to shake his hand and say, "Behave yourself." He laughed and gave me that look, the look that says—well, you know exactly what it says.

They tell you the numbers but not what they mean. In hospitals, they check your blood pressure about every three minutes it seems. After a few times, when the numbers were announced, I asked, "Is that good?" I received responses such as, "Good? It's nearly perfect." and "I wish mine was that good." Every time. More often than not, they'd take it again to make sure the machine was working properly.

One afternoon, as I was passing the Nurses Station, one of them accused me of being younger than I was claiming. "You can't possibly be that old and have consistent blood pressure readings that good." Others agreed. I did not have my wallet with me; my license, credit cards, etc. were being safeguarded by family back home. I had no way to prove my age, so I took the easy way out: "You're right. I'm only 27, just did a lot of meth back in college." (Of course, they knew I was kidding, but I'd swear a couple of them found the improvised explanation easier to believe than the facts.)

It's nice to have at least one bragging point, especially when we're feeling vulnerable and when all present are way too familiar with our flaws. "Okay, I may not be able to walk down the hall unassisted or speak integibll... intelibagl... clearly, but let's forget all that nonsense and check our blood pressure. I've got a baggie full of quarters and a sack of Cheez Doodles that say mine's best."

Almost every time I parade one of my woes down Main Street, I meet or am reminded of someone who is dealing or has dealt with far worse.

Somewhere along the line—probably from Wayne Dyer—I picked up the notion that what we focus on is what expands in our lives; what we dwell on is what we get more of, so my challenge to myself is to think about only what I want. I'd rather have more improvement, more progress than more misery, so I try to lead (inwardly and outwardly) with what's going right.

It's mighty tempting to put the emphasis on what's wrong, and that's a natural response because what's wrong is often what's uppermost on our minds. Before long, we realize that hey, everyone has had tough times; there's nothing unique about that, so why bore people with it? Besides, it's no fun to find yourself in the goofy position of telling Noah about the flood. After a while, we have to honestly ask ourselves what it is we want most.

At the various hospitals, I noticed that the happiest patients, the ones who were the most pleasant company, were the ones who talked and bragged about their progress more than their problems. I noticed how hard they worked on their exercises and therapy projects, working so hard while shedding tears of pain and determination. It was inspiring; it made me want to do my best too. I was feeling sorry for myself because I had to relearn some of the most basic human functions, but how much sympathy could I seek from someone who did not have all (or any) of those options?

I want to focus on and increase what I can do instead of lamenting my limitations. The mental exercises help every bit as much as the physical ones, maybe more.

Hale Yes

"Way to go, Tom!" "Lookin good, Mr. Hale."

What's the big deal? All I was doing was walking, pushing my trusty Rollator, past the Nurses Station. All I was doing was...walking. Oh, okay. It was the first time most of them had seen me vertical. In their previous dealings with me, I'd been either horizontal or sitting in a wheelchair. (Hey, I may have actually looked tall for once.)

All that encouragement and support from folks who had mostly seen me when I was feeling and looking (and sometimes behaving) my worst, was special, mighty special.

They didn't give two hoots what I looked like outwardly (pajama bottoms, wrinkled T-shirt; grooming was not exactly a priority), but they really did care that I was getting better. They cared about me as a person. That got me to rethinking a few things, starting right then and lasting through—what time is it now?

There's nothing better than a good (fill-in-the-blank) when you need one. I met some good ones this year. They were all good; some were extraordinary. When I thought to do so, I asked the extraordinary ones, "If you could go back and do it all again, what line of work would you go into this time?" Every one of them—every physical therapist, every nurse, every specialist, every technician, every over-and-above helper I had—said they'd make the same choice.

They were no-nonsense about their jobs, to be sure. They also had a warmth and a humor about it. I could tell that they truly cared whether I (and everyone else) got better or not. They were demanding, demanding my best effort even when I didn't feel like giving it. They would not compromise, but they would celebrate each little improvement. With those people, in that atmosphere, the only option is success.

When my doctor and I were going over my hospital release paperwork, I said, "I feel like all the characters in *The Wizard of Oz* all rolled into one." She hugged me and said, "Me too."

Even as I said it, I had no idea what I meant by it, but it somehow made sense. I've had some time to think about it and come up with a few parallels.

For example: The Physical Therapist, Occupational Therapist, and Speech Therapist represent the circumstances that, as difficult as they may and must be, reveal that we already possess what we need, what we may have perceived to be lacking—a brain, a heart, courage, strength, stamina, patience.

Sometimes we have to learn, sometimes we learn best, the hard way.

It was a strange, sometimes scary, magical place. The experience was not without its intrigue and fascination; even so, all I really wanted was to go home.

Back home at the local Physical Therapy Clinic:

Who comes up with these questions? A physical therapy assessment can have its amusing moments.

"Would you have any problem hopping up a flight of stairs?"

Yes.

"Why's that?"

First of all, there are not any stairs where I live. This experience has been weird enough without finding myself hopping up stairs that don't exist. Second, I've been on a lot of stairs in my day; never once did I hop up them. That, along with this not being able to walk unassisted thing, have made hopping of any kind less of a priority.

"Would you have any difficulty lifting a bag of groceries over your head?"

Certainly.

"Why?"

Why, exactly. Why on Earth would anyone lift a bag of groceries over their head? Have you ever done that? I have always found it easier to take items out of the bag before putting them away, over my head or at any level. Lifting a whole bag of groceries over my head would be difficult—difficult to explain.

It's easy to imagine that they ask such questions just for fun. But what do I know? They may have some assessment value. (Keep an eye on anyone who says they could easily hop up a flight of stairs.)

♫ "Where seldom is heard a discouraging word..." ♪

Aye, that's the place to be (roaming buffalo optional). I'm beginning to see and appreciate the true power of encouraging words.

A neighbor—who has recovered from his own physical setbacks—and I were visiting. He said I seemed to be feeling better. Instantly, I started to feel better. We talked about how the changes, the improvements, can come about so gradually that we often do not notice them until they're pointed out by others. The more I thought about it, the truer it got. Someone said I seemed stronger and steadier on my feet. I immediately felt stronger and steadier on my feet. Someone said my enunciation was improving, and sure enough it was, and continues to. Maybe their comments helped me become aware of the positive changes. Could it be, at least partly, the power of suggestion? Sure. The mind-body connection is strong. What matters is that, for whatever reason(s), it works.

As a result of these observations, the plan is to be alert for opportunities to offer encouraging words. I'm betting/praying it will help. Who knows? It might even do more good than carping about politics or the weather.

Chatting with a neighbor yesterday. He said, "I used to be a paramedic, and I saw a lot of people who didn't make it after going through what you did. When I saw them wheel you outta here that last time, I didn't figure we'd ever be talking again."

Several folks have told me, "You're obviously still here for a reason." We would be hard pressed to prove or disprove that or to identify exactly what the reason is. I personally believe that we are all still here for a reason...until we're not. We can't say with certainty what those reasons are, but we can guess PDQ what they are not.

Being able to use our talents and passions to earn a living is a mighty blessing and a big plus, but I'll bet you it's when we use those talents and passions to serve others and not just ourselves that they count the most. That's something else I can't prove, but don't you just know it? Doesn't it ring true?

If you sell me a sandwich, adjust my brakes, or convince me to buy a copy of your book, by all means take my money. And don't forget to give yourself a raise, a reminder that you just improved the life of a fellow traveler. That's reason enough for me.

At the Physical Therapy Clinic last week, they started me practicing with a walking cane. It's not that tricky, but there is a definite technique. The Physical Therapist offered this helpful advice: "Instead of watching your feet, you should watch where you're going."

Hey, good plan. Yeah, I like that.

I lifted my head and got into the rhythm, confidence growing with each step. That's when I dang near walked into the wall. My eyes were open, but I was thinking about what a fine metaphor this would be for ... Every teacher, every speaker has seen it: Someone is looking right at you, but you can tell their mind is far, far away.

There's a difference between watching and paying attention, isn't there?

My 12-year-old nephew really likes my purple walking cane. The first time he was playing with it, he said, "I can't wait to get old."

I wanted to tell him, "You don't have to show any I.D. to buy a cane. All you need is a website and your mom's credit card." But I feared the aforementioned mom might demonstrate another use for a walking cane, how it can also put a knot on someone's head.

It's a milestone day, my last trip to the physical therapy clinic.

During my visit yesterday, I noticed a bell hanging in a corner. Being a very curious fellow, I asked, "What's with the bell?"

One of the therapists said that people ring it after their last appointment if they are satisfied with the treatment they've received.

Another one said that not many people ring it anymore.

Another question came to mind: "Would anyone have mentioned it to me if I hadn't asked about it?"

"Probably not."

That may help solve the mystery of why so few ring it. I explained: "I try to avoid ringing bells if I don't know their significance, especially in a medical setting, especially if I don't even know they're there."

Today, I shall ring the bell with gusto, for I am most satisfied with the treatment. (They might want to brush up on their communication skills, but the PT part was really good.)

"Significant improvement." That's what the physical therapist said I've made. We both already knew that, but it's still fun to hear out loud.
"Did you ring the bell?"
Yes, and enthusiastically so.
"Cling-clang."
Walla-walla-bing-bang.
"I know that's right."

English can be rather awkward at times, eh? Especially when we're not sure what to say. The people at the local Physical Therapy Clinic and I didn't become fishing buddies; we didn't go camping or join a bowling league. We did, however, over the last month or so, develop something of a relationship that deserved to be acknowledged.
As I was leaving after my last appointment yesterday, one of the therapists said, "We enjoyed having you."
I said, "Thank you. I enjoyed being had (gads!)."
Another one said, "I hope you'll come back. Oh, not because you need us, but just, you know, for a visit."
If I could get a take-two on that klutzy exit, I'd say, "You have an admirable blend of humor, savvy, and professionalism. Thank you for all your help. You're good folks. I wish you well."
It's true. (And it sounds a lot better than "I enjoyed being had.")

It's the best lotion. They gave me a small bottle of it at a hospital in Illinois years ago. I rationed it, planning to pick up some more along the way. I couldn't find it in any stores, so ordered some online. And made it last. When it got down to the squeeze-it-with-vigor-for-little-return level, it was time for another online purchase, but it sure would be nice to have some handy, right here, right now.

Along with my belongings, the hospital sent me home last June with a plastic bag full of stuff. I tossed the bag aside without looking in it. Yesterday morning, just for fun, I opened the bag. Among the stuff was a big bottle of the best lotion. I'd been wishing I had something that was sitting right there, not far away, for the last four months.

Guardian Angel: (eyeroll) You got your wish, but you were too lazy to notice? C'mon, man.

After my medical adventures of last spring and summer, blood tests have been a routine feature in my world. A nice nurse just called to give me the latest results: "Wonderful." She said that my potassium level is in the "normal" range. I've been called many things in my time, but normal? Almost never. That will take some getting used to. Another miracle may be necessary to make that adjustment.

Tom Hale

The Finish Line

Is that the finish line? I recognize that tree.
I cannot separate soon-to from used-to-be.
We've run a million miles, but not so very far
From where those two limbs fork, where our initials are.
Is that the finish line? I recognize that smile.
Be back where it all began in just a little while.

Is that the finish line? I recognize that face.
No need to hurry now; there is no second place.
That vicious circle ran me ragged now and then,
But it's a hoot now that I have my second wind.
Is that the finish line? Got here but don't know how.
I know you still have the map, so can we go home now?

Is that the finish line? Look there: I see the time—
That priceless thing you did that cost me not a dime.
I've kept it in my heart, wrapped in a golden dream.
Reminding me bad times are more than what they seem.
Our walk around the block detoured to everywhere.
You brought back a ton of memories and love to share.

Is that the finish line? Your secret's safe with me—
It is my template for true grit and sanity.
It's how the bees spell buzz; it's what the new bird sings.
I pray, "Dear Lord, deliver me from lesser things."
The finish line: Ain't that a fine how-do-you-do?
If you'll hold my hand, I'll walk the final steps with you.